STELLA R QUAH

HOME AND KIN

Families in Asia

EASTERN UNIVERSITIES PRESS
by Marshall Cavendish

© **2003 Times Media Private Limited**

Published 2003
by Times Media Private Limited
(Academic Publishing) under the imprint
Eastern Universities Press
by Marshall Cavendish

Times Centre, 1 New Industrial Road,
Singapore 536196
Fax: (65) 6284 9772
E-mail: tap@tpl.com.sg
Online Book Store:
http://www.timesacademic.com

Printed by Vine Graphic Pte Ltd, Singapore
on non-acidic paper

National Library Board (Singapore)
Cataloguing in Publication Data
Quah, Stella R.
Home and Kin: Families in Asia / Stella R. Quah. –
Singapore: Eastern Universities Press, 2003.

p. cm.
ISBN: 981-210-214-0

1. Family – Asia – Cross-cultural studies.
2. Asia – Social conditions.
I. Title.

HQ663
306.85095 — dc21
SLS2003016089

London • New York • Beijing • Shanghai
• Bangkok • Kuala Lumpur • Singapore

Contents

About the Author

Stella R. Quah is Professor of Sociology at the National University of Singapore. She has published numerous journal articles and chapters in books on social policy, medical sociology, and sociology of the family. She is also author and contributing editor of eleven books and monographs including *Between Two Worlds: Modern Wives in a Traditional Setting* (1988); *The Triumph of Practicality: Tradition and Modernity in Health Care Untilisation in Selected Asian Countries* (1989); *The Family as an Asset: An International Perspective on Marriage, Parenthood and Social Policy* (1990); *Social Class in Singapore* (1991); *Family in Singapore* (1994 and 1998); and the *International Handbook of Sociology* (2000). She was elected Vice-President for Research and Chairman of the Reseach Council of the International Sociological Association and served in that capacity from 1994 to 1998. She is Associate Editor of *International Sociology*, member of the International Advisory Board of the *British Journal of Sociology*, and member of the International Board of the *Journal of Sociology*, the official journal of the Australian Sociological Association.

Preface

Families in Western countries have received a great deal of attention by social scientists but there is less information on how families in other regions of the world are doing. In this book I offer a comparative study of East and Southeast Asian families with the aim of documenting and explaining the importance of home and kin in our lives as we journey from the 20th to the 21st centuries.

This volume is a natural expansion of my interest in the family life of various cultures which began in the 1980s with the analysis of the influence of the state on family life. A study I conducted with a team of international sociologists on marriage and parenthood policies in Western and Asian countries was published in 1990. My attention then turned to families in Singapore in the 1990s. Out of that interest came the book *Family in Singapore: Sociological Perspectives*. The first edition was published in 1994, and the revised and expanded second edition, in 1998.

The idea of writing this book was inspired by questions raised about Singapore families. My students and readers often ask me if Singapore families are different from other Asian families and if there is such thing as a 'typical' Asian family. No definitive answer could be given to those questions. On the one hand, I personally observed important differences and similarities across the region. On the other hand, personal observations could not be confirmed or denied by existing literature. A comparison of findings from country-specific studies gives ambiguous signals of similarities and differences mainly because of the different objectives, methodology and nature of evidence they utilise. Thus, the wide gap in our knowledge of contemporary Asian families motivated me to investigate how different or similar family life is across Asia by conducting this systematic comparative analysis of specific countries. My original intention to cover the entire region was restricted by the scarcity of comparative data. Consequently, this book covers only ten countries, four in East Asia (Japan, China, Hong Kong, and South Korea) and six in Southeast Asia (Indonesia, Malaysia, the Philippines, Singapore, Thailand, and Vietnam).

As far as possible, I have organised the analysis of Asian families in this volume along the same central themes of the second edition of *Family in Singapore* in order to facilitate cross-national comparisons. The selection of themes in the 1998 edition of *Family in Singapore* reflected the aspects of family that were of major importance at the twilight of the 20th century. The relevance of these themes in Asia continues and, in some cases, has become even more important today. These themes are: the relevance of marriage and parenthood in family formation, ageing and the transmission of values, gender issues, divorce and conflict resolution, and pressures that socio-economic development imposes on families.

I discuss these themes from three perspectives concurrently: historical, conceptual and comparative. The historical perspective is attempted by tracing the roots of current family situations whenever feasible. The conceptual or theoretical perspective is attained through the application of family sociology theories and concepts. And using a comparative perspective, I bring together data and studies from ten nations in East and Southeast Asia in order to identify main trends in the region. Moreover, as far as permitted by available data, the policy implications of the findings are highlighted and discussed. An additional and important product of the application of these three perspectives is the extensive bibliography at the end of this volume. Considering these features, this book is relevant to a wide readership including social scientists, policy-makers, family researchers, university students, and readers interested in the impact of socio-economic development in Asia.

I was able to work on this research project and complete the book thanks to the cooperation and support of many people. I was prompted to pursue the investigation by discussions with my students in family sociology and by queries from international colleagues. I am indebted to the people in different countries for the generous gift of their time and willingness to share with me their experiences; and to respondents of surveys I have conducted on family life in Singapore.

I considered the idea of a comparative analysis of Asian families for a long time but had not been able to find the time to do it. The time to collect data and do further field research was generously granted by the National University of Singapore. I am indebted to the then Head of the Department of Sociology, Associate Professor K.C. Ho and the Dean of the Faculty of Arts and Social Sciences, Professor Lily Kong, for approving a five-month sabbatical leave during the second half of 2002 that released me temporarily from teaching duties. I wish to express my thanks to Professor Ron Duncan, Director of the National Centre for Development Studies (NCDS), Asia-Pacific School of Economics and Management (APSEM) of the Australian National University (ANU) in

Canberra, for his kind invitation to spend my sabbatical at NCDS/ APSEM as a Visiting Fellow. I am grateful to the Librarians at ANU's J.B. Chifley Library and R.G. Menzies Library. The collections of Asian documents in these libraries were extremely useful for this comparative study. I am also very appreciative of the access I was given to their electronic databases by the Family Division of the United Nations and their permission to use some of the data for this study. I wish to thank the editorial team at Eastern Universities Press for their book publishing expertise and cordiality with authors.

Above all this, the enduring encouragement and understanding of my husband Jon in the demanding process of researching and writing, and of my family, particularly my father and my sister Carmenza, continue to be my most significant inspiration.

Stella R. Quah
Department of Sociology
National University of Singapore
July 2003

List of Tables

List of Charts

1

Studying Families in Asia

The objective of this book is to provide a comparative analysis of family trends in Asia by focusing on the most important aspects of family and kin, from the process of dating to the impact of economic development on homes and family life, as they are experienced in ten Asian countries. I begin the story by highlighting the efforts made by researchers over the past 50 years to study Asian families. This background information helps the reader appreciate the details of studies and findings discussed in the other chapters.

The study of families in Asia has experienced a slow but unambiguous shift over the past decades. While most studies up to the 1960s were authored by European and North American researchers, today there is a definitive presence of researchers in Asia analysing family structure and behaviour in their own countries. This development has produced a wider range of themes and research approaches to the study of families. Three main questions are explored in this chapter: 1) What are the dominant themes in the study of families in Asia?; 2) What are the theoretical perspectives most commonly applied?; and, 3) What are the most common methodological approaches used? But before dealing with these three questions, we need to clarify what 'family' means in this book.

DEFINING FAMILY

Family, like beauty, is in the eye of the beholder. We would be happy settling the matter that way, except that to study families accurately we need clear and systematic definitions. Now, systematic definitions of family abound as shown in comprehensive reviews of family research such as the two volumes on "A Sixty-Year Review, 1930-1990" by Stephen Bahr,[1] and the second edition of the *Handbook of Marriage and the Family.*[2] But sociologists David M. Klein and James M. White[3] provide one of the most useful definitions of family. These authors propose that we think of **family** as a social group that is substantially different from other groups

1

such as co-workers or close friends. In their view, four characteristics distinguish the family from other social groups. First, "families last for a considerably longer period of time than do most other social groups." Second, "families are intergenerational." Third, "families contain both biological and affinal (e.g., legal, common law) relationships between members." And fourth, these relationships link families "to a larger kinship organisation."[4] In sum, these four features make the family a unique social group.

In addition to being unique, the social group known as family displays a wide variation in form, structure, and internal dynamics across time and space. In Europe, North America, Australia, and New Zealand, analysts and policy makers have recognised for some time now, the existence of a multiplicity of family forms.[5] To appreciate this variation we need to distinguish between **ideal** family and **actual** family forms. This conceptual distinction introduced by M. J. Levy[6] based on his study of the family in China, is highly relevant to Asian countries in general. I discuss this distinction further in Chapter 3 but the notions of ideal and actual families are relevant at this point.

Over the decades, Asian communities have continuously followed and transmitted to their children their image of the ideal family as dictated by their respective cultural traditions. For example, studies of families in China,[7] Japan,[8] Korea,[9] Malaysia,[10] the Philippines,[11] Singapore,[12] Taiwan,[13] Thailand,[14] and Vietnam,[15] indicate that, notwithstanding the cultural differences across Asian countries, they are all inclined to regard as their ideal family the extended family, understood as a tightly knitted group involving at least three generations where parents, their married children — all, some, or only one child — and their children's children and spouses live in the same household or compound or at least in the same neighbourhood. Thus, the concept of the ideal family has undergone comparably minor variations in Asia across time.

The actual family, however, is that which people can 'afford' to have according to the specific circumstances of their lives. During the past decades the ideal family has remained a cultural icon of Asian tradition while the actual family has been reshaped by the changing tides of social, political, and economic development, as documented in the chapters that follow. Today, the legal arrangements covering housing, income tax, inheritance, child maintenance, adoption, health care, and other aspects, suggest that there is a certain awareness of the actual presence of different types of families such as three-generation families, nuclear families, and single-parent families born out of widowhood, separation or divorce. Yet, these tend to be perceived as variations of a sole socially recognised legitimate family where parents are legally married and the children are born within such a legal union. Other family forms not based on, or derived from, a legal marriage are denied the same social recognition.

One additional aspect of the definition of family is the personal or subjectively perceived family. This aspect refers to the affective meaning we give to family in our personal lives, a meaning that determines our subjectively marked family boundaries of inclusion and exclusion. For a child rescued from a decaying orphanage by an adopting couple, her loving adopted parents may be her true parents even if she knows she is adopted and has met her natural parents. You may not see the son of your divorced parent as your 'half-brother' because you feel as close to him as you are to your 'full' brother. The subjective perception of family boundaries encapsulated in the concept "boundary ambiguity" proposed by Pauline Boss[16] in her study of divorced families, and developed by her and Kay Pasley,[17] is a very important concept in family sociology. This concept illuminates the affectual and subjective definition of family in each person's life.

Families as unique social groups, therefore, may be studied from a wide variety of angles of analysis. Researchers may investigate the ideal, actual or affectual (subjectively defined) family forms either at the individual's or small group's level (that is, micro-level analysis) or focusing on the societal implications for larger groups, institutions or socio-cultural or economic structures (that is, macro-level analysis). Besides these various levels of analysis, family sociology offers a rich body of theories and methodological techniques that, as it should be, are constantly under critical appraisal. In addition, family sociologists also do collaborative research with other social scientists, such as economists, political scientists, and psychologists.

DOMINANT THEMES IN THE STUDY OF FAMILIES IN ASIA

As it happens around the world, topics of family research in Asia have changed over time. The selection of research themes is commonly determined by many factors including the researcher's personal interest. Because most of these sociological studies are conducted at universities or research institutions, other factors affecting the selection of research topic are institutional agreement on the relevance of the topic and the availability of financial support and research facilities. These potential obstacles to research on families were well documented in the 1970s and 1980s in Indonesia,[18] the Philippines,[19] Thailand,[20] Malaysia and Singapore,[21] and continue today in these and most other Asian countries.

Personal interest and the availability of financial and logistic support are factors influencing scientific research everywhere, including Japan[22] and South Korea.[23] Studies of the family in China, on the other hand, were drastically curtailed by the revolutionary change in the political system. According to Chinese sociologist Tan Shen,

> ... sociology and anthropology were abolished in the readjustment of the institutions of higher education at the beginning of the 1950s, thus suspending for nearly 30 years the study on family through actual examples. Even till now, there have not been specialised studies of this period. I can only make a preliminary depiction of it in the light of the relevant documents issued by the Party and the government at the time.[24]

But three features of Hong Kong, Malaysia, Indonesia, the Philippines, Singapore, and Thailand, have been particularly influential in shaping the type of family research conducted in these countries. These features, all derived from the history and level of wealth of these countries, are: (a) colonial background; (b) flow of foreign scholars; and (c) restricted access to sources of financial support.

Colonial background features prominently in the description of the development of sociology and other social sciences in several Asian countries[25] including Indonesia, Malaysia, the Philippines, and Singapore. According to Isabel Panopia and Ponciano Bennagen,[26] Spanish missionaries during the 19th century and American missionaries and scholars during the first half of the 20th century exerted a significant influence upon the introduction and development of a research tradition, first in anthropology and later in sociology, in the Philippines. Both Spanish and American colonial administrators, missionaries and scholars were keenly interested in the study of indigenous peoples' culture, religion, social structure and language, among other things.

These topics dominated the research scene in sociology before the Second World War. The interest in indigenous culture produced studies of family structure and family behaviour such as kinship systems and marriage customs.

E. K. M. Masinambow and Meutia Swasono[27] describe a rather similar scenario with respect to the role of the Dutch colonial government in Indonesia. From the mid-1800 until the 1940s, the Dutch colonial government was interested in understanding the culture and the level of assimilation of Indonesian peoples. Among the first research themes explored by officially sponsored studies were "land tenure, land ownership, migration … child marriages … prostitution"[28] and other aspects that were related, directly or indirectly, to the traditional family system of different Indonesian communities. Given the historical period, it is understandable that none of these studies were conducted by what the authors refer to as "trained sociologists" who were available only "after Independence"[29] that took place soon after the Second World War.

Vietnam and Cambodia were French colonies in the later part of the 19th century and first half of the 20th century. Three other countries with a colonial past are Brunei, Malaysia and Singapore. They share a common history and the same British colonial rule with Hong Kong. The presence of the British colonial government in Malaysia and Singapore began in 1819, when the British Crown acquired the island of Singapore. In 1826, the territories of Penang and Malacca — in Peninsular Malaysia — together with Singapore became the British or "Straits Settlements." Malaysia gained full independence from Britain in 1963 with Singapore as one of the states of the Federation. Singapore separated from Malaysia and became an independent republic in 1965. Given this shared background as a unified British colony, there were no significant distinctions in the sociological research scene between these two countries before the Second World War. It appears that the British colonial government was less concerned with collecting systematic information on the cultures of indigenous peoples in the Straits Settlements than were the Spanish or American colonial administrators in the Philippines or their Dutch counterparts in Indonesia. But there were interested British and European scholars and missionaries who investigated various aspects of local customs and behaviour during the late 1800s and the first half of the 1900s. Following the trend reported in Indonesia and the Philippines, pioneer researchers during this period were foreigners not formally trained in sociology,[30] but their descriptions of customs, daily life and places provided data of great sociological interest. Japan and Korea have also a history of Western influence although it is more recent, briefer, and the circumstances of the American presence in both countries were different. Nevertheless, following the same trend of British colonies, American researchers also initiated systematic studies of social and family life in these countries. In contrast to other Asian countries, Thailand does not have a colonial past.

In addition to the presence or absence of colonial background, the country variation in selection of research themes on family sociology is also influenced by the flow of foreign scholars. To illustrate: the colonial status of Hong Kong, Indonesia, Malaysia, Philippines and Singapore before World War II helps to explain the steady flow of Western scholars to these countries, eager to explore and analyse exotic cultures, religions and different ways of life. The research themes selected by foreign scholars during the colonial period were thus focused on the social organisation, customs, and beliefs of indigenous peoples as well as their adaptation to change. This early trend in research topics determined by American and European scholars' choices and interests is illustrated by the studies they conducted in Singapore,[31] the Philippines,[32] and Indonesia.[33] Although Thailand was not a colony, the presence of foreign scholars was also felt during the first half of the 20th century but, judging from Amara Pongsapich's account, not with the same intensity experienced in the former British or French colonies.[34]

After the former colonies obtained independence, the changing political conditions affected the flow of foreign scholars. In some countries, such as Singapore and Malaysia, the flow of foreign researchers continued while in other countries foreigners could no longer enjoy the same easy entry. But the seriousness of the obstacles they faced, and the consequences for local research, varied from country to country. Radical changes took place in Vietnam, Cambodia, and North Korea. One earlier example of radical change was Indonesia. Masinambow and Swasono wrote:

> As a result of the West Irian crisis almost all scholars from the Netherlands who came to Indonesia after the Second World War left Indonesia in 1957 and 1958 causing the universities to be depleted of most of their senior and experienced specialists. While

research activities of the Dutch came to a standstill, those of non-Dutch expatriate researchers continued ... sponsored by a variety of foreign institutions.[35]

The presence of American, British and other European researchers in the Philippines, Malaysia, Singapore, and Thailand has continued but has varied somewhat from the 1950s onwards. The American presence has been more obvious in the Philippines and Thailand and, since the 1970s it has increased in Malaysia, Singapore, and Indonesia. British, German, French, and other European scholars, together with a rising number of Japanese scholars are also found today in many Asian countries. The foreign influence on the range and selection of family research themes is narrower now than in the past and the current trend is towards collaboration between local and foreign researchers and increasing research work by local researchers.[36]

The types of studies conducted before 1990 are illustrated by a meta-analysis of family studies published in English between 1950 and 1989 in Indonesia, Malaysia, the Philippines, Singapore, and Thailand.[37] As described in Table 1.1, five main research themes were identified: population, marriage, gender roles, and family structure. The category "Population" covers studies dealing with family planning and control of population growth including fertility trends, KAP (knowledge, attitudes and practice) studies of fertility behaviour, the value of children, husband-wife decision-making on contraception, number of children, and nuptiality patterns among other aspects. The category "Marriage" refers to studies on the institution of marriage including mate selection, courtship and marital dissolution or divorce. The category "Gender roles" covers studies on gender or sex-role stereotypes and the status of women in society. The category "Family structure" encompasses studies on the family as a social unit and the analysis of family relations from a variety of angles including kinship systems, family networks, family policy, studies on parent-child interaction, child socialisation and problems faced by families who migrate together or separately within or outside their country of origin. As the number of publications for each of these subtopics was small, they are classified in Table 1.1 under the theme "Family structure."

7

TABLE 1.1   FAMILY RESEARCH PUBLISHED IN ENGLISH IN
FIVE ASIAN COUNTRIES, 1950-1989, BY THEME, COUNTRY
AND TIME PERIOD (IN %)

| Country | Time Period | Research Themes | | | | All themes % (N) |
		Population	Marriage	Gender roles	Family structure	
Indonesia	1950-1980	40	30	0	30	100 (5)
	1981-1989	31	15	31	23	100 (26)
Malaysia	1950-1980	28	36	0	36	100 (11)
	1981-1989	33	15	20	32	100 (40)
The Philippines	1950-1980	18	20	8	54	100 (51)
	1981-1989	29	10	10	51	100 (51)
Singapore	1950-1980	43	25	17	15	100 (53)
	1981-1989	32	18	18	32	100 (28)
Thailand	1950-1980	58	5	5	32	100 (19)
	1981-1989	38	23	4	35	100 (26)

Source: Table 4.4 in Quah (1993:84). Data are from a meta-analysis of family
studies published in English from 1950 to 1989 and that dealt with family in
Indonesia, Malaysia, the Philippines, Singapore and Thailand alone or in
combination. A total of 310 publications met these criteria (Quah, 1993:69-93).
The complete bibliography listing the 310 studies is provided in Quah
(1993:107-125).

The aspect of family research that captured the attention of most
researchers in the four decades from 1950 to 1990 was the control of
population growth also known as family planning research. With the
exception of the Philippines, family planning was the most active field
of research compared to other family research topics in Indonesia,
Malaysia, Singapore, and Thailand. During the period 1950-1980,
family planning research was most salient in Thailand (58 per cent of
all family sociology publications in English), Singapore (43 per cent),
and Indonesia (40 per cent). The number of this type of studies
decreased after 1980 in these countries. Malaysia experienced the
opposite trend: only 28 per cent of all studies were on family planning
in the period 1950-1980 but this proportion increased to 33 per cent
for the period 1981-1989. Studies on marriage became popular in

Thailand in the 1980s. However, while this has been a subject of interest to a good number of family sociologists in the region, the proportion of marriage studies in the other four countries declined in the period 1981-1989. Indonesia and Malaysia have been the focus of studies on gender roles and the status of women only in the past two decades. This topic has occupied the attention of researchers in Singapore, the Philippines and, to a lesser degree, Thailand, for much longer.

The theme on family structure studies in these five Southeast Asian countries as well as in other countries in Asia deal with legislation and policies affecting families; kinship networks in rural and urban areas; and styles of child socialisation, among other topics. But there are differences in emphasis across countries. About one out of every two family studies on Filipino families from 1950 to 1989 was a study of family structure. Reflecting on the economic and political situation in the country, the most common problem in the minds of Filipino researchers was migration. Migration studies became prominent in the 1980s. These studies deal with the problems faced by Filipino families who, for primarily economic reasons, migrate to other countries either as a family or individually. Researchers discuss the problems faced by heads of households, their spouses and children when one of them becomes a guest worker in another country. This preoccupation with migration and guest workers (primarily in construction and domestic work) continues to be in the current research agendas of Filipino researchers.[38] The impact of migration on families is now pursued by many researchers in other Asian countries as illustrated by the work published in the *Asian and Pacific Migration Journal.*[39]

THEORETICAL AND METHODOLOGICAL PERSPECTIVES

Are there discernible theoretical or methodological approaches that distinguish Asian research on families from family research conducted elsewhere, say in North America or Europe? The meta-analysis discussed above indicates that the majority of the 310 studies published in English from 1950 to 1989 were mostly descriptive and exploratory rather than theoretical pieces or tests of theoretical propositions. As presented in Table 1.2, the proportion of descriptive studies conducted

9

in the five Southeast Asian countries (Indonesia, Malaysia, Philippines, Singapore, and Thailand) ranged from 56 per cent in Indonesia to 63 per cent in Thailand. This characteristic is confirmed by the reports of senior Asian scholars to UNESCO on the development of Sociology and Anthropology in Southeast Asia up to the mid-1980s. In their opinion, studies conducted by non-Asian scholars were more likely to deal with theories and concepts while studies conducted by Asian researchers were typically descriptive.[40] Table 1.2 groups the 310 publications into three categories according to the author's approach with respect to concepts and theories. The category "Description" refers to purely descriptive studies where the authors' main objective was to make a representation of the situation they observed as detailed as possible without getting involved in a conceptual discussion. The category "Concepts" refers to studies where the discussion and application of concepts was the main objective but the authors did not test specific conceptual propositions or hypotheses. The third category, "Theoretical assumptions" covers studies where the authors formulated and tested theoretical assumptions or hypotheses.

TABLE 1.2   FAMILY RESEARCH PUBLISHED IN ENGLISH IN
FIVE ASIAN COUNTRIES, 1950-1989, BY APPROACH TO
CONCEPTS (IN %)

Approaches	Indonesia	Malaysia	The Philippines	Singapore	Thailand
Description	56	61	61	59	63
Concepts	22	12	18	17	16
Theoretical assumptions	22	27	21	24	21
All studies	100	100	100	100	100
(Number)	(27)	(49)	(94)	(80)	(43)

Source: Table 4.5 in Quah (1993:87). Data are from a meta-analysis of family studies published in English from 1950 to 1989 and that dealt with family in Indonesia, Malaysia, the Philippines, Singapore and Thailand alone or in combination. A total of 310 publications met these criteria (Quah, 1993:69-93). The complete bibliography listing the 310 studies is provided in Quah (1993:107-125). This table excludes 17 studies for which no information on conceptual approaches was available.

It is relevant to look into the type of authorship when discussing theoretical and methodological approaches in studies carried out between 1950 and 1989. Mostly foreign scholars conducted studies involving concepts and theories. Foreign scholars authored 81 per cent of the Indonesian studies published in English from 1950 to 1989; 57 per cent of the Malaysian studies; 44 per cent of the Philippines studies; 17 per cent of the Singapore studies; and 47 per cent of the studies in Thailand.[41] Not surprisingly, studies by foreign scholars reflected the stage of social sciences in Europe and North America at that time by addressing conceptual assumptions about family structure (for example locality, fertility, family size, marriage patterns) and examining the impact of socioeconomic and demographic variables (e.g., income, education, occupation, religion, age, gender). Following Robert K. Merton's[42] classification, the 'mini' theories tested in some of these studies were "middle-range theories" but most studies presented only "working hypotheses" or empirical generalisations. In the 1970s and 1980s, the research emphasis was mostly on procreation and family planning decisions as this type of studies were actively promoted by American and international funding agencies. Foreign and local researchers conducted jointly a smaller proportion of studies (3 per cent of all studies in Indonesia, 8 per cent in Malaysia, 10 per cent in the Philippines, 20 per cent in Singapore and 40 per cent in Thailand).[43] Some of these studies tested conceptual assumptions while others were only descriptive.

Concerning methodological approaches used in the 310 studies, there was a significant variation among the five countries. The studies were classified into five categories: (a) "Quantitative" studies referred to studies that collected and analysed first-hand information on representative samples of a target population and used structured questionnaires, attitudinal scales, and statistical analysis of correlations among variables; (b) "Qualitative" studies were those using methods such as participant or non-participant observation, ethnographies, in-depth interviews and other qualitative techniques of data collection and analysis; (c) "Historical" studies were those based on secondary documents and material whether historical or contemporary; (d) A fourth category of studies was labelled "Mixed" because it involved studies that combined more than one of the previous three approaches, quantitative, qualitative or historical; (e) Finally, the category "Other" comprised studies that were not research-based or did not use empirical data, for example bibliographical essays, essays presenting personal opinions on family matters or on conceptual issues.

The classification of the 310 studies into these five categories revealed the following features. Quantitative studies on the family were most prominent in Thailand (78 per cent of all publications on Thai families), the Philippines and Malaysia (64 per cent each), and Indonesia (52 per cent). Only 34 per cent of the Singapore studies were quantitative. Although less popular, qualitative studies were more common in Indonesia and Malaysia (24 per cent each) than Singapore (14 per cent), the Philippines (13 per cent), or Thailand (10 per cent). In comparison to quantitative and qualitative studies, historical and mixed studies were less common in most countries except Singapore where the historical approach was used in 20 per cent and the mixed approach in 18 per cent of all studies.[44]

Compared to the period 1950-1989, the nature of sociological studies on families conducted after 1990 suggests a dual trend. First, there is an increasing involvement of local scholars as sole or principal investigators and a rising sophistication in the selection of conceptual premises to be tested and methodological techniques applied to data collection and data analysis. This improvement is to a large extent a reflection of larger numbers of Asian scholars with advanced training in North America or Europe working in Asia and a large number of Asian graduate students doing their thesis research on Asian themes in American, Canadian, British and other European universities, or in universities in Australia or New Zealand. Second, a small number of researchers show an interesting circular trend concerning conceptual and methodological approaches. This type of researchers bring to mind their early 20th century counterparts as they eschew conceptual analysis to concentrate exclusively on descriptive narrations of a few selected individual cases.

THE BOOK

The focus of this book is Asia, but it is not possible to cover the entire region. Asian countries vary widely in terms of population and geographical size, ethnic composition, level of socioeconomic development, and political system, among other aspects. In addition to this diversity, a second major constraint to the comparative analysis of all countries in Asia is the unevenness of data reporting, of available population statistics, and of published studies on families. Some countries publish periodic and detailed figures on a wide range of population characteristics and census data, but other countries publish only general indicators irregularly or sporadically.

Thus, the comparative analysis presented in this book involves ten Asian countries. Four are East Asian countries: China, Hong Kong,[45] Japan, and South Korea.[46] The other six are Southeast Asian countries: Indonesia, Malaysia, the Philippines, Singapore, Thailand, and Vietnam. These are the ten countries for which comparative data are available. Correspondingly, as far as permitted by available comparative data, the spotlight is on developments in those countries over the past decade 1990/93-2000/03. But a longer historical view is provided whenever possible.

Two dimensions are covered in each chapter, a macro-level analysis of family trends based on demographic and survey data as well as the role of the state and social policy; and a micro-level analysis of home and kin situations based on my own interviews and analysis of cases from other studies. The comparative analysis of the ten Asian countries begins in Chapter 2 with the process of family formation, including dating, weddings, and marriage. Chapter 3 pursues the analysis looking into parenthood in the context of culture and social policy. The theme of parenthood is extended to grandparenting in Chapter 4 where the social perception of age and the situation of the senior generation are examined. Following the theme of Chapter 4 on the social restrictions faced by the senior generation, Chapter 5 moves on to discuss the social restrictions imposed on women and men based on gender roles and how gender roles affect families. Chapter 6 deals with the theme of conflict and its manifestation in marital breakdown, and examines critically one social arrangement, the family court, set in place in some societies to deal with family conflict. The book concludes with the analysis in Chapter 7 of the impact of socioeconomic development on homes and family life and the role of the state in assisting families to deal with social change.

As I discuss Asian families in the chapters that follow, I have endeavoured to cover a wide range of relevant family studies from various levels of theoretical and methodological sophistication. The bibliography at the end of the book offers details of those studies for interested readers.

ENDNOTES

1. See Bahr (1991).
2. See Sussman, Steinmetz and Peterson (1999).
3. See Klein and White (1996:20-24).
4. See Klein and White (1996:20-23).
5. See Rapoport and Rapoport (1982); Sussman and Steinmetz (1987); Moen (1989); Kamerman and Kahn (1989); Edgar (1990); Koopman-Boyden (1990).
6. See Levy (1949, 1965).
7. See Cheung and Liu (1997) and Yi (2002),
8. See Sasaki and Wilson (1997).
9. See Inoue (1998).
10. See Ngin and DeVanzo (1999).
11. See Medina (1991).
12. See Quah (1998).
13. See Lu (2000).
14. See Schvaneveldt, Young and Schvaneveldt (2001).
15. See Thi (1999) and Knodel et.al. (2000).
16. See Boss (1977, 1988).
17. See Pasley (1987, 1993).
18. See Masinambow and Swasono (1985).
19. See Panopia and Bennagen (1985).
20. See Pongsapich, (1985).
21. See Quah (1998).
22. See Fuse (1996).
23. See Cho and Shin (1996)
24. See Tan (1996).
25. See Kumar and Raju (1981) and Quah (1998:3-12).
26. See Panopia and Bennagen (1985:220-224).
27. See Masinambow and Swasono (1985:182-195).
28. See Masinambow and Swasono (1985:183-184).
29. See Masinambow and Swasono (1985:183).
30. See for example Buckley (1902) and Reith (1907).
31. See Quah (1998:7-12).
32. See Panopia and Bennagen (1985).
33. See Masinambow and Swasono (1985).
34. See Pongsapich (1985).
35. See Masinambow and Swasono (1985:187).
36. See Quah (1993:80-82).
37. See Quah (1993:69-94).

38. See Asis (2002).
39. See for example Tyner (2002); Yeo, Graham and Boyle (2002); and Hugo (2002).
40. See Masinambow and Swasono (1985:180-201); Panopia and Bennagen (1985:232); and Pongsapich (1985:165).
41. See Quah (1993:80).
42. See Merton (1968).
43. See Quah (1993:80).
44. See Quah (1993:87-89).
45. Hong Kong is a Special Administrative Region of the People's Republic of China. I refer to Hong Kong as a country in this book to facilitate the presentation and discussion of findings.
46. I refer to the Republic of Korea as South Korea or briefly as Korea in this book, to facilitate the presentation and discussion of findings.

2

"I Do", "We Do": Forming and Extending Families

A new family begins when two people get married. Or so it is believed in some regions. In other cultures and places marriage signals the expansion of an existing family, as a stem sprouting from a growing tree buttressed by deep ancestral roots. In spite of differences in the way marriage is seen by different communities from East to West, it is clear that the worldwide changes permeating social life at the dawn of the 21st century have also, inevitably, involved the meaning and structure of family and marriage everywhere.

Still, while change is relentless, the nature of change varies and the pace of change is faster in some communities or nations than in others. Let us consider the case of Montaillou, a small farming village perched in the Pyrenees, a mountain range between France and Spain. Fourteenth-century family life in Montaillou reaches us through records of personal accounts by the farmers themselves, studied by E. L.R. Ladurie[1] and Frances and Joseph Gies.[2] In Montaillou, families remembered their ancestors by name "up to as many as four generations." The extended family was very important although the constituting conjugal or three-generation families could live in separate households.[3] The head of the family was the husband and this role was taken very seriously as one husband put it: "A man is worth nothing if he is not his wife's master."[4] Parents had to provide dowry for their daughters, an obligation that could ruin poor families; but marriage was a norm, so the village "had no old maids." Marriages were arranged mostly seeking a good match in financial terms but a love match was possible, mostly for the man, who could make a choice. Women in the village "married as early as fourteen, men not until they were established in life, sometimes in their early thirties. The differential in age meant many young widows, and frequently second and even third marriages for women."[5]

We have advanced a great deal in science and technology since those Montaillou villagers were around. Yet, as we shall see, the century and the location are different but this portrayal of the 14th century European village approximates the values, beliefs, the perception of marriage, and the role of wives and husbands in some rural and urban communities of the third millennium. To appreciate the intricate designs woven by threads of past and present in the fabric of social life, let us consider four aspects of family life related to marriage: spouse selection, main motives of marriage, wedding celebrations, and marriage trends.

THE PATH TO MARRIAGE: SPOUSE SELECTION

Dating styles and how young people get to meet potential marriage partners are complex subjects that would require a separate book. But some general and tentative trends may be identified at this juncture. A key feature of the search for a marriage partner in most cultures is permanence in the midst of change. Just as it was for the villagers at Montaillou, it is not uncommon for young people in many Asian countries, especially in rural areas, to be assisted by older adults and peers in meeting suitable marriage partners. The older adults are mostly parents and other senior family members, but they may also be family friends, higher-ranking co-workers, or professional matchmakers. The idea of romantic love is regarded as a Western notion by senior generations of Asians for whom love is either constructed day by day over a lifetime, or replaced by a sense of responsibility and obligation. At the same time, young educated Asians seem to be rather inclined to make their own choice of spouse, even if they need some assistance in meeting eligible people.

The styles of matchmaking, the role of older adults and peers, and their relation to the young person they help as matchmakers, vary across cultural and religious communities, rural and urban settings and the community's or country's level of economic development. But one aspect found practically everywhere is the importance given to the process of identifying an eligible marriage partner. Who are eligible partners? The field of eligibles is defined individually and collectively. For the individual man or woman, the field of eligibles is that category of people that he or she considers the most appropriate potential marriage partners. Who would be an appropriate spouse is decided subjectively by the person seeking to get married, based on a wide variety of desirable attributes or criteria. Often, however, that person cannot ignore or may not wish to ignore, the family's and community's definition of his or her field of eligibles. For example, let us assume that in the case of single educated women, the most basic collective definition of her field of eligibles would be single university educated men. Yet, single educated women may very well find themselves in good jobs but surrounded by married male colleagues, and with a steadily decreasing circle of eligible single male friends. A single educated person's field of eligibles becomes even narrower with additional requirements such as religion and ethnic background. The parents of a young man or woman from an ethnic minority may be advised by kin and friends to reach out to the country of their ancestors if the pool of eligible marriage partners at home for their daughter or son is depleting or inadequate.

Variations in the community's definition of the field of eligibles take place over time to accommodate changing circumstances. Similarly, as a person becomes older or better educated, and goes through difficult life experiences, his or her subjective definition of an eligible spouse may be altered. Yet, single people and their parents strive to meet explicit and implicit social requirements even when changing demographic, socioeconomic, or political conditions make it more difficult for them to reach their field of eligibles. The modern version of matchmaking illustrates this effort well.

Young Japanese prefer a *ren'ai* (romantic love) marriage. A marriage may be seen as *ren'ai* if the couple fall in love irrespective of the circumstances that brought them together, that is, whether they met on their own or were introduced by parents, friends or matchmakers.[6] But if parents assist with a *miai kekkon* (arranged marriage) their style is subtler than that of commercial matchmakers. Parents may request a mediator, usually a friend of the family, to recommend a suitable partner and a background check is conducted discreetly. The parents provide the information and photograph to their son/daughter for examination and the first meeting of the two young people is arranged, usually with both sets of parents present.[7]

The assistance from parents, informal social networks and dating or matchmaking agencies appears justified in modern times given the difficulties that single Japanese face in meeting suitable marriage partners. The *o-miai* custom is "still highly esteemed as the 'official' way to meet a prospective husband" and it refers to "rounds of blind dates premised on marriage" arranged by family or friends of women in their late 20s or early 30s who are seen as "getting closer to the cut-off age of eligibility" for marriage.[8] In his analysis of the changes in the timing of marriage in Japan for the past three decades, James M. Raymo[9] found that "marriage market opportunities" have decreased mainly for highly educated women and lower educated men. Considering the weakening enthusiasm for old fashioned arranged marriages among the singles, various measures are taken. A group of five Japanese mothers in Nagoya decided to form "The Wedding Society Asahi" in 1990. By 1991, the society had reached 1,000 members. The society "holds meetings at which parents exchange information" such as age, level of education, occupation, physical characteristics of their unmarried children "in the hope of finding suitable marriage partners for their sons and daughters."[10] The Wedding Society mothers represent the personal, direct involvement of parents.

On the opposite side of the scale are the commercial dating or matchmaking agencies resorted to by the singles themselves. In modern, industrialised, and urban Asian settings, friends are crucial although informal matchmakers. But just as important are commercial agencies. Commercial matchmaking services (for example computer-dating services and marriage bureaus) like those found in Western countries are common. Commercial matchmaking services have a long history, can be very lucrative,[11] and tend to have a clear sense of what customers want. Illustrating the customer-friendly attitude of commercial matchmaking services, A. Levy quoted a matchmaking agency manager:

> The little lady wants a blue-eyed, six foot, 35-year-old peanut vendor with a passion for the Italian Renaissance? She's been looking for him for ten years? We can find him in five minutes if we've got him! And if we've got him, she can have him![12]

Commercial dating and matchmaking agencies today continue to display this can-do attitude. Interesting illustrations of tradition and modernity in dating and matchmaking are found in Asian global cities like Tokyo, Hong Kong, and Singapore.

The range of matchmaking agencies in Tokyo alone is enormous including and exceeding the types of agencies described by Bob Mullan[13] in the United States. The Japanese agencies are very well advertised through all available media including cyberspace. Assessing matchmaking services in Tokyo, journalist Emma Kelly writes "Given the price of a beer in Roppongi and the cost of an evening out, even though an agency can't promise they'll find your Ms Right, they might be able to make the process a little easier."[14] Japanese farmers, whom cyberspace advertising may not reach, are getting assistance from other quarters. Japanese provincial and local governments "have started to double as marriage agencies" by facilitating the travel of young women from South Korea and various countries in Southeast Asia "to Japan to marry Japanese bachelor farmers"; but it is costly as "farmers seeking foreign wives spend as much as US$20,000 on marriage broker fees, trips abroad and presents for the prospective bride" and "the 'bride price' paid to the woman's family can run up to US$3,000."[15]

The ancient tradition of *mendang hudui* (equal status) marriage in China made it essential for parents to search for appropriate marriage partners for their sons and daughters. Dai Keijing[16] reports that *mendang hudui* marriages were discredited as "feudal and evil" by the Communist regime. She describes the situation after the Communist revolution in 1950 as one of radical change with young people establishing intimate relationships before marriage and being introduced to potential partners by friends and co-workers. On the other hand, Richard E. Barrett and Li Fang[17] present a more varied picture: while young people were given more freedom from parental supervision by the communist revolution, "no true dating culture emerged" because "it was hard for young people to be alone together, especially for those who lived in villages full of nosy kinfolk." More importantly, the Cultural Revolution that took place from 1966 to 1976 was a period of "Communist asceticism ... when virtually no interest in the opposite sex was allowed."[18] This era was followed by a slow but steadily increasing interest in capitalist-style romance and dating promoted by old and new love novels, and modern music and romantic songs "smuggled in from Hong Kong, Taiwan and the West."[19] Comparing 1990s data from surveys on dating, Barrett and Li conclude that although "Chinese youth have, on average, far fewer boyfriends or girlfriends than do their American counterparts, the networks and introduction mechanisms that lead to marriage are remarkably similar." In both countries, one's network of friends and family members are the most important introduction mechanisms and between 25 to 35 per cent of young people in both countries "find their marriage partners on their own."[20]

Although the high value given to a traditionally proper match is still acknowledged in China,[21] young adults are losing faith in the traditional matchmakers or *mei po* and searching themselves for a romantic love match or turning to commercial matchmaking agencies. Commercial agencies have become popular not only in large cities but also in rural areas. In 1998, the Queqiao Marriage Service Centre in Zhongpingle Village, Hebei Province, reported receiving "between 20 to 50 inquiries from young farmers on a daily basis."[22] Matchmaking and dating agencies are even more active and accessible in Hong Kong. Many of those agencies offer international choices advertising the chance to find possible partners in China, Taiwan, and Western countries. But, as in China and other rapidly developing nations, traditional and modern values on marriage coexist in Hong Kong.[23]

Marriage is seen as a very important life transition by South Korean singles and a source of emotional security and happiness although they are inclined to believe that getting married means losing some personal freedom.[24] However, the timing of marriage has changed. Just as in the case of other Asian countries, the age at marriage has been rising steadily over the past decades. This is in part a result of the steady increase in the level of education of South Koreans. In particular, the women's level of education has increased dramatically since the establishment of the Republic of Korea in 1948, leading to the corresponding increase in the proportion of single women holding jobs.[25] Finding the right marriage partner is a problem for South Korean singles, especially for educated women, given the perceived attributes of the ideal spouse: educated men believe that a wife should be less educated than her husband; and educated women believe that the wife should be at least three years younger than her husband.[26] Another side of the Korean situation is the trend away from arranged marriage and towards romantic love,[27] a trend also evident in other rapidly developing Asian countries with the corresponding presence of commercial matchmaking agencies and the informal involvement of family and friends in arranging casual introductions.

In contrast to other Asian countries, Singapore offers an interesting example of open state patronage of matchmaking through various agencies. Commercial matchmaking agencies are popular today but the idea was introduced by the government, prompted by the increasing number of educated singles above the age of 30. The first matchmaking agency, set up in 1984 under the umbrella of the Public Service Division of the Ministry of Finance, was the Social Development Unit (SDU). Initially, the SDU reached its target population — single university graduates in the labour force, mostly in the public sector — through their employers, but it later changed to direct invitations to fresh university graduates to join its activities. SDU expanded its activities beyond social gatherings to include educational and cultural activities such as personal effectiveness workshops, supervisory management skills courses and photography classes among other subjects[28] and four core areas or services namely, "Take Flight activities," "Computer Matchmaking," "Choice Match," and "Tele-Pal."[29] The latter service renamed "I-Pal" in 1997, was an electronic mail "self-help programme for finding friends of the opposite sex," that allowed the user "to select friends based on your personal preference," and it was open to both SDU members and non-members who meet basic requirements such as being single and having a tertiary education.[30] The continuous upgrading of SDU matchmaking services has kept pace with the leaps and bounds of technological innovations to facilitate communication with the field of eligibles among university educated singles. By 2003, SDU members could select from a wide catalogue of options to "get acquainted with their new found friends" in a private and easy manner. The options include "SMS [short messaging service through mobile phones], e-Notes, i-Date (SDU's very own instant messaging service) ... i-Chat (the Internet Relay Chat service that is available around the clock)," and "Table 4 Two" which is a computer matching service that allows a subscriber "to browse through the profiles of members of the opposite gender online through eBrochure" using a search function to identify the best matches according to his or her own specified criteria.[31]

Government subsidy was high in the early years of the service, as an added incentive for young adults to attend the activities organised by SDU. The fees are still reasonable in 2003 as the SDU is a non-profit organisation, but participants pay the cost of most of the events they attend or services they use, including the SDU's computer matching service. The participation fees for workshops and courses may range, for example, from a few dollars to a few hundred depending on the type of social activity. Still, with the aim of removing obstacles for young educated employees to participate, all SDU activities are "provided at cost" and at times "SDU has to underwrite cost overruns."[32] The system of payment of SDU services now incorporates electronic banking facilities[33] following the lifestyle of its target population which is the highly educated 20-40 age cohort of single professionals and white-collar income-earners.

As people became more used to the idea of matchmaking, SDU transformed its earlier low profile style into an open and trendy image. These efforts, apparently, have been fruitful. The number of single graduates participating in the SDU's activities increased from 1,395 in 1984 to 6,972 in 1988.[34] SDU membership went up to over 16,000 in 1995 with private sector participants comprising 64 per cent in 1990 and 74 per cent in 1994,[35] and has increased steadily to 26,000 in 2003.[36] The SDU expanded its services by setting up the "A-Level Programme" in 1985 geared to young adults who have completed their post-secondary school education.[37] That service is now the Social Development Service or SDS and is designed to increase the opportunities to meet their field of eligibles for single adults aged 20 to 40, who are not university graduates. The SDS has followed SDU in improving its range of matchmaking services and smartening up its image to attract upcoming generations of single young adults.[38]

The degree of freedom in dating enjoyed by young people in Thailand varies depending on whether they are male or female and on their social class, among other factors. According to Thai ethnographer S. Ratarasam,[39] in contrast to young men, young women in both rural and urban areas are traditionally chaperoned by their families but stricter control in dating is exercised by parents from upper class families. Legislation in force since 1932 waives parental consent for the marriage of people over the age of 18. Nevertheless, Ratarasam observes that although young people tend to select their own marriage partners, socially it is still expected that they "secure the approval of their parents."[40] A similar situation is found in Indonesia where the traditional trend of marrying girls at a very young age necessarily involved the parents as matchmakers. The timing of marriage for women has been changed by legislation to the minimum age of 16 and there is a discernable trend towards romantic love rather than arranged marriages even in rural areas of Indonesia.[41]

MAIN PURPOSE OF MARRIAGE

Historical records from different communities around the globe[42] suggest that marriage is considered an important life event for many reasons but two motives stand out, one personal and the other social. The personal motive is to secure a keel for the emotional life of the individual.[43] The social motive is to ensure the socioeconomic stability and progress of

23

family, kin, and community. Historical examples of the social motive abound. In his analysis of ancient and medieval Western civilisations, the renowned historian Fernand Braudel[44] labelled "political marriages" those marriages arranged around communal or national interests and gave numerous examples from European monarchies. Political marriages are but high profile illustrations of reciprocity, a principle found in marriages across the social class spectrum. Claude Levi-Strauss[45] suggested that marriage falls within the area of reciprocity, particularly in traditional societies: "The inclusion of women [as brides] in the number of reciprocal transactions from group to group and from tribe to tribe is such a general custom that a volume would not suffice to enumerate the instances in which it occurs." He also saw reciprocity in modern marriage: "marriage is everywhere considered as a particularly favorable occasion for opening a cycle of exchanges" where the bride is "the supreme gift amongst those that can only be obtained in the form of reciprocal gifts."[46]

The concept of reciprocity is implied in exchange theory as a relevant criterion in spouse selection. Using exchange theory to explain the influence of kin on spouse selection, sociologist F. Ivan Nye argued that "the greater the anticipated economic and social interdependence of the conjugal pair and their families of orientation, the greater control exercised by the family of orientation over the choice of spouse."[47] This assumption is widely supported by historical records of family and kinship network relations in Eastern and Western societies with one important proviso: the kinship network intervenes in spouse selection when the choice of spouse is seen as directly affecting the power, prestige and wealth not only of the groom and bride but of their respective families and kin. Borrowing from Gary R. Lee's[48] study of the effects of social networks on families, and observing families in traditional and "modern capitalist societies," Nye maintained that "the greater the control of economic and status resources by the family of orientation, the more effective [its] control of spousal partners" selection.[49]

This exchange theory assumption is supported by the situation in China during the Eastern Chou dynasty,[50] the Ming dynasty,[51] among aristocratic families in the sixth to ninth centuries,[52] the Sung period,[53] the Ch'ing period,[54] and even during the Communist regime.[55] The goal of a correct matching is found also in arranged marriages — which are the norm — in the Muslim countries in Southeast Asia, Brunei Darussalam, Myanmar, Malaysia and Indonesia and in the Muslim communities of China, Thailand and the Philippines.[56] The influence of kin on the selection of spouse when the socioeconomic status of the family of orientation is in the balance continues to be evident in contemporary societies.[57]

The fast pace of change is affecting parental influence on spouse selection although the relevance of socioeconomic status may not be completely relinquished. This seems to be the case in the global cities of Singapore and Hong Kong, and among urban families in South Korea, the Philippines, Thailand and Vietnam. South Korea is distancing from tradition. Confucian beliefs among South Korean families up to the mid-20th century supported parental authority and arranged marriages. But, as discussed earlier, it appears that the current South Korean trend is towards relative autonomy of the young person in his/her search for a suitable marriage partner. This conclusion is suggested by the findings from South Korean surveys on marriage conducted in the 1990s.[58] The main principle in spouse selection among urban families in the Philippines is romantic love and thus selecting a spouse is a decision that can only be made directly by the man or woman who wants to get married. As Belen T.G. Medina put it "Parents and kinsmen used to have complete control over ... when, whom and under what circumstances their children should marry" but values and beliefs have changed and "today ... young people themselves pick their mates and decide when to get married."[59]

This move from parental to personal choice of spouse does not mean distancing from the exchange theory concepts of reciprocity and gain. A distinctive situation in the Philippines shows that reciprocity and gain are serious considerations. The Filipino situation is, in Medina's words, "the mushrooming of the mail-order bride system" facilitated by a thriving "marriage market" involving agencies and clever use of international mass media advertising. Following reports of unhappy outcomes, Medina lamented,

> This long-distance match-making through catalogues and videotapes involves thousands of Filipino brides every year who leave for such countries as Australia, Germany, Belgium, Italy, Switzerland, England, and the United States to start a family. This commercialized form of mate selection has a socio-economic rather than a romantic basis since most brides expect financial or economic security out of their marriage. ... Congress has recently enacted a law banning the mail-order bride system ... With the strict enforcement of this law, it is expected that this commercialized mate selection system will be at least regulated.[60]

25

Understandably, state vigilance is not perfect and the Philippines' market of mail-order brides although less entrenched in the past few years, has not been eradicated. Similar market-driven international matchmaking services are found in other Asian countries. The changing economic nature of marriage choices is common in cities but it is also reaching rural areas in Asia. For example, attitudes towards marriage and spouse selection are changing among young people in Thai villages.[61] In Vietnam, the process of change has been driven by the state while traditional values on home and kin still persist. Describing the marriage situation in her country, Thi Le, a Vietnamese researcher, explains

> Regarding freedom of marriage, in general, young people nowadays have the right to decide on their marriage, consulting their parents and obtaining the latter's approval. This demonstrates the reconciliation or mutual concession between the old and the young generations, between tradition and modernity. According to Vietnamese custom, a marriage should be testified by the parents who usually take up the main expenses of the wedding ceremonies. If the parents do not agree with the marriage, it is very difficult to be organized, and may be regarded as legal but not conformable to common rule.[62]

There are two interesting departures from the general trends on the role of kin and personal and social reasons for marriage discussed in the preceding pages. One of these departures is the phenomenon of polygamy. In Asia today polygamy is found almost exclusively among Muslim communities where marriage is regulated by the Syariah law.[63] Although acceptable under Islamic law, the practice of polygamy creates difficulties for the spouses but especially for the wives. Being married to more than one spouse simultaneously may not necessarily represent reciprocity and emotional or socioeconomic security for all spouses in that union. In their study of contemporary polygamous families, Irwin Altman and Joseph Ginat found that many of their respondents "described life in a plural marriage as an unending struggle: everyday is a challenge, and one never completely resolves the conflicts, jealousies, and stresses that inevitably arise."[64]

The other departure regarding reasons for marriage and the role of kin is represented by the political upheavals of the first half of the 20th century involving the Communist revolutions. Most Asian countries have a traumatic history of wars, invasions and colonisation but it was the communist revolution leading to the creation of the Soviet Union that heralded radical and rapid changes in family structure and family relations in all the nations under Soviet domination or tutelage.[65] The impact of communism on the family was acutely felt in Vietnam and China where the traditional Confucian emphasis on family hierarchy, filial piety, and parental authority were essential in spouse selection, the timing of marriage and the locality of the wedded couple, among other aspects.

Referring to the changes in the Vietnamese family brought about by the Communist regime, Lai Tuong[66] recollected ancient Confucian traditions dictating a strict kinship hierarchy giving parents and the family a great deal of control over the individual. This traditional family system survived the prolonged colonisation by the French. But, Lai stresses, "Since August 1945 social turbulence [has] shaken the foundation of the ancient family institution."[67] In a similar vein, C.K. Yang described vividly the seriousness of the communist State intrusion into family relations in China and the disruption of the traditional role of parents in the marriage of the young. Writing seven years before the tumultuous role of the Red Guards youth in the Cultural Revolution, Yang lamented,

> Under the Communist regime young men and women are recruited in large numbers as paid workers or volunteers for a great variety of public activities which take them away from home part time or full time at an age from the early teens to the twenties, an age in which they would have remained very close to home in the traditional system ... [thus] the superiority of age [is] seriously undermined, with the young tending to move out of the range of family education and discipline, with the legal support of filial piety gone ... the basic concept of the marriage of the children [is] changed.[68]

In her analysis of the situation in China three decades later, Dai Keijing describes the same ideological and policy changes brought about by the Chinese Communist regime but asserts that "the old values and customs formed over thousands of years die hard" and "they tend to remain ... in people's minds" and influence their "daily life and behaviour."[69] The resilience of Chinese ancient traditions is also reiterated by married couples' decisions on the location and composition of their homes,[70] as I shall discuss later. Still, the communist regime gave women access to formal education and paid employment. These changes contributed to the subsequent increase in the age at marriage, which was reinforced by the rise in the legal marriage age. The Marriage Law set the minimum marriage age at 20 for women and 22 for men in 1987, up from 18 and 20 respectively in 1950.[71] It is highly possible that changes akin to those in China and Vietnam occurred in North Korean families as well. However this remains an educated assumption until sociological studies of North Korean families become available.

CULTURE AND WEDDING CELEBRATIONS

Before dealing with weddings and official marriage, let us consider briefly situations where these practices are circumvented. For a variety of personal reasons, some couples may decide to forgo the official marriage registration completely, or to postpone it briefly or indefinitely. They cohabitate instead. Is cohabitation in vogue today? Specific figures on cohabitation are not available for most countries around the world. There are no figures for Asian countries. The European Observatory on National Family Policies (EONFP) compiles statistics from the 15 Member States of the European Union on "non-married couples" and it appears that non-married couples are still a minority but their numbers may be increasing particularly in Denmark. However, the EONFP recommends caution when making inferences from their data because of two main problems: "the difficulty of establishing the nature of living together relationships"; and "because it [cohabitation] is not well accepted in some [European] countries, there is likely to be a degree of under-reporting."[72] The same two reasons seem to explain the dearth of information on cohabitation in Asia.

Having bypassed marriage registration, do cohabiting couples also evade the announcement of their decision to live together as a couple? Anecdotal evidence calls attention to the social and emotional significance of this announcement. A 32 year-old man was so infuriated by the attention his female cohabitating partner was receiving from another man at his company's party that he decided to inform the group she was his wife. She was surprised that he broke their agreement to keep their marital relationship private but, she revealed in the interview, she was at the same time very pleased to be acknowledged by him as his wife in front of their friends and colleagues. To her, his announcement made their marital relationship "official." Upon hearing the announcement, everyone congratulated them; some good friends brought 'wedding' gifts later. Both of them felt his impulsive public announcement had settled their 'marriage'. This situation might not be uncommon among cohabiting partners. They may not follow official marriage procedures or hold a wedding party, but the necessity to establish the boundaries of their relationship is compelling and may lead them to tell at least their closest friends about it, if and when they feel their relationship is relatively stable. A main obstacle to a social announcement is precisely the inherent instability of cohabitation, a contrasting feature compared to the typical long-term intention of partners in regular marriages. This brings us to wedding celebrations.

In addition to the importance of spouse selection, the wedding celebration is another aspect of marriage that illustrates permanency in the midst of change. The celebration of marriage as an important life event is well documented in accounts of ancient civilisations and throughout history.[73] A common and crucial thread across the rich tapestry of marriage rituals and customs around the world is the imperative to announce publicly as a joyous occasion the commitment of two persons to live together as husband and wife and, traditionally, the commitment of their respective families to support the newlyweds in keeping that pledge according to the customs of the community. This social meaning of marriage ceremonies is pursued even in cases when couples elope: the couple is expected to return and announce their wedding eventually, so that they can take their proper place as a married couple in the community and within their kinship network.

In his ethnography of Japanese weddings, Walter Edwards[74] describes the efforts of both the bride's and the groom's families to celebrate a wedding in a culturally appropriate manner. Depending on the cost of an elaborate ceremony, families may use a variety of affordable arrangements for the wedding celebration but doing away with the celebration is seldom, if ever, an option taken. The selection of a propitious date for the wedding is a very important part of the preparations. Ako Nanakarage[75] asserts that "the precise day" is chosen depending "on the *koyomi*, the astrological calendar, which is used for choosing days for special events" and spring and fall are the most preferred seasons for weddings. She estimates that, although modern features are common, about nine out of every ten weddings follow the "Shinto ceremony, a successful blend of ancient and relatively modern elements." These elements include the exchange of rings, "sharing of sake cups," "speeches by *nakodo*, very important guests, and several rituals including the cutting of the wedding cake," the *kanpai* or toast, and the banquet. Nanakarage reports that the average cost of a wedding is about five million Yen (in 1998) and could range from two million for a *jimikon* or simple wedding, to ten million Yen for a *hadekon* or "fabulous" wedding.

While Japanese families decide on their own if a given wedding celebration style is affordable or not, in the People's Republic of China, expensive customary wedding celebrations were prohibited by the state "as a waste of resources and because they were a feudal custom."[76] The practice is slowly returning particularly in the more affluent special economic zones in the South. Interestingly, in Communist Vietnam, the old custom of elaborate wedding celebrations has been revived lately.[77] W.R. Rishi offered a detailed description of traditional Asian marriage rituals and celebrations that were enforced up to the second half of the 20th century.[78]

Today the cultural home rituals particular to the couple's ethnic community are practised in a simplified form if at all, while close attention is placed on the public celebration. In addition to the purely secular aspect of the public celebrations, couples that are members of a religious community conduct a ceremony in their official place of worship (a church or temple) usually preceding the social celebration. Wedding celebrations in Taiwan, Hong Kong, Malaysia and Singapore typically involve a very large number of guests and elaborate banquets. Parents of the couple take the opportunity to invite not only the extended kin and personal friends but also work and business relations, people in important positions or perceived to be influential in the community, and well-placed acquaintances. The wedding dinner is the main public celebration of the marriage in Hong Kong, Taiwan, and for Singaporean Chinese families. They have a tea ceremony at home involving the close and the extended family and kin; and the religious ceremony (if any) is normally held in church amid family and fellow church members. Malay and Indian wedding celebrations in Singapore and Malaysia are typically larger in terms of the number of guests. It is common for Malay wedding banquets to be held in a large hall or location from mid-morning to late afternoon, so that the numerous guests can be well attended as they arrive individually or in groups continuously throughout the day. The immediate family members take turns with the hosting duties. Indian weddings also tend to involve a very large number of guests and large quantities of food, but in contrast to the Malay weddings, they are held for fewer hours.

MARRIAGE TRENDS

Patterns of family formation are revealed by trends in three aspects: the timing, postponement, and prevalence of marriage. Put as questions, these three aspects are: What is the age at which most people tend to marry? For how long do most people stay single? Is marriage popular? Before proceeding with the answers, I reiterate at this junction the cautionary note made in Chapter 1 about comparative statistics. The study covers China, Hong Kong (SAR of China), South Korea, Japan, Indonesia, the Philippines, Singapore, Thailand and Vietnam. These are the ten countries in Asia with the most accessible population data, although not all family-related data are available in all ten countries for the same time periods or years and at the same level of specificity. Still, for comparative analysis, the most reliable sources of population information on the ten countries are the statistics from the United Nations and other international agencies and their national population censuses.[79] An additional note of caution is that the use of total population census data precludes fine distinctions across ethnic communities and religious affiliations and between rural and urban residents.

Under normal circumstances, when one person proposes marriage to another, and the latter accepts the proposal, each one would assume it was an individual decision. Yet, there is a social dimension to the timing of the decision to marry. Sociological studies over the past 50 years have shown that level of education, job or career considerations, income generating opportunities, housing availability, and other factors, are relevant considerations. More importantly, kinship and social networks tend to influence the young person's decision by signalling the socially appropriate time to get married through social pressure and the subtle or open expression of approval or disapproval. This social pressure is the manifestation of cultural norms and beliefs on the meaning and purpose of marriage for the individual and the community. Examples of negative and positive social pressure are conveyed by A. B. Shostak's[80] description of the situation of never-married people in early and mid-20th century America. Single men were seen as "self-centered, irresponsible sowers of wild oats" who could "be redeemed only by marriage, and that as soon as possible" while the single women were regarded with pity as spinsters. Positive pressure to marry was exerted by presenting "wedded bliss" as the only route to happiness.

31

As the product of cultural values and norms, the socially defined appropriate age at marriage is altered over time with changes in social values. European and North American figures on marriage patterns over the past three decades show that despite variations across countries (for example, Spain, Portugal and Italy tend to differ from their Northern neighbours), there is a sustained trend towards later marriages and a slightly decreasing proportion of people getting married while, as indicated earlier, there is a hint of preference for cohabitation either as a prelude to marriage or as a permanent arrangement.[81,82] Reflecting value changes in Western countries, these arrangements are typically consensual unions. In contrast to the Montaillou villagers of old whom we visited at the beginning of this chapter, by the end of the 1990s cohabitation and marriage in Europe were "characterized by low female domesticity, a higher age at marriage, higher female education levels, more career-oriented individuals and careful mate selection processes"[83] carried out by both men and women. Reversing a traditional pattern, the Swedish experience of late is that cohabitation may lead to parenthood and eventually to marriage, in that order. [84]

Is the timing of marriage different in Asia? Speaking of Asia as a unit must be done with caution because both diversity and similarity lend blasts of colour to the Asian landscape reflecting a rich ethnic and religious mosaic. For example, differential legal procedures in marriage registration and other family matters exist in Singapore, Malaysia and other Southeast Asian countries with Muslim and non-Muslim communities such as Indonesia, Brunei, the Philippines and Thailand.[85,86] Singapore and Malaysia for example have two legal systems, English Common Law, and the Islamic or Muslim law governing "the Muslim community in religious, matrimonial, and related matters."[87, 88] As far as possible, it is advisable to examine data on family life transitions such as the registration of marriages and divorces closely in terms of ethnicity and religion. Let us use Singapore to illustrate this point. The analysis of local variations across ethnic and religious groups in Singapore shows that the average age at marriage of Muslim brides and grooms is lower than that of non-Muslim Chinese, Malay, and Indian grooms and brides. Still, these ethnic communities and religious groups shared the same steady trend towards later marriages in the last three decades of the 20th century.[89] They are converging towards a common pattern of later marriages among Singaporeans: grooms are still older than brides but the ethnic and religious differences in the actual age at marriage seen 30 years ago are diminishing[90] and the timing of marriage continues its upward trend among both men and women irrespective of their ethnicity or religious affiliation in Singapore.[91]

Unfortunately, there are no comparative data on ethnicity and religion for all Asian countries or even for the ten countries in this study. The comparable data are from the total populations of the ten countries but the figures reveal trends worthy of note, nonetheless. Chart 2.1 illustrates the situation of singlehood in seven of the ten Asian countries (China, Malaysia, and Vietnam are not included in Chart 2.1 because there are no data for 1995/96). Reading the chart from the bottom up you find each country's figures first for men in 1990-91 and 1995-96 and then for women in 1990-91 and 1995-96. The proportions of single men and women in the age cohort 30-34 changed from 1991-1992 to 1995-1996, but not with the same intensity and in the same direction in all countries. Hong Kong, Japan, and Singapore had the highest proportion of single men and women in both time periods while Indonesia had the lowest.

CHART 2.1 PROPORTION OF SINGLE MEN AND WOMEN IN AGE COHORT 30-34: CHANGE FROM 1990/91 TO 1995/96

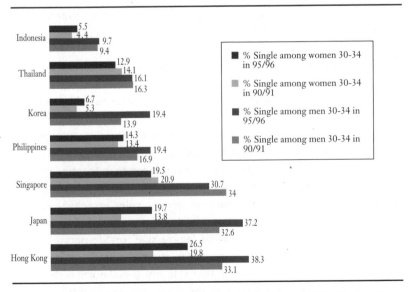

Source: Calculated from United Nations Statistics Division (2002). No data for 1995/96 were available for China, Malaysia and Vietnam.

Another noteworthy detail in Chart 2.1 is that there was an increase in the proportion of single men and women from 1990-91 to 1995-96 in all the countries except Singapore, where the trend was reversed, and Thailand, where it was halted. The decrease in the proportion of singles among Thai men aged 30-34 was negligible, from 16.3 per cent to 16.1 per cent. Among Thai women aged 30-34, the decrease was from 14.1 per cent to 12.9 per cent in the same time period. The decrease was slightly more evident among Singaporean women aged 30-34 (from 20.9 per cent in 1990-91 to 19.5 per cent in 1995-96) but was significant among their male counterparts (from 34 per cent to 30.7 per cent). Singapore has a distinctive approach to the promotion of marriage as indicated earlier, and this decrease in the proportion of singles may tentatively be seen as an indication that the efforts of the state in promoting marriage are bearing some fruit, particularly among men. To find a marriage partner when you are in your 30s is apparently easier if you are a man than if you are a woman. An alert observer of cultural nuances would not find this surprising because, if there is one generalisation about Asia that may be made with just a very slight risk of being wrong, it is that men are expected to initiate a serious relationship and are given more flexibility in their approach, while women still shy away from taking the initiative in a conspicuous manner as they have narrower structures of opportunity. I elaborate on this gender issue in Chapter 5.

In contrast to the situation in most Western countries, this gender-role distinction on socially acceptable behaviour for men and women still prevails despite advances in many aspects of life, even in high income economies like Japan[92,93] and Singapore[94] or in ideologically egalitarian countries such as Vietnam or China. A study on marriage patterns in rural China found that although the goal is to marry someone better off outside one's village, "it is almost inconceivable for an unmarried woman to show up in a distant rural village as a stranger and try to arrange for her own marriage."[95] Social values on gender roles are changing but everyday language throughout Asia reveals the persistence of traditional norms. A woman would be labelled 'aggressive' or 'desperate' if she ventured to propose marriage instead of waiting (demurely or not) to be approached with the question. Another relevant social norm is that men prefer to marry younger women thus the attractiveness of a single woman as a potential bride diminishes as she ages. The Japanese refer to the right age to marry (it was 23 to 25 for women in the late 1980s) as *tekireiki* or *konki* and the unflattering term *Kurisumasu keri* meaning "Christmas cake" is applied to a "woman who doesn't marry when the time is ripe" because "nobody wants either one after the twenty-fifth."[96] The youngest generation of adult women in Asian cities today (the 20-25 cohort) are portrayed in the media as determined to set their own agenda and to demolish restrictive gender values. Looking on, many of their older sisters remember they entered adult life with the same resolve.

The average age at marriage provides a glimpse of what is happening to the socially acceptable timing of marriage. Chart 2.2 indicates that for the period 1991-1997, the average age at marriage for women in the ten Asian countries ranged from 22 (in China, Malaysia and Indonesia) to 28 (in Hong Kong). The average age at marriage for men ranged from 24 (China and Vietnam) to 30 (Hong Kong, Japan and Singapore). As most people in the ten Asian countries get married between the ages of 22 and 30, the marital status of people aged 30 to 34 is significant as the unmarried in this age cohort would be a minority who are pushing the subtle boundary of singlehood beyond socially acceptable limits. The social pressure to marry intensifies for single men, and more so for single women, over 30. The timing of marriage may appear to be an individual's decision but it is not entirely so. Chart 2.2 illustrates the impact of socioeconomic factors on the age at marriage using the Human Development Index (HDI).[97] The HDI scores range from 1 (lowest) to 100 (highest) in a scale of human development. The HDI scores of the ten countries vary significantly, from 67.2 (Indonesia) to 92.8 (Japan).

As shown in Chart 2.2, socioeconomic factors represented in the HDI scores play an important part in the timing of first marriage. The correlation between HDI and the average age at marriage is positive and very strong, both for men ($r = .957$; $p = .0001$) and for women ($r = .904$; $p = .0001$). The higher a country's HDI scores, the higher the age at first marriage. Countries with high HDI scores offer better technical and tertiary educational opportunities to young people and overall improved life chances compared to countries with low HDI scores. Accordingly, young men and women in high HDI countries have a better and wider range of educational and job opportunities when starting their lives as adults. They may choose to postpone marriage in favour of upgrading their skills, finding a suitable job, and embarking on their careers. As a country moves up the socioeconomic ladder, norms are transformed. In the more developed

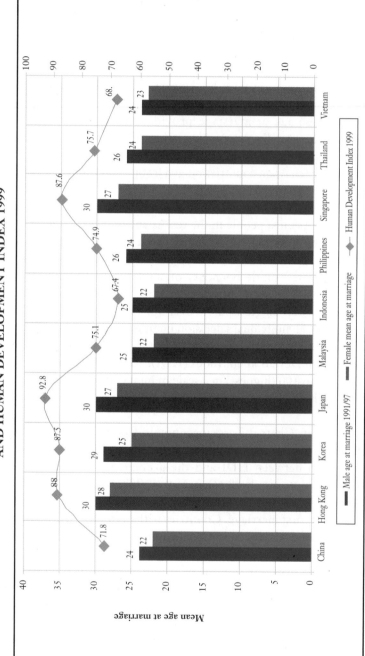

CHART 2.2   FEMALE AND MALE MEAN AGE AT MARRIAGE 1991/1997,
AND HUMAN DEVELOPMENT INDEX 1999

Sources: Female and male mean age at marriage calculated from United Nations Statistics Division (2002) except the Malaysian figures that were estimated from other sources. The Human Development Index 1999 scores are from ESCAP (2002).

Note: Pearson correlation of Human Development Index 1999 with female mean age at marriage r = .904, with male mean age at marriage r = .957; p = .0001 for both correlations.

countries (those with high HDI scores) marriage may be a crucial personal life goal for young men and women but, receiving a diploma or degree, getting the first paid job, or obtaining the first career-track promotion, become important pre-marriage rites of passage into adulthood. In contrast, educational training and job opportunities are fewer or non-existent in less developed countries (those with low HDI scores), especially in the rural areas. Thus marriage has less competition as *the* rite of passage into adulthood for young people in these countries. Marriage actually becomes an advantage in farming communities or in the informal urban economy (cottage industries, produce and cooked food hawking, and the like) where family members collaborate in income-generating activities.

The second marriage trend is the postponement of marriage ascertained by the proportion of single men and women in the age cohort 30-34. I use the term 'postponement' to suggest that the proportion of single people in a country's population at any given time is not an indication of the demise of marriage but rather of the dynamic nature of family formation as it responds to and influences other aspects of social life. Charts 2.3 and 2.4 illustrate this point with the combined influence of wealth and level of urbanisation on the proportion of single women and single men aged 30-34.

The level of urbanisation of the ten Asian countries is closely associated with their level of wealth as measured by the gross domestic product (GDP) per capita.[98] With the exception of Vietnam, and of the global cities of Singapore and Hong Kong,[99] all the other seven countries saw an increase in urbanisation from 1990 to 2000. But the pattern of differentiation remains: the least urbanised country (and thus that with the largest rural population) in 2000 was Thailand (only 19.8 per cent of its population was living in cities) followed closely by Vietnam (24.1per cent) and then China (32.1 per cent) and Indonesia (40.9 per cent). At the top of the urbanisation scale are Singapore (100 per cent) and Hong Kong (100 per cent), followed by South Korea (81.9 per cent) and Japan (78.8 per cent). Malaysia (57.4 per cent) and the Philippines (58.6 per cent) are in an intermediary position. Countries with high levels of urbanisation tend to be relatively richer than others ($r = .810$; $p = .0001$). But people living in cities are subjected to positive aspects (such as proximity to jobs, services, and to social networks) as well as to negative aspects (environmental pollution, space restrictions, crime, high cost of living, among other things).[100]

Still, as far as finding a marriage partner is concerned, one would assume that cities offer a better bet than rural areas. By the sheer number of people and the variety of social networks, cities appear to offer a better chance of making contact with the field of eligibles. Why, then, are the proportions of 30-34 years old single men and women higher in countries with the highest level of urbanisation? The answer lies in the level of economic development and increased opportunities for educational training and career advancement found in more urbanised countries, as explained earlier. Charts 2.3 and 2.4 confirm the findings in the two previous charts: wealthier, more advanced and urbanised countries offer young people appealing alternatives to *early* marriage not found in less developed countries.

CHART 2.3   WEALTH, URBANISATION, AND PROPORTION OF SINGLE WOMEN AGED 30-34

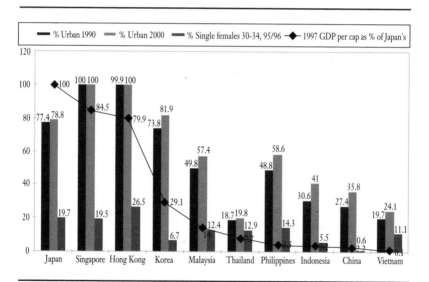

Source: Calculated from United Nations (2000); and United Nations Development Programme (2002). Per cent urban is the proportion of total population living in cities as defined by the respective countries. Single women percentages for China, Malaysia and Vietnam are for 1990/91 as their figures for 1995/96 were not available. Pearson correlation of 1997 GDP per cap and per cent single females 30-34 in 95/96 is r = .767; p = .044. No significant association with level of urbanisation was found.

CHART 2.4   WEALTH, URBANISATION, AND PROPORTION OF
SINGLE MEN AGED 30-34

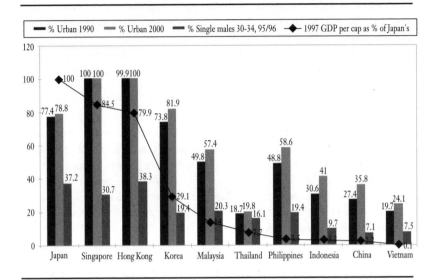

Source: Calculated from United Nations (2000) and United Nations Development Programme (2002). Per cent urban is the proportion of total population living n cities as defined by the respective countries. Single men percentages for China, Malaysia and Vietnam are for 1990/91 as their figures for 1995/96 were not available. Pearson correlation of per cent single males 30-34 in 95/96 with 1997 GDP per cap and is r = .938; p = .002. And with level of urbanisation in 2000 is r = .777; p = .040.

An important additional finding in these charts is the different role that socioeconomic factors play on men and women's marriage postponement. The level of urbanisation influences significantly marriage postponement among men (Chart 2.4) but not among women in the age group 30-34 (Chart 2.3). The association is significant only among women aged 20-24 as shown in Chart 2.5. A brief note on this issue is in order. Chart 2.5 compares marriage postponement among younger (20-24) and older (30-34) single women in terms of the ten countries' scores on the Gender-Related Development Index (GDI). The GDI measures inequalities between men and women in life expectancy, adult literacy, combined primary, secondary and tertiary education enrolment, and estimated earned income.[101] The GDI ranges from 0 (lowest gender equality) to 100 (highest gender equality). Chart 2.5 illustrates the strong correlation (r = .982; p =.0001) of GDI with the proportion of single women aged 20-24 and the absence of correlation with the proportion of single women aged 30-34. This means that women in their early 20s are inclined to postpone marriage to get further education and job experience. But these reasons are no longer influential among older single women (those over 30 years of age) who may have already attained their desired educational qualifications and job experience. The reasons for their postponement of marriage are likely to be in the realm of gender values and gender stereotypes. The self-improvement opportunities found in more developed and urbanised countries influence significantly men's postponement of marriage well into their 30s. A highly educated single man holding an important career position is considered a very valuable marriage partner. But the opposite could be said about a woman with similar attributes. This is because by virtue of their education and jobs, professional women contradict traditional gender norms on the subordination of women whereby wives should be younger and less educated than their husbands. This difference in the situation of men and women is congruent with the gender values dominant in Asia discussed earlier (see also Chapter 5).

CHART 2.5   PROPORTION OF SINGLE WOMEN IN AGE COHORTS 20-24 AND 30-34, 1995/1996 AND GENDER-RELATED DEVELOPMENT INDEX

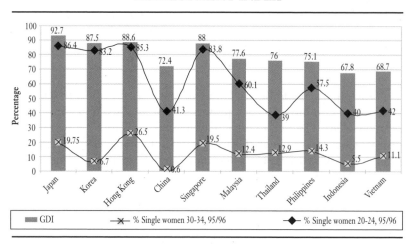

Source: United Nation Development programme (2002: 222-225) for GDI. Data on single women calculated from United Nations Statistics Division (2002).
Notes: Single women percentages for China, Malaysia and Vietnam are for 1990/91 as their figures for 1995/96 were not available. Pearson correlations: Proportion of single women 20-24 with GDI is $r = .982$, $p = .0001$; Proportion of single women 30-34 with GDI is not statistically significant.

The final question on marriage trends refers to the prevalence of marriage: Is marriage popular? Numerous voices have been heard over the past half a century forecasting the demise of marriage in Western countries. Some contemporary writers assert the future of marriage (and of the family) is bleak even in Asia, referring to figures on fertility decline, proportion of single people, and increasing divorce rates in Japan[102] and even Indonesia.[103] Other observers see hope in state intervention to stop and even to reverse these trends.[104] Against this background, the population figures from the ten Asian countries in Chart 2.6 responds to the question "Is marriage popular?" with a resounding "Yes." Between eight to nine out of every ten men and every ten women aged 40-44 are married in all the ten countries. These high proportions of married people confirm that marriage is not forgone but postponed. The figures on younger men and women (30-34 years old) correspond to the trend in postponement: the proportion of married people in these age groups is slightly lower in most countries but significantly lower in Japan, Hong Kong and Singapore. These are the three countries with the highest HDI scores. Postponement of marriage among people in their early 30s is lowest or negligible in China and Vietnam.

CHART 2.6 PROPORTION OF MARRIED MEN AND WOMEN IN AGE COHORTS 30-34 AND 40-44, 1995-1996

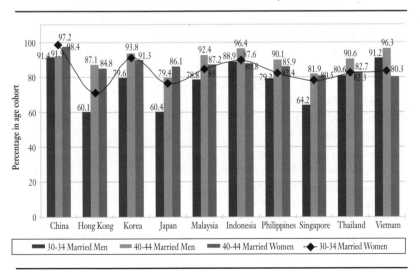

Source: Calculated from United Nations Statistics Division (2002). Figures for China, Malaysia and Vietnam are for 1990/1991 as the 1995/96 figures were not available.

SUMMARY

This chapter has offered a portrayal of dating, spouse selection, and marriage in ten Asian countries: China, Hong Kong, South Korea, Japan, Malaysia, Indonesia, the Philippines, Singapore, Thailand, and Vietnam. These countries are richly varied in many respects but similar features are discovered when one pays attention to the process of family formation across the region. Some relevant sociological concepts and approaches have been applied to facilitate our understanding of the relevance and significance of marriage in Asian communities. Socioeconomic development and concomitant changes in values and attitudes are taking place but some fundamental aspects of family formation, such as the importance of marriage, remain.

ENDNOTES

1. See Ladurie (1978).
2. See Gies and Gies (1987:178-185).
3. See Gies and Gies 1987:179-182).
4. See Gies and Gies (1987:181).
5. See Gies and Gies (1987:184).
6. See Edwards (1989:53-58).
7. See Edwards (1989:58-76).
8. See Miyamoto (2001:12).
9. See Raymo (2001).
10. See *Sunday Times* (1991:12).
11. As aptly explained by Bob Mullan (1984).
12. See Levy (1965:72) cited by Mullan (1984:ii).
13. See Mullan (1984).
14. See Kelly (2002).
15. See Martin (1997).
16. See Dai (1990:182-185).
17. See Barrett and Li (1999:66-68).
18. See Barrett and Li (1999:67).
19. See Barrett and Li (1999:79).
20. See Barrett and Li (1999:67).
21. See Higgins, Zheng, Liu and Sun (2002); and Pimentel (2000:44).
22. See *Straits Times* (1998).
23. See Ting and Chiu (2002).
24. See Inoue (1998:25).

25. See Choe (1998:46-56).
26. See Choe (1998:56-59).
27. See Bumpass and Mason (1998:242-243).
28. As explained in the SDU's newsletter *Link* (1988).
29. See *Link* (1996:18).
30. See *Link* (1997:7).
31. As advertised in the Civil Service newsletter *Challenge* (2003).
32. See Chan (1997:18).
33. See SDU (2003).
34. See *Straits Times* (1988).
35. See Ang (1995:17).
36. See SDU (2003).
37. See Quah (1998:113-115).
38. See SDU (2003).
39. See Ratarasam (1990:291-295). This trend is confirmed by Bumroongsook (1995: 172).
40. See Ratarasam (1990:293).
41. See Jones (2001:75-77).
42. See Braudel (1973); Habakkuk (1974); Yang (1959); Gies and Gies (1987); Casey (1989); Dai (1990); Ratarasarn (1990); Kumagai (1990); and McDaniel and Tepperman (2000).
43. See Quah (1998:84-101).
44. See Braudel (1973).
45. See Levi-Strauss ([1957] 1974:9-12).
46. See Levi-Strauss ([1957] 1974:11-12).
47. See Nye (1979:28-29).
48. See Lee (1979).
49. See Nye (1979:29).
50. See Thatcher (1991).
51. See Holmgren (1991).
52. See Ebrey (1991).
53. See Chaffee (1991).
54. See Rawski (1991) and Mann (1991).
55. See Lavey (1991) and Ocko (1991).
56. See for example Heaton (1996); Hassan (2002); and Kling (1995).
57. See Adams (1986); Goody (1990); and Klein and White (1996).
58. See Choe (1998) and Inoue (1998).
59. See Medina (1991:243).
60. See Medina (1991:244).

61. See Jackson and Cook (1999); Schvaneveldt, Young and Schvaneveldt (2001); Bumroongsook (1995: 21-67).
62. See Thi (1999:63).
63. See Hassan (2002).
64. See Altman and Ginat (1996:436-437).
65. See Yang (1959); Boh (1990); Dai (1990); and Horna (1990).
66. See Lai (1991:5-6).
67. See Lai (1991:6).
68. See Yang (1959:102-103).
69. See Dai (1990:175).
70. See Yi (2002).
71. See Dai (1990:177); and Barrett and Li (1999).
72. See Ditch, Barnes, Bradshaw and Kilkey (1998:12)
73. See Gies and Gies (1987); Casey (1989); Middleton (1972); Reiss (1972); Habakkuk (1972); Rishi (1970); and Dai (1990).
74. See Edwards (1989:36-42).
75. See Nanakarage (1998).
76. See Barrett and Li (1999:67).
77. See Thi (1999:62).
78. See Rishi (1969).
79. This section covers data on marriage trends compiled into its Common Database by the United Nations Statistics Division from population censuses of the ten countries. See United Nations Statistics Division (2002).
80. See Shostak (1987:355),
81. See Ditch, Barnes, Bradshaw and Kilkey (1998).
82. See McDaniel and Tepperman (2000).
83. See Gonzalez-Lopez (2002:25).
84. See Bjornberg (2001).
85. See Jones (1994:44-58).
86. See Hassan (2002:23-24).
87. See Chan (1986:20).
88. See Ahmad Ibrahim (1984).
89. See Quah (1998:87).
90. See Quah (1998:88-89).
91. See Quah (1998:35-44).
92. See Joseph (1993:40).
93. See Cherry (1991:40-41; 52-54).
94. See Quah (1998:145-175).
95. See Gilmartin and Tan (2002:209).
96. See Cherry (1991:53).

97. The Human Development Index is "a composite index" of a country's average achievement in life expectancy at birth, adult literacy rate, the "combined gross enrolment ratio" in primary, secondary and tertiary education, and the Gross Domestic Product per capita in US$. For a detailed explanation of the HDI calculation see United Nations Development Programme (2002:253).

98. For the definition and calculation of GDP see World Bank (2003:247).

99. For a comparative analysis of Hong Kong and Singapore as global cities see Quah (1997).

100. See World Bank (2003:107).

101. For the definition and calculation of the GDI see United Nations Development Programme (2002:255-256).

102. See Ochiai (1997).

103. See Hull (2003:61).

104. See Ogawa (2003).

CHAPTER 3

Parenthood Under Siege?

As every parent knows, the birth of a child is extraordinarily meaningful. It is seldom, if ever, a neutral event and under certain circumstances, it may not necessarily be a happy one. Besides this personal dimension, parenthood has also a social dimension: procreation has become a national issue in an increasing number of countries around the world. To appreciate the nuances of parenthood, both its personal and social dimensions are considered jointly in this chapter after presenting the main trends in parenthood in ten Asian countries. I begin by reviewing, albeit briefly, a few relevant concepts or ideas on social policy and on family.

IDEAS ON SOCIAL POLICY

Three basic assumptions on social policy are pertinent to the discussion of parenthood.[1] First, who is serving whom? Developments in the past century show that social policy in most countries has been characterised by their governments' attempt to use the family as an instrument of social change and economic development. Second, the appeal that families have for the state as vehicles of socioeconomic change does not ordinarily induce governments to formulate a comprehensive and consistent policy agenda or plan of action to serve families. Third, in the absence of a consistent policy agenda to bolster people's family life, families are typically confronted by disparate and even contradictory policies designed to attain political or economic goals.

These assumptions are best examined in the context of family policy. The common meaning of the term family policy is 'anything governments do that affect families.' I follow a more specific definition. Family policy is defined in this discussion as a comprehensive plan of action formulated to reflect shared social values and to attain defined social goals concerning the nation's families. While examples of a comprehensive family policy are rare, it is more common to find countries with an array of policies and regulations that affect the family either directly (when their main goal is to modify or change family behaviour) or indirectly if their main target is not the family.[2] In reference to the ideas of Lasswell[3] and Kahn,[4] I propose that the formulation of public policy on families requires first, explicit and defined social goals concerning the nation's families; and second, that these goals be based on relatively clear and shared values on the type or types of families that the country wants to maintain and encourage. Thus, family policy encompasses plans of action formulated to reflect these social values and to attain these social goals.[5]

In most contemporary societies the decisions to get married and to become a parent are regarded as entirely private matters normally pondered on and made in the intimacy of a couple's relationship. Thus, it is not easy for people to be confronted with the idea that their private decisions might have negative consequences for the society at large. In addition to this sensitive issue of the boundary between the private and public domains, there is another serious concern. To wrestle with the collective consequences of these private decisions is to bring marriage and parenthood into the realm of public policy, an action that assumes the population's consensus not only on social goals and family types as indicated earlier, but also on the principle that such type(s) of family could not be attained without the modification of private choices concerning marriage and/or parenthood. Given the great internal diversity in ethnic, religious and ideology values and norms in most countries in the 21st century, bringing private family decisions into the public arena is highly controversial. The likelihood of reaching consensus on the type (or types) of family to support and on the acknowledgement of the public consequences of private marriage and procreation choices decreases as the level of ethnic, religious, and ideological diversity of the population increases.

Fuelling the controversy is the idea of government intervention. One extreme view is that legislation of whatever kind is intrinsically harmful to family life. The opposite position is that only the state is powerful enough to mobilise the resources needed to solve serious problems affecting families today such as poverty, marital breakdown, single parenthood, child support, family violence and other crises. There are, of course, many moderate views between these two extreme positions. For example, I. Tallman[6] rightly asserted that policies should provide the necessary conditions or "opportunity structure" to ensure the well-being of the family and, at the same time, to protect the family from excessive interference or restrain by the state. The key arguments in the controversy[7] may be summarised by focusing on some of their best-known representatives.

On the side of the opponents of state intervention one may find Lasch[8] and Donzelot[9] who stress the undesirability of social control or policing of the family; and Steiner[10] and Henslin[11] who are concerned about what in their view is the almost certain inability of any complex society, including its politicians and scholars, to identify family goals and to formulate ways of attaining them in a manner that would satisfy everyone. On the part of the advocates of family policy, the most prominent pioneering work is that of Kamerman and Kahn[12] who documented and discussed the rich variety of family policies found around the world addressed to different types of families and family problems. While theirs was a minority position in the 1970s and 1980s, well-known sociologists have followed their lead and reassessed the potentially valuable contributions of informed social policy in democratic societies.[13]

The moderate position in this controversy states, basically, that social policies may be an effective instrument to help families facing certain kinds of problems but that, in order to avoid blunders and excesses, the limits of state intervention should be clearly demarcated. Three of the representatives of this view are Brigitte Berger, Peter Berger and Nathan Glazer. Berger and Berger[14] add an important qualification to the use of family policies as a vehicle to help families in need: priority must be given to family support networks already present in the community and thus legislation should be applied only as a last resort. Glazer's[15] reflections on the limitations and pitfalls of social policy add significance to the Bergers' recommendation. From the moderate perspective, family policies may be beneficial to families only if they are applied judiciously at two levels, general and specific. At the general level, government legislation may prevent the disruption of family life by providing or reinforcing the social conditions needed for family growth (employment opportunities, affordable housing, sanitary conditions, educational facilities, basic healthcare and the like). At the specific level, legislation may be applied to provide special services (for example, income supplements, medical insurance, counselling, child care services, transport allowances, home care for the aged sick, and other welfare services) to families facing precise problems.

Most people would agree with the need for the general level of intervention. After all, governments are there to manage resources and to help to distribute them fairly according to the predominant ideology of the nation. However, the second level of intervention is more controversial. It is worth repeating that perhaps the most significant feature of these specially tailored policies ought to be the element of choice. Even the best planned welfare policies might have unexpected and negative consequences. The good intentions of policy planners become a red tape nightmare for unemployed parents searching for ways to feed their families; or single working mothers in need of reliable and safe child care services; or adult children unable to cope with chronically ill parents. Because of inflexible rules or absence of choice, anxious individuals may discover at the bureaucratic counter that the price of state assistance to their families may be too high (it may range from giving up their privacy to losing custody of their children).

These are, in broad brush strokes, the main positions in the controversy on family policy. Analysts who hold moderate views are more aware of the dangers of legislation even when applied to specific services, than the proponents of state intervention although the latter group acknowledges the double edge of legislation. Also, contrary to those who oppose legislation, the moderates agree that there are situations under which certain policies may be, at least the best, if not the only, available way of helping families.

The trend towards a positive perception of family policy by societies that were traditionally opposed to state intervention in family life became evident in the 1990s. A good illustration of the recognition of family policy as a potentially useful instrument to enhance and secure family well-being was the establishment in 1989 of the European Observatory on National Family Policies as a "collaborative venture" among social scientists from Member States of the European Union. In 1996, the Committee of Experts appointed by the European Union recommended a "European Bill of Rights" which includes "the right to protection for the family" and the recommendations "to enhance the European model of citizenship" including "the need for practical proposals which will enable men and women to reconcile family responsibilities with paid employment."[16] Central to that preoccupation is the need to improve the level of child care assistance required by working parents but some European countries are currently concerned with declining fertility as well.

The concept of family policy is applied in this chapter to the discussion of population growth policies in Asia as those policies impinge upon the couple's private decisions and behaviour on procreation.

IDEAS ON FAMILY

Sociology offers a wealth of conceptual insights or analytical tools relevant to the study of family. Four sets of conceptual insights are particularly useful for the analysis of family in general and parenthood in particular. They are Max Weber's[17] *ideal type* and *household*; James Coleman's[18] *primordial structure* and *social capital*; Marion Levy's[19] *ideal* and *actual* family forms; and Pauline Boss'[29] and Kay Pasley's[21] concept of *boundary ambiguity*.

Weber[22] proposed the "ideal type" as a "methodological device" that would solve his dual concern for fruitful theoretical and methodological approaches to the understanding of the meaning of social action. By identifying the essential or "conceptually pure" elements of social action, the ideal type helps to elucidate "deviations" and the richness in variations of social action under changing conditions and among different social actors and groups. Applying the ideal type method to the concepts of household and marriage, Weber considered "the relationships between father, mother and children, established by a stable sexual union" as fundamentally "natural" relationships. Nevertheless, he clarified,

> ...separated from the household as a unit of economic maintenance, the sexually-based relationship between husband and wife, and the physiologically determined relationship between father and children are wholly unstable and tenuous....Of all the relations arising from sexual intercourse, only the mother-child relationship is "natural" because it is a biologically based household unit that lasts until the child is able to search for means of subsistence on his own.[23]

Weber conceived the household as primarily an economic organisation, and marriage as an institution embedded in the household but also serving as a bridge between the household and the larger community. These, then, are two important contributions made by Weber to our understanding of parenthood: (a) the idea that the most explicit and direct way in which community regulations penetrate the household is through the social sanctioning of legitimate marriage and, correspondingly, the legitimating of children; and (b) the suggestion that of the four main relationships observed within the household (husband-wife, father-child, mother-child, and sibling relationships) in society, the mother-child relationship is the most significant and enduring family relationship. [24]

The second set of relevant analytical tools is offered by James Coleman's[25] theory of purposive action, particularly his concepts of "primordial structure" and "social capital." Coleman sees modern societies as composed of "two parallel organisational structures." One is "a primordial structure based on, and derived from the family." The second one is "a newer structure composed of purposive corporate actors wholly independent of the family" and consisting of "economic organizations [...] single-purpose voluntary associations, and governments."[26]

A related concept is "social capital" (also discussed in Chapter 4) which Coleman defines by contrasting it to "human capital" thus: "Social capital...is created when the relations among persons change in ways that facilitate action" but "human capital" is "embodied in the skills and knowledge acquired by an individual; social capital is even less tangible, for it is embodied in the relations among persons."[27] Perhaps the most useful of Coleman's ideas to the analysis of parenthood is the loss in social capital brought about by the changes undergone by the family in modern industrial societies. Coleman[28] argues that the necessary social capital required by children and youth for their development is provided "in three aspects of social structure" that support the parent-child relationship: the strength of the parent-child bond; the shelter provided by a solid connection between the parents; and "closure," that is, the steadfastness and continuity of that tripartite relationship over time. Coleman explains "closure" in this manner:

> Closure is present when [...] the adults are able to observe the child [...] compare notes, talk to each other about the child, and establish norms. The closure of the network can provide the child with support and rewards from additional adults that reinforce those received from the first and bring about norms and sanctions that could not be instituted by a single adult alone.[29]

Coleman was of the opinion that increased economic development and modernisation tend to weaken all or some of these three aspects to the detriment of family social capital.

Weber[30] focused on the household and identified the mother-child relationship as the essential component of family. In contrast, Coleman[31] asserts that the child needs significant relationships with both parents and, at any rate, with more than one dependable adult. One of the key reasons for the difference in views between Weber and Coleman is their different angles of analysis. Coleman's attention is not on constructing an ideal type of the household, as Weber's was, but on the needs of children and youth in modern societies. Coleman suggests that the social arrangements distinctive of the modern industrial society, or "new social structure," produce negative consequences for children and youth due to a drastic reduction in the social capital they should receive from the child-adult relationship. As working fathers and working mothers occupy most of their time in the purposive or corporate structure and away from the family, the "intensity" of the child-adult relationship diminishes. This process "takes away from the child some of the psychic investment in the child by mother and father" who "transfer" that psychic investment to their jobs.[32]

Some critics may take Coleman's view on the negative consequences of a reduction in social capital children should receive as an indictment on beleaguered working parents who are simply trying to overcome the constraints of the social system. It appears as if structural constraints affecting parents as well as the parents' motivations and attitudes, do not receive due consideration in Coleman's framework. In spite of these and other questions, Coleman's ideas are an important conceptual contribution towards the elucidation of the social meaning of parenthood in contemporary societies. Just as with any theory, his concepts need to be tested and refined through further conceptual analysis and empirical research. In this connection, Coleman offers six suggestions on how to grapple with the problem of measurement of social capital. His six indicators are: (1) the presence of both parents, where absence indicates 'low intensity' of social capital; (2) number of siblings, whereby a small number means large social capital per child; (3) parents-children talk about personal matters whereby lack of talk would mean low attention given by parent to child; (4) mother's employment outside the home before child enters school with a 'yes' meaning less time given to child and lower strength of the relationship; (5) parents' interest in the child attending college, with a 'yes' answer indicating parental interest in the child's future; and (6) the number of times a child has changed school because the family has moved, as "an indirect measure of all three forms of closure."[33] A methodological expansion of these indicators would be to ascertain the level or degree of social capital investment of mothers compared to that of fathers and how to detect changes in social capital investment by both parents over time.

The third set of conceptual tools I want to discuss is Marion Levy's[34] dual typology of *actual* and *ideal* family forms. By applying Weber's ideal type method to his cross-cultural study of family structures, Levy was able to identify two co-existing types of family forms. In any society, the *ideal* family form is that type of family most people wish to have; it is a vision of the family's structure and relationships (for example, what is a good parent and a good spouse, what is the most desirable number of children, what is the best family living arrangement, and who are the closest members of one's family), forged by the community's prevalent cultural values and ideology, whether political, religious, or both. In contrast, the *actual* family form is the type of family ordinary people in the community can 'afford' to have, given the real constraints of their socioeconomic and political situation and their society's level of technology.

Levy illustrated his concepts of ideal and actual family with examples from China. He found there that the mandate of cultural tradition emphasised the feudal ideal of the extended family based on the economic organisation of the household-cum-family business (approximating Weber's ideal type of the household described earlier) under centralised patriarchal authority, and following the distribution of authority and power strictly along the principles of gender (with males dominant) and age (with older members dominant). Historical records indicate that, as expected, this ideal family form requiring land ownership and an expanding family business to accommodate and feed the growing extended family, could only be afforded by the wealthy and the aristocracy in ancient China. The actual family type among the overwhelming majority of the Chinese population up to the early part of the 20th century was most likely smaller and sustained primarily by the hired manual labour of its adult members, both males and females, and among the very poor, even by the contributions of child labour or by the sale of young daughters to other families.[35]

In addition to his specific typology of ideal versus actual family forms, Levy[36] contributed another insight relevant to this discussion. He suggested that actual structural conditions in a society may facilitate or impede the realisation of the ideal family form. An inference from this assumption is, of course, that the ideal and actual family forms in any society are not static but are subject to change, just like any other form of social action. Moreover, if Festinger's[37] principle of cognitive dissonance is extended to collectivities, we may expect that in societies where the discrepancy between ideal and actual family forms exceeds a certain level of tolerance in the community, people's vision of the ideal family will become more attuned to the real structural conditions in that community. The ideal vision of the mother's and father's roles (including features such as the mother's constant presence at home and complete domesticity) is thus expected to change seeking a match with actual family forms as a country moves to post-industrial occupational structures and patterns of employment that involved both men and women.

The fourth set of relevant concepts includes role identity, role salience, and the theoretical contribution to the analysis of parental roles by Boss[38] and Pasley[39] represented in their concept of *boundary ambiguity*. Pasley has studied the situation of stepfamilies using the concept of boundary ambiguity that Boss[40] developed from stress theory and symbolic interaction theory. The term 'family boundary' alludes to "system and subsystem rules regarding ... who, when, and how members participate in family life." Accordingly, *boundary ambiguity* is "the uncertainty among family members" concerning "who is in or out of the family and who is performing what roles and tasks within the family system."[41] Boundary ambiguity results from the possibility that a family member could be "psychologically present" or "psychologically absent" as well as "physically" present or absent in terms of his or her role performance. Moreover, the subjective *salience* or prominence of a given role identity may vary among social actors enacting that role. LaRossa and Reitzes[42] suggest that the perceived salience of the parental role is higher for women than it is for men. If their assumption is correct, one would expect that *boundary ambiguity* affects more the parental role of fathers than the parental role of mothers because mothers would have a higher likelihood of being psychologically and physically present for their children.

There is a common thread weaved through the four sets of concepts. Current scholarly and popular literature suggests that over the past decade, young parents see the psychological absence of a parent (whether father or mother) as undesirable deviation from the *ideal* parent-child relationship (in Levy's terms). Similarly, the psychological absence of a parent may be seen from Coleman's perspective as the lack of closure of the family network and, correspondingly, a dire loss of social capital needed by the child. In contrast, Weber's conceptualisation of the parent-child relationship is characterised in the affective sense, by the psychological presence of the mother and the psychological absence of the father.

Ample historical evidence suggests that the prevailing cultural values and socioeconomic structures existing in Weber's own lifetime (Europe in the late 19th and early 20th centuries) put emphasis on the physical and psychological presence of mother. For example, if these concepts are applied to the early years of Max Weber's childhood, it could be said that his father was psychologically absent while his mother was devotedly present both psychologically and physically. According to the biography written by his wife, Marianne Weber,[43] Max became very ill when he was about two and a half years old. From that time onwards,

> The young mother now tended her child constantly ... She had always been uncommonly conscientious, and several years of caring for her firstborn child made her totally self-sacrificing with all her younger children as well. She was never again able to understand that a mother could entrust her small children to strangers for more than an hour during the day, let alone at night.[44]

Meanwhile Max's father was a member of parliament and consequently, "His public life, his position, his politics, and his social life claimed his attention. He was busy with meetings all day, went on election trips, and often spent his vacations traveling alone."[45] The father's role changed slightly when the children reached adolescence: "Although he left their upbringing largely to their mother, he hiked and traveled a great deal with his children and thus offered them a stimulation that is given to few."[46] But, in general, the relationship between father and son was strained and came to a critical point when Max Weber was about 33 years old and teaching at Heidelberg.[47]

In addition to the preceding four concepts, three other sociological considerations are useful to the study of parenthood: networks, socialisation agents, and gender. The network of social relationships formed by the spouses, parents-children, and siblings relationships constitutes a dynamic and evolving social system, the family *system*.[48] Accordingly, the social actors in the parent-child relationship are not restricted to birth relations. Most of the time, the parent-child relationship is represented by the relationship between parents and their birth children. Yet, that relationship need not have a genetic basis as it refers fundamentally to a *social* relationship rather than a genetic one. The parent-child relationship under discussion could be that of children with their parents or grandparents by birth, as well as that established by adoption, step-parenting, or any other social arrangement that bestows the relationship with the legitimacy of a parent-child relationship as understood and sanctioned by the community and/or as mutually perceived by the main social actors involved, the adult(s) and the children. In their study on human bonding, Rossi and Rossi[49] found in stepfamilies a type of relationship that demonstrates this point. The authors reported "relatively high obligation ratings" expressed by both stepparents and stepchildren "suggesting it is the position of parent or child that was of major salience to our respondents overriding the fact that these are affilial kin" and not consanguineal kin.

On the matter of socialisation agents, we must distinguish between parent and socialisation agent. Most of the time parents play the role of socialisation agents. But a person may be a socialisation agent without being the child's parent in any sense, legal or otherwise. Moreover, there may be many socialisation agents, but there is only one mother and one father in the parent-child relationship I am discussing, that is, the relationship as perceived by the parent and the child. For this reason, a modification is needed in Coleman's argument on who may be the significant adult in the parent-child relationship. Coleman[50] believes that two adults perform the socialisation job better than one, and that a variety of adults may take the place of one of the parents, including non-kin such as a friend of the parent, a teacher, a neighbour, or even "an adult youth leader." Indeed, it has been demonstrated that children may receive positive nurturing socialisation from a multiplicity of socialisation agents. Every child encounters a variety of adults that may become his or her significant others and role models (in fact, this process may continue throughout a person's life cycle). However, the presence of those adults together with all other external influences upon the child's character formation (mass media, school curriculum, peers, and other factors) does not represent a unique and enduring part of the family as a social group. The parent-child relationship is a primary *dyadic* relationship. Consequently, the significant element here is not a collectivity of caring adults. A child may establish an affective attachment to one or two caring adults to form the father-child or mother-child relationship he or she lacks. But the child focuses only on *one* adult to take the place of *one* absent parent, not on a group of adults, however caring they may be.

Regarding the gender of the parent, findings from cross-cultural studies suggest that the mother-child relationship tends to be closer compared to the father-child relationship. This assumption is not to be confused with the "motherhood mystique" that is, "the belief that mothers, not fathers, are uniquely suited to raise children" which is a social myth aptly criticised by R.A. Warshak.[51] Moreover, it is evident that both norms and "the roles they compose" undergo constant change propelled by factors such as age of the social actors and "the interactional structure of the family."[52] Accordingly, the characteristics of the parent-child relationship and, in particular, of the mother-child relationship, fluctuate in strength over time, across the social actors' life cycle and across generations. Therefore, the time dimension is a very important aspect of this relationship.

More specifically, the assumed difference in resilience between the mother-child and the father-child relationship finds conceptual support in the work of Weber and Coleman. Weber considered the father-child relationship as primarily dependent on the economic nature of the father's role as the household provider. He stressed that even when the father is the economic provider, "the father relationship may not always be of great import."[53] Coleman's views on the role of the father are based on his concept of continuity. He argues that if the parent-child relationship is to provide social capital that is, to be positive to the child, it must guarantee continuity. Coleman sees fathers as more inclined than mothers to discontinue that relationship.[54] It appears that in the past two decades, the *ideal* family form (in Levy's sense) held in Western and some Asian countries prescribes a close relationship between the child and both parents, mother and father. But the socioeconomic, political, cultural, and other constraints faced by most contemporary nations have shaped the *actual* family form as one sustained by the mother, with the father-child relationship showing a weaker resilience. This pattern is expected to continue changing in Asia as countries advance in economic development.

Although the basic approach to the family as an instrument of social change still permeates policy formulation in most Asian countries, some significant improvements began taking place in the 1990s. Efforts at economic development have been accompanied by a growing awakening on the part of some political leaders to the social significance of the family as an institution in itself, and to the need to increase family well-being. Thus, in societies like Japan, Singapore, Hong Kong, and

South Korea, there is now a tendency towards more explicit reference to family well-being in the planning and formulation of economic and social policy. In some countries (for example, Singapore and Taiwan) there is also an increasing official interest in sociological research findings on the family for the purpose of policy formulation and policy evaluation. However, in most countries the focus of state interest is still the same of the past three decades: procreation patterns and their implications for population growth.

PARENTHOOD TRENDS

There is an increasing concern on the part of some Asian governments, particularly in Japan, Singapore and Hong Kong, about people postponing marriage and not having children. Government leaders worry that singlehood and childlessness are becoming fashionable among the younger generations and particularly among the well-educated. Are those fears justified? As shown in Chapter 2, marriage is still very much in fashion except that young people marrying for the first time are postponing the decision to wed until they feel well prepared to take on the responsibilities of marriage in terms of maturity and financial security. The same situation applies, in general, to parenthood but as we shall see, there are some additional aspects to consider.

This section discusses data on the contemporary situation. Although the pace and scope of local sociological research on the family and the recording of relevant official statistics have expanded considerably during the past ten years in most Asian countries, it is necessary to reiterate the cautionary note made in Chapter 1 on the limitations of comparative data. This study covers only the ten Asian countries for which comparable data were available: China, Hong Kong, Japan, South Korea, Indonesia, Malaysia, the Philippines, Singapore, Thailand, and Vietnam.[55]

The situation today is the outcome of a historical process of development where individual choices, policy decisions and intangible demographic and economic changes are closely intertwined. Thus, the analysis of parenthood must take a historical perspective. The most basic statistic associated with parenthood is the crude birth rate, that is the number of live births per 1,000 persons in the population. The change in crude birth rates from 1960 to 2000 has been evident and varied across the ten Asian countries. Chart 3.1 includes data for United Kingdom and United States for comparison. This chart highlights the magnitude

CHART 3.1   FORTY-YEAR CHANGE IN CRUDE BIRTH RATES, 1960-2000

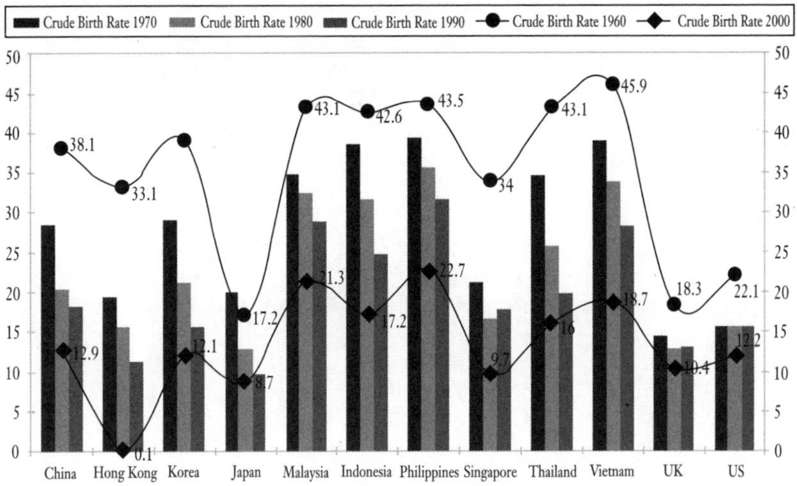

Source: Calculated from United Nations Statistics Division (2002). Crude birth rate is the number of live births per 1,000 population occurred during the period indicated.

of the fertility change in each country by presenting the figures for the extreme years (1960 and 2000) of the 40-year comparison as curves and the data for the intermediate years as bars. A glance at the size of the gap between the two curves conveys the contrast between two groups of countries. The fertility rate change was modest in developed countries (Japan, United Kingdom, and United States) as they already had low fertility in the 1960s. The change in fertility rates was substantial in all the other Asian countries but it was highest for Hong Kong, Thailand and Vietnam, and lowest for the Philippines. Chart 3.2 illustrates another interesting aspect of the same phenomenon. The trend in all the ten Asian countries, the United States and the United Kingdom has been the same: steady decline in the crude birth rate (number of live births per 1,000 population). This similarity stands in sharp contrast to the significant variation in economic development and socio-cultural values of these countries.

There are indications that the factors motivating people to modify their private decisions on the number of children they wish to have are

CHART 3.2 CHANGE TRENDS IN CRUDE BIRTH RATES, 1960-2000

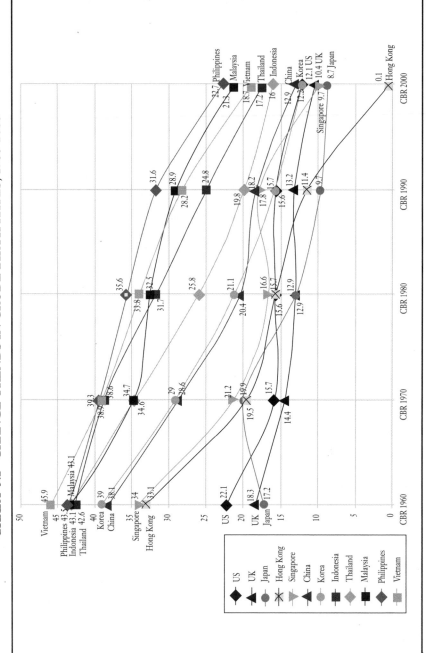

Source: Calculated from United Nations Statistics Division (2002). Crude birth rate is the number of live births per 1,000 population occurred during the period indicated.

mostly socioeconomic rather than direct state intervention. The possible exception to this trend is China where state intervention on fertility control has been unyielding and comprehensive. Chart 3.3 provides clear evidence of this link: the total fertility rate for the period 1995-2000 is closely associated with a key indicator of socioeconomic development, the Human Development Index (r = -.681; p =.04). The HDI ascertains life expectancy at birth, adult literacy rate, the combined gross enrolment ratio in primary, secondary, and tertiary education, and the gross domestic product (GDP) per capita in US dollars.[56] Chart 3.3 includes two additional socioeconomic indicators, the female combined enrolment ratio in primary, secondary, and tertiary education; and electric power consumption (kW per capita) as an indicator of level of industrialisation. The total fertility rate for the period 1995-2000 was lowest in the four countries with the highest 1999 HDI scores: Japan (92.8), Hong Kong (88.0), Singapore (87.6) and South Korea (87.5).

CHART 3.3   LINK BETWEEN SOCIOECONOMIC
DEVELOPMENT AND FERTILITY, 1995-2000

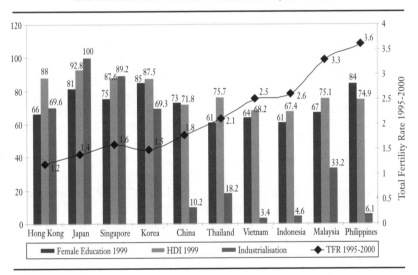

Definitions and Sources: The indicator of industrialisation is electric power consumption (kwpc), compiled from World Bank (2002). The indicator of female education is the combined school enrolment in primary, secondary and tertiary education, compiled from United Nations Development Programme (2002). TFR (total fertility rate) is the average number of children a woman would bear if age-specific fertility rates remained unchanged during her lifetime, compiled from United Nations Development Programme (2002).

CHART 3.4 GENDER DEVELOPMENT INDEX, WEALTH PRODUCTION, AND FERTILITY, 1995-2000

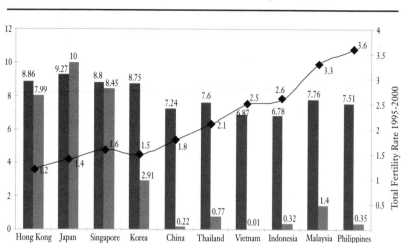

Definitions and Sources: GDI (Gender-related Development Index) is a composite measure of gender equality as reported in United Nations Development Programme (2002). TFR (total fertility rate) is the average number of children a woman would bear if age-specific fertility rates remained unchanged during her life time; calculated from figures reported in United Nations Development Programme (2002). The 1997 GDP (Gross domestic product) per capita as percentage of Japan's GDP was calculated from figures in United Nations (2000).

Chart 3.4 offers additional information confirming the influence of a country's socioeconomic conditions upon people's procreation decisions and outcome. This chart includes the 1997 GDP as a percentage of Japan's GDP to reflect the regional disparity in economic development or wealth creation, and the Gender-related Development Index (GDI). The GDI measures the inequalities between men and women in three aspects: health status (life expectancy at birth); education (adult literacy and combined primary, secondary and tertiary gross enrolment ratio); and standard of living (estimated earned income).[57] The total fertility rate increases in inverse proportion to a country's level of gender equality (r = -.620; p =.032) and level of wealth (r = -.676; p =.032). In contrast to low income countries, in high income nations young people (particularly women) enjoy better opportunities to acquire education and to join the labour force, are more likely to postpone marriage and parenthood, and when married, they are more inclined to have only one or at the most two children. Such is the case of Japan, Hong Kong, Singapore, and South Korea.

It is clear that an important aspect of parenthood decisions is the impact of the status of women. Their level of formal education as conveyed by the Gender-related Development Index (Charts 3.3 and 3.4) influences the number of children they have. When the average number of children among ever-married women is examined in terms of the mother's level of education, the figures fit the pattern found around the globe: the more educated a woman is, the fewer children she is likely to have. This correlation is a worldwide phenomenon. Singapore is a direct illustration. The number of children per woman at all levels of education decreased considerably between 1970 and 1990 but the same pattern remains. Women with no formal education have more children than women with university education who had, on average, two children. The figures on the impact of education have remained relatively stable since 1980.[58] I discuss the influence of economic development on family patterns further in Chapter 7.

From the perspective of family policy, the case of China is noteworthy. China has used state intervention to attain low fertility (as shown in Charts 3.1 to 3.4), while many Western countries and Japan and Hong Kong have achieved the same outcome through socioeconomic development. Singapore, on the other hand, is an illustration of a combination of both sets of factors, government policy, and socioeconomic development.

PARENTHOOD AND THE STATE

In the realm of parenthood, the boundary between the private and the public hovers on the delicate and intimate moment of conception. A private act gets under the spotlight because of its public ramifications. Three decades ago, most governments around the world were unconcerned about the size and rate of growth of their population or were ideologically reluctant to discuss childbearing decisions, a matter generally judged to be of a fundamentally private nature. That has changed. In 1976, 52 per cent of the country members of the United Nations had a policy of **no intervention** in childbearing decisions of their citizens. By 2001, 68 per cent of the UN member nations were monitoring the situation and have an active policy position on the matter.[59]

But, although the perceived problem is the same (their citizens' procreation decisions), the reasons for concern differ drastically between developed nations and the rest of the world community. Manifesting the prevalent values on marriage and parenthood, developed nations have experienced a steady decline in their population growth below replacement level. In contrast, governments in less developed nations are concerned about reducing their high fertility rates.[60] Table 3.1 illustrates the situation in eight Asian countries. The wide range of economies represented in the region comes across in the governments' appraisal of the situation: Japan and Singapore consider their fertility rates "too low" (1.4 and 1.7 respectively) while similar fertility rates in South Korea and China (1.7 and 1.8 respectively) are seen as "satisfactory" by these governments. The other four countries — Indonesia, Malaysia, the Philippines, and Vietnam – see their fertility rate as "too high." With the exception of Japan, all the other countries have a policy of intervention to deal with the problem as they see it.

Table 3.2 presents the situation on a more drastic form of population growth control, abortion. The grounds under which abortion is permitted, vary among the nine countries listed. Information was not available for Hong Kong. Following an international trend, all the nine countries allow abortion to save the life of the woman. Indonesia and the Philippines are the only two countries that do not permit abortion for the less drastic reason of "preserving physical health." Abortion is available on demand in China, South Korea, Singapore, and Vietnam. While the chances of women using abortion as a contraceptive method are higher when it is available on demand, it appears that it is in Japan where abortion is used more as a contraceptive method, given that "oral contraception was illegal in Japan until 1999,"[61] and the widespread perception that oral contraceptives have harmful side effects.[62]

TABLE 3.1   MAIN PARENTHOOD-RELATED POLICIES IN EIGHT ASIAN COUNTRIES

Country	Policy area	Government	
		Position	Intervention
China	**Population growth** (% annual rate, 1995-2000 = 0.9)	Too high	Lower the rate
	Fertility and family planning		
	Fertility level (1995-2000 = 1.8)	Satisfactory	Maintain fertility
	Contraceptive use	Direct support	Direct support
	Adolescent fertility	Minor concern	—
	Policies & programmes on adolescent fertility	—	Yes
	Health and mortality		
	Mortality under five (per 1,000 births) 1995-2000 = 48	Acceptable	—
	Maternal mortality ratio (per 100,000 live births), 1995-2000 = 95	Acceptable	—
South Korea	**Population growth** (% annual rate, 1995-2000 = 0.8)	Satisfactory	No intervention
	Fertility and family planning		
	Fertility level (1995-2000 = 1.7)	Satisfactory	No intervention
	Contraceptive use	Direct support	Direct support
	Adolescent fertility	Minor concern	—
	Policies & programmes on adolescent fertility	—	Yes
	Health and mortality		
	Mortality under five (per 1,000 births) 1995-2000 = 13	Unacceptable	—
	Maternal mortality ratio (per 100,000 live births), 1995-2000 = 130	Unacceptable	—
Japan	**Population growth** (% annual rate, 1995-2000 = 0.2)	Satisfactory	No intervention
	Fertility and family planning		
	Fertility level (1995-2000 = 1.4)	Too low	No intervention
	Contraceptive use	Indirect support	Indirect support
	Adolescent fertility	Minor concern	—
	Policies & programmes on adolescent fertility	—	Yes

TABLE 3.1   MAIN PARENTHOOD-RELATED POLICIES IN EIGHT ASIAN COUNTRIES (cont'd)

Country	Policy area	Government	
		Position	Intervention
	Health and mortality		
	Mortality under five (per 1,000 births) 1995-2000 = 6	Unacceptable	—
	Maternal mortality ratio (per 100,000 live births), 1995-2000 = 18	Unacceptable	—
Indonesia	**Population growth**		
	(% annual rate, 1995-2000 = 1.4)	Too high	Lower the rate
	Fertility and family planning		
	Fertility level (1995-2000 = 2.6)	Too high	To lower rate
	Contraceptive use	Direct support	Direct support
	Adolescent fertility	Major concern	—
	Policies & programmes on adolescent fertility	—	Yes
	Health and mortality		
	Mortality under five (per 1,000 births) 1995-2000 = 63	Unacceptable	—
	Maternal mortality ratio (per 100,000 live births), 1995-2000 = 650	Unacceptable	—
Singapore	**Population growth**		
	(% annual rate 1995-2000 = 1.4)	Satisfactory	Maintain the rate
	Fertility and family planning		
	Fertility level (1995-2000 = 1.7)	Too low	Raise fertility
	Contraceptive use	Direct support	Direct support
	Adolescent fertility	Minor concern	—
	Policies & programmes on adolescent fertility	—	Yes
	Health and mortality		
	Mortality under five (per 1,000 births) 1995-2000 = 6	Acceptable	—
	Maternal mortality ratio (per 100,000 live births), 1995-2000 = 10	Acceptable	—

TABLE 3.1   MAIN PARENTHOOD-RELATED POLICIES IN EIGHT ASIAN COUNTRIES (cont'd)

Country	Policy area	Government	
		Position	Intervention
Malaysia	**Population growth** (% annual rate 1995-2000 = 2)	Satisfactory	No intervention
	Fertility and family planning		
	Fertility level (1995-2000 = 3.2)	Too high	—
	Contraceptive use	Direct support	Lower fertility
	Adolescent fertility	Major concern	Direct support
	Policies & programmes on adolescent fertility	—	Yes
	Health and mortality		
	Mortality under five (per 1,000 births) 1995-2000 = 15	Acceptable	—
	Maternal mortality ratio (per 100,000 live births), 1995-2000 = 80	Acceptable	—
The Philippines	**Population growth** (% annual rate 1995-2000 = 2.1)	Too high	Lower the rate
	Fertility and family planning		
	Fertility level (1995-2000 = 3.6)	Too high	Lower fertility
	Contraceptive use	Direct support	Direct support
	Adolescent fertility	Major concern	—
	Policies & programmes on adolescent fertility	—	Yes
	Health and mortality		
	Mortality under five (per 1,000 births) 1995-2000 = 44	Unacceptable	—
	Maternal mortality ratio (per 100,000 live births), 1995-2000 = 280	Unacceptable	—
Vietnam	**Population growth** (% annual rate 1995-2000 = 1.6)	Too high	Lower the rate
	Fertility and family planning		
	Fertility level (1995-2000 = 2.6)	Too high	Lower fertility
	Contraceptive use	Direct support	Direct support
	Adolescent fertility	Minor concern	—
	Policies & programmes on adolescent fertility	—	Yes

TABLE 3.1 MAIN PARENTHOOD-RELATED POLICIES IN
EIGHT ASIAN COUNTRIES (cont'd)

| Country | Policy area | Government | |
		Position	Intervention
	Health and mortality Mortality under five (per 1,000 births) 1995-2000 = 56	Acceptable	—
	Maternal mortality ratio (per 100,000 live births), 1995-2000 = 160	Unacceptable	—

Source: Compiled from United Nations Population Division (1999) and (2003).

TABLE 3.2 GOVERNMENT POLICY ON ABORTION

| Country | Grounds on which abortion is permitted | | | | | | |
	To save the life of the woman	To preserve physical health	To preserve mental health	Rape or incest	Foetal impairment	Economic or social reasons	Available on request
China	Yes	Yes	Yes	Yes	Yes	Yes	Yes
South Korea	Yes	Yes	Yes	Yes	Yes	Yes	Yes
Japan	Yes	Yes	No	Yes	No	Yes	No
Indonesia	Yes	No	No	No	No	No	No
Singapore	Yes	Yes	Yes	Yes	Yes	Yes	Yes
Malaysia	Yes	Yes	Yes	No	No	No	No
The Philippines	Yes	No	No	No	No	No	No
Thailand	Yes	Yes	Yes	Yes	No	No	No
Vietnam	Yes	Yes	Yes	Yes	Yes	Yes	Yes

Source: United Nations Population Division (2003)

It is possible that the decline in the crude birth rate could have taken place as an spontaneous response to industrialisation and to a higher educational level of the female population as demonstrated in the preceding section. Yet, systematic and forceful state intervention in the form of family planning programmes is an important part of the population growth equation. The two well-known styles of state-led fertility control are China and Singapore.

Numerous studies have been published over the past two decades on China's efforts to control its population growth. China's case is notable given the radical interventionist approach taken and two major obstacles faced by its population policy: the traditionally strong preference for sons[63] that was still evident in the 1990s; and its low level of economic development.[64] The policy of population growth control began in the early 1950s and a comprehensive plan of action was enacted in 1979 as the "Later-Longer-Fewer" (*Wan-Xi-Shao*) campaign, that preceded the now well-known "one-child-per-couple policy."[65]

The Singapore experience is different. The family planning programme implemented in Singapore during the 1960s and 1970s had an important role to play in the decrease in the number of children born in Singapore after the mid-1960s. The impact of that programme was due not so much to the fomenting of contraceptive use[66] as to the promotion of the benefits of small families and a change in the preference for sons.[67] However, the desired control of population growth turned out to be unevenly successful in the minds of policy makers.[68] Since the early 1980s, the two related trends of later marriages and fewer children per married woman have been presented to Singaporeans by the political leadership as social problems that require prompt measures. Why, exactly, do these trends constitute problems for Singapore? Explaining this has been the earnest task of the top political leadership. Briefly, the three main reasons given are: (1) the serious reduction in the already limited talent pool is a problem because of the small size of the country;[69] (2) a reduction in the size of Singapore's labour force would "seriously limit the GDP growth rate";[70] and (3) there would be an imbalance in the proportion of aged dependents per adult worker.[71]

Following their well-tested style of institutional intervention,[72] the first step taken by the Singapore political leaders to deal with these three demographic problems was to distribute objective information. Most of the speeches by the top political leaders on these matters were broadcast through all mass media and accompanied by clear and detailed tables and charts documenting the nature and size of the problems. While the first step of institutional intervention presents the given social problem to the target population, the second step involves the suggestion of solutions to the problem, usually introduced as appropriate patterns of behaviour or social goals to be attained. In the case of the dual problem of late marriages and fewer children, the political leaders have outlined explicitly the desirable social goals which, necessarily, involve the family and private choices of individuals, and have addressed the key target populations namely, all women of reproductive age, particularly the better educated, and all men eligible for marriage and parenthood, particularly the better educated. Singapore illustrates a situation where the formulation of public policy is preceded by the leadership's introduction and promotion of social goals in order to gain consensus. In many countries, the opposite process evolves whereby pressure groups and organisations seek by various means the government's recognition of their needs and agendas.

The solutions or social goals proposed by the Singapore government to counter these problems are straightforward albeit sensitive or even explosive in any other context. One is the encouragement to young educated adults to get married, and the other one is the new population policy introduced in the 1980s: "Have three, and more [children] if you can afford it."[73] But information and admonitions are not sufficient to change people's behaviour. Another characteristic of institutional intervention in Singapore is its third step namely, the introduction of incentives to reinforce the suggested pattern of behaviour in the target population. If incentives do not get the expected results, the other steps may be the introduction of disincentives and sanctions as was the case of the first population policy which became an international example of success in the control of population growth.[74] The multi-pronged approach and the various incentives and disincentives put in place by the Singapore government, and its efforts to avoid contradictory policies, are discussed elsewhere.[75] How do people negotiate these social goals with the attainment of their own personal goals and life plans? This brings us to the personal dimension of parenthood.

RECONCILING THE PRIVATE AND PUBLIC SPHERES OF PARENTHOOD

The fertility rates and other population growth figures show a clear decline in birth rates associated with high economic development. Does this mean that parenthood is not a personal goal for people in affluent societies today? Put differently, smaller families appear to be the norm in economically dynamic countries where women are better educated. Why do educated women have smaller families? This question was one of the most researched by social scientists during the 1970s and 1980s when generous funding was available to study the control of population growth. Reviewing the main findings of such studies, S.H. Cochrane[76] summarised the answer thus: Compared to women with no or low education, educated women have a more positive perception of their own fertility, are more likely to marry later, have living standards more conducive to child survival, are better informed about contraception, and through their wider life goals, they tend to perceive greater benefits in having a small family.

Consequently, it would be inaccurate to interpret the trend towards smaller families among educated women as an indication that these women are rejecting motherhood. Available evidence indicates that such an assumption is wrong. There are indications that educated couples wish to give the best to their children; that educated mothers want to be physically and psychologically present in the lives of their children; and that the vision of the ideal family is changing in the more advanced countries in Asia, from the traditional extended family to that of a smaller family unit functioning more or less autonomously within a kinship network of mutual aid.[77]

The question of parenthood is a complex one. The chores and daily responsibilities of child care are burdensome particularly for the increasing proportion of women who hold jobs outside the home and may not be able to afford childcare services. These are typically women who wish or need to remain in the labour force.[78] At the same time, research has shown that the mundane dimension of parenthood (including the feeding, cleaning and all other prosaic aspects of childcare) does not cloud the fact that having children is a desirable and rewarding experience for most women, including women in industrialised countries,[79] as well as in Asian societies.[80]

One possible exception to the positive view of parenthood in Asia may be Japan, if one estimates Japanese attitudes by the rapid decline in fertility rate. The figures could be seen as an indication of a change in cultural values shaping the vision of the ideal family. However, some Japanese social scientists give alternative interpretations. In her investigation of the fertility decline, Akiko Fuse[81] found that the "priority put on rationalization during the period of rapid economic growth" led to a single-minded effort to succeed at all levels and, consequently, "the principle of 'efficiency first' became all powerful." She suggests that these dominant values lead Japanese men and women to dedicate themselves to work leaving little room for family life and procreation, even though children are highly valued. Her data show that "the number of children desired by young married couples is greater than the actual fertility."[82] A related interpretation is provided by Emiko Ochiai:[83] "The reason [Japanese] people have fewer children is not because they value them less; on the contrary, it seems that people limit their families so that they could love the children they had all the more." Naohiro Ogawa[84] explains Japan's current low fertility rates as a reaction of women to "the economic slowdown in the 1990s" as married women foresee economic difficulties ahead, their plans to have children are adjusted accordingly. This, Ogawa says, is more evident among urban married women, as the cost of raising children is higher in urban areas.

These explanations are all in terms of the cost of rapid economic growth. The situation these and other Japanese authors depict appears to fit Coleman's assumption of the loss of social capital brought about by people's concentration on the demands of corporate structures in modern industrial societies. Japan and other upper income countries in Asia (Singapore, Hong Kong, Taiwan, and South Korea) may be facing the struggle of reconciling the *ideal* family form of more than two children with the *actual* smaller family they can afford given the pressures of a rapid economic growth. These pressures are specially felt by salaried Asian women who would like to be mothers and to be physically and psychologically present in the lives of their children but are unable to do so. The most evident illustration of the high cost of economic survival for parents is the thousands of Filipino fathers and mothers who have to leave their children behind for prolonged periods of time to work in foreign countries. Considering that cultural values in Asia stress the mother-child bond (that Weber deemed a universal trend), the price of a foreign job is particularly high for Filipino mothers and their children.

In sum, while procreation trends are heading towards smaller families, parenthood continues to be an important personal goal in Asian societies. At the beginning of this chapter I indicated that bringing private matters such as parenthood into the realm of public policy is controversial and it presupposes a certain level of collective agreement on the type or types of family the country wants to encourage (a shared vision of the *ideal* family or *ideal* range of families); and at least a modicum of collective acknowledgement that private choices have consequences for the community. Seeing family policy as a comprehensive plan of action to attain shared social goals, it is then interesting to explore how governments in Asia deal with fertility rates, later marriages, and **changing** family goals, among populations that, as a whole, are marrying later and apparently are leaning towards the small family norm. With the exception of China and Singapore, there is no clear evidence of state intervention to introduce or promote family goals in the other eight Asian countries. As indicated earlier, the process of institutional intervention involves the distribution of objective information and advice followed by incentives, disincentives, and sanctions, for the purpose of changing people's behaviour. In the case of Singapore's current population policy, so far only the first three steps of institutional intervention have been applied, that is, the dissemination of objective information on the negative demographic consequences of low reproduction and marriage rates, advice, and a full package of incentives.

The second assumption made when private choices are brought into the public arena, is that people would show a basic consensus on important social goals that cannot be attained unless private choices on marriage and parenthood are modified. Studies conducted in some of the eight countries suggest different trends. On the one hand, in Japan and Singapore people tend to accept the social (that is, national) need to provide incentives to stimulate young couple to have more children. But at the same time they are inclined to regard the individual as autonomous in making decisions on marriage and procreation as these are life aspects of a completely private nature. As a 25-year-old Japanese woman told me, "What the government does is its duty, but I don't let officials decide for me. I have my own plans."

In contrast to Japan and Singapore, the other eight countries have a problem (actual or potential) of rapid population growth. The state offers people in these countries information and incentives to prevent pregnancy and to limit their number of children, an effort that goes against some of the community's cherished cultural and/or religious values shaping their vision of the *ideal* family. Citizens who have a 'helicopter view' (typically the better educated minority) can appreciate the long-term effects of rapid population growth and, more importantly, of economic downturns. They may begin to modify their own personal goals based on the *actual* type of family they can afford. But the majority of the population is not likely to agree with the idea that their right to have children interferes with the state's long-term development plans. Population growth control measures are not popular. It is not surprising then that those measures are not pursued with vigour by the political leadership in the countries concerned.

Singapore has experienced a shift in policies and public attitudes. In contrast to the situation in the early 1980s, the later part of the decade witnessed an improvement in the public attitude towards the new policy goals on marriage and reproduction. There were signs that the target population accepted as national goals the officially identified need for more marriages and larger families: marriage and fertility rates increased in 1987 and 1988. Yet, the increase was not sustained, most likely because of the predominance of personal goals among the increasingly better educated population. Marriage rates declined between 1980 and 1990 (Chart 3.4) and crude birth rates declined for all ethnic groups from 1988 to 1995.[85] Studies indicate that both marriage and parenthood are top personal goals for Singaporeans[86] thus the lower figures in marriage and birth rates reflect people's changing subjective perception of the appropriate or desirable time and conditions to become a spouse and parent. Moreover, there is no sign that pain has been inflicted to the target population by encouraging them to modify their private choices on the decision and timing of marriage and on the number of children they should have. No comparable information on the population's attitudes towards the fertility control policy are forthcoming from China, the only other country with an explicit procreation agenda.

The study and open discussion of demographic projections of population trends is a basic and indispensable task of governments everywhere. One of the outcomes of that exercise is the well-known finding that low-income families with *small* number of children have significantly better chances of getting out of the poverty trap than large families. For example, research conducted in the United States have found that not only "about one in five families with minor children lives in poverty" but, more importantly, "low-income families are frequently driven into poverty by the addition of family members...family size and poverty are closely related, as half of families with five or more children are poor."[87]

Official statistics show that some countries have managed to keep demographic and economic growth in balance. The factors that I suggest have contributed to the people's acceptance of the old and the new population policies in Singapore may be unique because, not notwithstanding the facts on demographic trends and poverty, government intervention into the private choices of individuals is considered, at best, undesirable in most modern democracies. Internationally, one of the main arguments against legislation is, as expressed by two American analysts, that "The right to bear and rear children has always been considered an inalienable right [...] Any attempts to legislate this privilege of procreation endanger a most fundamental freedom."[88] Others point to the problem of the "futility of family policy" due to the diversity of family forms and individual choices and the obvious fact that "families are neither monolithic nor unchanging."[89] Yet another reservation has to do with the assumed hidden agenda of governments:

> ...there are no grounds for feeling that family policies are *necessarily* a good thing...history shows that 'family' policies have often been disguised attempts by governments to manipulate families for 'national' interests [for example]...the Third Reich...the Soviet Union...China...Hungary and Kenya...[90]

An additional fear of official intervention, clearly put by an American sociologist, goes beyond the obvious difficulties of defining what is best for our families into the question of how to avoid the negative and often unforeseen consequences of well-intentioned policies.[91]

In spite of all these imponderables, the reality and the magnitude of social problems affecting the family in countries from all corners of the globe is undeniable as it is the incapacity of individuals or isolated groups to deal with and solve many of those problems. There is, therefore, a perceivable trend among social scientists to take a fresh look at what governments could contribute. After a very good discussion of the complex problems faced by families headed by women without husbands, Kamerman and Kahn conclude their study by acknowledging that:

> Society has begun to see that its economic future and national well-being require new commitment to rearing responsible, competent, creative citizens...we cannot afford to 'waste' any citizens...There is no excuse for not acting--on a larger scale, in a basic and decisive sense, and now.[92]

The underlying premise of what these well-known scholars are advocating has been part of the Singapore approach to social problems for the past two decades. It is a matter of priorities: in the face of serious dangers to the community's well-being, the collective consensus may determine that the common good takes precedence over individual preferences. The Singaporean position differs from that of other nations, in terms of the definition of what constitutes the common good or national interests and the need for social discipline to override individual choices.

Features similar to Singapore's position may be found in other new industrialising nations in the East, for example South Korea and Taiwan, while it is common to find strong reservations against government policy in Western Europe, North America, Australia, and New Zealand. Thus, the contrast in outlook between East and West is, among other things, the product of a difference in ideology and culture, an issue beyond the scope of this chapter but I continue the analysis of the role of the state in Chapter 7. Suffice it to say at this point that the acknowledgement of these differences should not prevent us all from learning from each other. It should, instead, work as an added inducement to continue exploring the cultural and ideological boundaries between public and private spheres of life and the roles and duties of governments and citizens in different nations around the world.

ENDNOTES

1. For a detailed discussion of family policy in a comparative perspective see Quah (1990b:1-22; 378-384) and Quah (1998).
2. See Quah (1981a); Quah (1990c); and (1990e).
3. See Lasswell (1968).
4. See Kahn (1969).
5. See Quah (1998).
6. See Tallman (1979:470).
7. These arguments as discussed in detail in Quah (1990d).
8. See Lasch (1979).
9. See Donzelot (1977).
10. Steiner (1981) and (1985).
11. See Henslin (1985).
12. See Kamerman and Kahn (1978) and (1988).
13. See for example, Jencks (1992); Wilson (1993); Etzioni (1993); and Etzioni (1995).
14. See Berger and Berger (1983).

15. See Glazer (1988).
16. See Ditch, Barnes and Bradshaw (1996:2).
17. See Weber (1978).
18. See Coleman (1990).
19. See Levy (1949) and Levy (1965).
20. See Boss (1977) and Boss (2002).
21. See Pasley (1987) and Pasley (1993).
22. See Weber (1978:6-7).
23. See Weber (1978:356-357).
24. See Weber (1978:357-358).
25. See Coleman (1990).
26. See Coleman (1990:584).
27. See Coleman (1990:304-305).
28. See Coleman (1990: 592).
29. See Coleman (1990: 593).
30. See Weber (1978).
31. See Coleman (1990).
32. See Coleman (1990:591).
33. See Coleman (1990:595-6).
34. See Levy (1949) and Levy (1965).
35. See Doolittle (1986); and Wolf and Huang (1980).
36. See Levy (1965).
37. See Festinger (1957:31).
38. See Boss (1977) and Boss (1993).
39. See Pasley (1987) and Pasley (1993).
40. See Boss (1977).
41. See Boss (1993:164); and Pasley (1987:206).
42. See LaRossa and Reitzes (1993:145-146).
43. See Weber (1988).
44. See Weber (1988:32-33).
45. See Weber (1998:34).
46. See Weber (1988:63).
47. See Weber (1988:230-233).
48. See Whitchurch and Constantine (1993).
49. See Rossi and Rossi (1990:490).
50. See Coleman (1990:590-592).
51. See Warshak (1992:14).
52. See Rodgers and White (1993:234).
53. See Weber (1978:357).

54. See Coleman (1990:590).

55. When data are not available for one or more of the ten countries, this is indicated in the respective tables or charts.

56. For a detailed description of the calculation of HDI see United Nations Development Programme (2002:253).

57. A detailed description of the GDI is found in United Nations Development Programme (2002:255).

58. See Quah (1998:105).

59. See United Nations Population Division (2003:6).

60. See United Nations Population Division (2003:4).

61. See United Nations Population Division (2002:79).

62. See Sugimoto (2003:165-166).

63. See Arnold and Zhaoxiang (1992).

64. See Greenhalgh and Bongaarts (1992).

65. See United Nations Population Division (2003:94-95).

66. See Chang, Ong and Chen (1980:77-78).

67. See Kuo and Chiew (1984:172-177); Quah (1981), Quah (1983); and Kuo (1987:9).

68. See Quah (1998).

69. See Lee (1982:8).

70. See Economic Committee (1986:106).

71. See Goh (1987:2).

72. For the definition and discussion of institutional intervention see Quah (1983:281).

73. See Goh (1987:2).

74. See Quah (1983:280-285).

75. See Quah (1998:111-118).

76. See Cochrane (1982).

77. See Quah (1999) and Quah (2003).

78. See Fawcett and Khoo (1980:562-565); Singapore Ministry of Labour, (1989:40, 57, 112) and (1997); Moen (2003); Abroms and Goldscheider (2002); Broadbent and Morris-Suzuki (2000).

79. See Coles (1986) and Moen (2003).

80. See Fawcett and Khoo (1980:575); Saw and Wong (1981: 32-37); Quah (1988); Singapore Ministry of Social Affairs (1984:55); Quah (1986).

81. See Fuse (1996).

82. See Fuse (1996:82).

83. See Ochiai (1997:47).

84. See Ogawa (2003:99).

85. See Quah (1998:58-62).

86. See Quah (1998), Quah (1999).

87. See Levitan, Belous and Gallo (1988:140, 143).
88. See Abbott and Walters (1985:190).
89. See Steiner (1985:494).
90. See Wicks (1987:122).
91. See Henslin (1985: 491).
92. See Kamerman and Kahn (1988:228).

4

Age, Grandparents, and Social Capital

It appears that the 21st century has caught us unprepared. We have advanced in knowledge far more rapidly than our ability to adjust and meet the challenges posed by scientific discoveries. Our sluggishness in transforming attitudes is evident in the way we deal with age. People's life expectancy is steadily increasing and with better standard of living and medical progress, the additional years gained are, for the most part, healthy and productive years. Yet, our collective image of senior generations is archaic. We use the term "greying society" and "the aged" dismissing the ability and desire of senior people to continue their contributions to family and society. The term "greying population" is a negative one. It conveys the image of a society with an increasing proportion of sick and dependent people; and it wrongly suggests that improving life expectancy creates social problems. As people reach the socially defined age of departure from their jobs, they are labelled "retired" and another negative stereotype sets in. "Retired" people are assumed to seek disengagement, not only from the work force but from active and productive life in general. This is a distorted perception of the senior generation that represents a valuable resource to any community. I will argue in this chapter that contrary to that negative tendency, the senior generation is *social capital* sustaining both community and family.

What is happening to this social capital in Asia? This chapter examines the situation from three angles: (1) conceptually, using the concepts social capital, value transmission, and value transformation, that enhance our understanding of the assets of the senior generation and of grandparenting; (2) historically, by ascertaining changes across time in the attributes of the senior generation; and (3) from the perspective of social space for the seniors as individuals, family members, grandparents, and members of the community. The main theme throughout this discussion is the bioethics principle of *respect for autonomy*. Advances in biological knowledge and socioeconomic development provide the senior generation with the ability to lead active and self-fulfilling lives. They ought to be treated as "autonomous" persons, that is, persons who act "in accordance with a freely self-chosen and informed plan"[1] rather than a generation of frail, dependent and lower educated individuals.[2]

RELEVANT CONCEPTS

The public image of the senior generation became negative around the second part of the 20th century. At the dawn of civilisation, the pioneers in the development of human intellectual discourse asserted the fundamental role that the senior generation must play in the advance of knowledge and values in society. One of the first articulated voices in the East was that of Confucius (551-479 B.C.) who stressed the wealth that the wisdom and values of the senior generation represented for the ordinary individual within the family as well as for the society at large. Ten years after Confucius' death, Socrates (469-399 B.C.) was born in Athens, the cradle of Western thought. As narrated by Plato (427-347 B.C.), one of his best students, Socrates said to his senior generation friend, Cephalus:

> There is nothing which for my part I like better, Cephalus, than conversing with aged men; for I regard them as travelers who have gone a journey which I too may have to go, and of whom I ought to inquire, whether the way is smooth and easy, or rugged and difficult.[3]

Studies of historical records of civilisations around the world confirm that this principle advanced by Confucius and Socrates has been applied for centuries as communities grow and advance from one stage of development to the next. The senior generation in the community transmits the body of experience it has received and accumulated to the younger generations together with those values that help the community to survive and prosper. This process of value transmission requires the presence of a network of relations involving young and old by which the members of each generation perceive the others as a vital resource for the prosperity of their community. It is this network of intergenerational relationships that forms the community's social capital.[4]

What is Social Capital?

There are many ways to say it. Social capital is "fraternity," "civic virtue," "civic community" or "Salem without witches"; it is "connections among individuals"; it means that "social networks have value," explains Robert Putnam.[5] As I point out in Chapter 3, the concept of social capital was first systematically formulated in 1990 by James Coleman[6] and has been actively argued and researched by social scientists over the past decade although the positive output of social bonds has been discussed for much longer.[7] Coleman had to use an elaborate conceptual definition of his idea because his was a conceptual argument. Putnam is reviewing and using work done on social capital, so he puts it across in simple terms:

> Whereas physical capital refers to physical objects and human capital refers to properties of individuals, social capital refers to connections among individuals — social networks and norms of reciprocity and trustworthiness that arise from them.[8]

Two important qualifications must be made. The first qualification is that social capital can be positive or negative. Given the rich diversity of social groups and social conditions in any society, social networks come in a wide range of shapes and forms, from ascetic communities doing welfare work, to friends playing cards, to terrorists' groups and secret societies of gangsters. It is easy then to agree with Putnam and others that the social capital generated by all these types of networks is not all positive and that the social capital of some networks is clearly destructive because "Social capital ... can be directed toward malevolent, antisocial purposes, just like any other form of capital."[9] The second qualification is that the counterpart of social capital, that is the counterpart of social network bonding, is exclusion.[10] If your group of close friends is tightly knit, chances are that it has developed an "us" mentality which is very good for the sense of belonging and well-being of all group members. But, if you and your friends are "us," everyone else becomes "them." This exclusionary feature of group identity has been studied by sociologists for a long time and one of the first to analyse its negative consequences was Max Weber in his study of "a consciousness of kind" in ethnicity and religion. Interestingly, the exclusion of "them" or "others" from "us" happens concurrently with the group's bonding of people of different (but to the group, unimportant) attributes.[11] For example, a fervent religious group may accept and even encourage membership from people of different ethnic backgrounds. This feature of social capital has been reported in several studies.[12]

Although the concept depicts small group relations, social capital may be applied to the analysis of societies and groups of any size by estimating its relative presence or absence. The main problem in ascertaining social capital is that while easy to put into words, it is not easy to measure. Putnam measures social capital through interview questions on political participation, membership in civic groups, work groups, and religious groups and organisations, in family and informal social networks, and through attitudes on altruism, volunteering, philanthropy, reciprocity, honesty, and trust, among others. He then reviews the situation of several types of organisations including family and kin relations in his critique of the impact of social change upon social capital in the United States[13] and other countries.[14]

Two Australian researchers, Wendy Stone and Jody Hughes, embarked on the difficult task of ascertaining social capital by focusing on what they saw as its two important manifestations: "networks, trust, and reciprocity" and "the quality and structure of social relations."[15] Their conceptual framework has two sets of variables: types of networks "where trust and reciprocity operate," and network characteristics. They propose that three types of networks are important: informal ties networks (family, kinship, neighbours, friends, and coworkers); networks of generalised relationships (local people, people in general and civic groups); and networks of institutional relationships. Stone and Hughes identify three types of network characteristics: size and extensiveness; density and closure; and diversity.[16] The objective of the Australian study, based on a nation-wide sample, was the construction of a valid and reliable measure of social capital. In the process of doing that, the researchers found a high level of trust and reciprocity (mean score of 9 or higher in a scale 0-10 where 10 is maximum trust and reciprocity) in family networks among people who live with their families.[17] They concluded that social capital is a multidimensional phenomenon. For example, people could have high social capital in informal networks (say, a cohesive family and kinship network) and yet enjoy no social capital from their place of work (no meaningful interaction, or trust, or reciprocity with employer and co-workers).

Political scientist Takashi Inoguchi examined social capital in Japan based on his own data and population surveys conducted by various

Japanese sociologists over the past three decades. He found that family size was an important determinant of social capital as ascertained by participation in civic and political activities. More specifically, three-generation families (those with one or both grandparents present) "exhibit the highest degree of participation and affiliation in general" as they tend to be long-term residents in their constituencies and thus "more likely to be firmly embedded in local networks of activities and institutions." In view of the twin trends of high physical and human capital on the one hand, and a decreasing size of Japanese families on the other hand, Inoguchi suggested that "an optimal size of city and family may be necessary to keep such an accumulated social capital from being rapidly depleted."[18] He reports that trust and a "a very strong sense of obligation" among the Japanese tend to be restricted to family and kin or at the most to "known small groups."[19]

Value Transmission and Value Transformation

Two additional notions are relevant to this discussion of age, grandparents, and social capital: value transmission and value transformation. The process of transmission of the community's stock of cultural traditions from one generation to the next takes place through many channels, some more important than others. But the principal channel of transmission is the socialisation of children by their parents and/or grandparents because it is the first and, commonly, the most constant form of culture transmission in a person's life. Once a person reaches adulthood, parental influence (intentionally or not) takes the form of forewarning and actual example. A person may evaluate the outcome of the application or neglect of cultural traditions in the lives of his or her parents. Other significant but less stable channels of transmission of the stock of cultural traditions in modern society are the school, the mass media and, under certain conditions, state-level institutions such as the armed forces particularly through the system of compulsory military service for young citizens. Irrespective of the presence and effectiveness of other vehicles of value transmission, the role of parents is indispensable for the process of transmission of a country's or community's stock of cultural traditions across generations.

The second process that shapes the stock of cultural traditions held by the new generation of young adults at any given time in the history of a community is the process of transformation of its original or earliest stock of cultural traditions. Of the many factors that transform the original stock, three are the most significant: educational progress, economic development, and political change.

(a) Educational Progress

In the historical path of a human collectivity from a primitive or traditional community to a post-industrial or global society, the educational progress of its members is a fundamental factor of value transformation at three levels. First, education helps the community to redefine its original stock of cultural traditions according to challenges posed by changing socioeconomic, political, and other aspects of the physical and social environment. Second, education helps the community to reassess the individual and collective goals of its members to meet new challenges. And third, education helps the community to create or discover new guidelines and procedures of action. These three main effects of the exposure to increasing levels of education upon the stock of cultural traditions are associated with, but not determined by, the community's formal school system. This is because people may use their initiative to acquire more knowledge from other sources, or to obtain higher education outside their community.

(b) Economic Development

Apart from its purely financial rewards, economic development also contributes to the transformation of a community's stock of cultural traditions in at least two ways. First, advances in economic development give prominence to the potential "profitability" of traditional values, beliefs, and practices, thus leading to the redefinition of some cultural traditions as either obstacles or assets to progress. An example of tradition as economic benefit is the community's emphasis on education as the best inheritance parents can give to their children to assure the latter's future financial security. On the other hand, an example of cultural traditions as obstacles to progress is the norm that an employer must hire workers based on personal affection, kinship obligations, or in return for favours received or expected, rather than on objectively assessed skills or qualifications for the job. An employer whose company is competing in the international market soon discovers that skirting expertise as a key employment criterion reduces drastically the company's competitiveness and thus the probability of financial success and profitability of his or her business. If tradition dictates 'kin-comes-first' and tradition predominates, this employer would hire a relative over a stranger even if the relative does not have the required skills to do the job.

The second main way in which economic development helps to transform the stock of cultural traditions is by determining the standard of living of each generation in the community. On the one hand, when the standard of living deteriorates compared to previous generations because of low or stagnant economic growth, individuals and families have to change or to postpone their dreams or self-fulfillment goals in favour of immediate concerns such as housing, food, and security (a reversal of Maslow's hierarchy of needs). The negative consequences of the forced postponement of life goals are mixed and volatile: from a return to traditional values such as frugality, savings and sacrifice, to a passive, aggressive, or even violent search for new ways of distributing wealth in society. On the other hand, when the standard of living improves compared to that of previous generations, it is accompanied by a higher level of education of the population and increased exposure to other societies (through high technology, mass media, and travelling, among other things). The stock of cultural traditions is consequently expanded by the borrowing of new values absorbed in full or adapted from other societies.

(c) Political Change

The third factor contributing to the transformation of the stock of cultural traditions is political change in the community. Changes in the political system, or in legislation, or in administrative directives, may rule out any changes in traditional customs or may even impose a return to ancient traditions (for example in Iran after the Shah), or may legitimise changes in traditional values (for example, the move against parental authority during the early years of the communist regimes in Russia, China, Cuba and North Korea whereby children, as little guardians of the revolution, were indoctrinated to spy on their parents). The acceptance or rejection of patronage in political representation, of nepotism in the appointment of public officials, or the rejection or support of a particular political ideology (for example, the supremacy of individual freedom over the community's well-being), and the support of meritocracy and honesty in public life, are some examples of values that a given political system or political party in power may introduce or prevent. In the same vein, government decisions also shape the framework and boundaries of action for the new generations (for example, by dictating their definitions of freedom and civil responsibility, among other aspects).

(d) The Partnership of Past and Future

Every new generation in a community possesses a stock of cultural traditions that is the outcome of the combined effect of the process of value transmission (where the family plays a fundamental role assisted by the school, the mass media and other institutions) and of the process of value transformation (taking place mainly through educational progress, economic development, and political change). The most active vehicles for the introduction of non-indigenous values are educational progress (of both parents and children) and economic development.

We may visualise the scope of the personal and collective horizons of each generation as the total set of values, goals, and aspirations for the growth of its members. Taking a historical perspective and barring natural and man-made disasters, we may envisage a continuous expansion of the scope of personal and collective horizons of each new generation of young adults compared to their parents' generation. For each generation, its scope of personal and collective horizons contains both a stock of cultural traditions (partly transformed in its journey across time), and new elements that are created by their members or that they borrowed and adapted from other cultures.

The present generation of 20- to 30- year-olds in developed parts of the world, including most parts of Asia, is experiencing the widest scope of personal and collective horizons of any generation before them. The educational, socioeconomic, and political changes experienced by each generation contribute to the shaping of those horizons. Another major influence is the current phenomenon of globalisation by which a person's or group's goals, aspirations and boundaries of action cease to be determined by the geographical borders of their country. Instead, the world is targeted as their sphere of action. Globalisation reaches homes through the media (television and the Internet being the most rapid vehicles particularly for the younger generations in Japan, Singapore, Hong Kong, South Korea and Taiwan), through the availability or depletion of jobs in an internationally-linked economy, and through consumer products, among other ways. The crucial challenge is to take advantage of the globalisation process at the same time that the core of the stock of cultural traditions is preserved and applied in daily life. The overall objective is a partnership of past and future. That is, a partnership of the junior, middle-age and senior generations to integrate the best of the old with the best of the new so as to create the optimum environment for human development (cultural, social, economic and political).

Together, the ideas of social capital, value transmission, and value transformation suggest two roles of the senior generation in the community. First, grandparents represent family social capital in their role as vital links bringing together the network of the comparatively autonomous smaller family units of their married children. This role of grandparents is particularly significant when a child's parents divorce or have to work away from home for extended periods. The latter situation is typically prompted by the demands of intense economic development and globalisation (or 'regionalisation') leading companies to relocate employees (and often their spouses and children) to wherever their skills are needed, or force people to migrate in search of jobs. Grandparents are vital nodes in the modified extended family network[20] connecting all their children and their grandchildren, far and near. Second, grandparents are a flesh-and-blood symbol of the stock of core community and family values to their grandchildren — especially if they are living in the same home or have frequent face-to-face interaction — thus serving as effective vehicles of value transmission and as a social anchor to the younger generations in the inevitable process of value transformation.

THE SENIOR GENERATION ACROSS TIME

Following the same ten countries covered in Chapters 2 and 3, I discuss in this chapter the situation of the senior generation in East and Southeast Asia drawing information from China, Hong Kong, South Korea, Japan, Indonesia, Malaysia, the Philippines, Singapore, Thailand, and Vietnam. However, as indicated in previous chapters, the discussion is limited to available comparable data. To dispel the outdated image of the senior generation, ideally we should compare some of its basic features at various points in the history of a community or society. Unfortunately this is precluded by the lack of comparable detailed figures for all the ten countries. Thus, I use the case of Singapore first as an illustration of the transformation of the senior generation. I then proceed to identify trends in all the ten countries.

The Singapore Case

Let us take the cohort of people 80 years old and older as the most senior generation. To approximate the comparison of the senior generation of Singapore residents who will be 80 years old or older four decades from 1990-2000 we could, tentatively, project the situation with data from 1990 and 2000, the years of the latest population censuses. Table 4.1 presents a comparison of Singapore's residents who were 80 years old or older in 1990 with people in the age cohort 40-44 in 1990 and those who were 40-44 years old in 2000. Based on their projected life expectancy, these two cohorts will be 80-84 in the year 2030 and 2040 respectively.

The differences between these three generations are striking. The most senior generation (80 years old and older) formed only 1.0 per cent of the total Singapore resident population in 1990. But demographic studies suggest that the 1990 and 2000 cohorts of 40-year-olds will reach their 80th birthday in larger proportions given the natural increase in life expectancy. Thus, the proportion of 80-year-olds in 2040 is very likely to be greater than that in 2030 and 1990. Numbers have social and political significance. The experience of industrialised countries indicates that their growing number, among other things, has given senior citizens greater visibility and weight in public affairs, for example on taxation, medical services, public transport, and social security policies.[21]

There is also a remarkable difference in education between the three senior generations. While only 2.7 per cent of the 1990 senior generation had secondary school or higher education, approximately a third of the 2030 and more than half of the 2040 senior generations will have secondary school or higher education. Correspondingly, the majority (65.7 per cent) of the 1990 senior generation was illiterate, but it is expected that less than 10 per cent of the senior generation in the year 2030 and less than 3 per cent of the 2040 seniors will be uneducated. With education comes the ability to be literate in more than one language. The expected outcome of the current bilingual educational system in Singapore is that about a fourth of the 2030 senior generation and over half of the 2040 senior generation will be literate in more than two languages, compared to only 2.8 per cent of the 1990 senior generation.

TABLE 4.1. ESTIMATED COMPARISON OF THREE COHORTS OF
SENIORS IN SINGAPORE, 1990, 2030, AND 2040 (IN PERCENTAGES)

Cohort Characteristics	Senior Cohorts		
	Seniors aged 80 and above in 1990	Seniors aged 80-84 in 2030 (40-44 in 1990)[1]	Seniors aged 80-84 in 2040 (40-44 in 2000)[2]
Number in actual cohort[3]	27,099 (100.0)	203,975 (100.0)	615,835 (100.0)
Proportion illiterate[4]	65.7	7.2	2.7
Proportion with secondary school or higher education[5]	2.7	35.9	53.8
Proportion literate in two or more languages[6]	2.8	27.1	51.7
Proportion who are Central Provident Fund contributors (compulsory savings from wages as financial security after retirement)[7]	10.6	57.8	75.7
Proportion born outside Singapore[8]	81.2	20.7	15.8

1. Information refers to the 1990 age cohort 40-44 which will be 80-84 years old in the year 2030.
2. Information refers to the 2000 age cohort 40-44 which will be 80-84 years old in the year 2040.
3. Figures on the third and fourth columns refer to the actual number of people aged 40-44 in 1990 and 40-44 in 2000. But the 2000 census figures for the education and literacy characteristics listed in this table are given for the combined age cohort 35-44 as no separate data are provided for the age cohort 40-44.
4. Singapore Department of Statistics (1993:34); and Leow (2001a:114).
5. Singapore Department of Statistics (1993:181); and Leow (2001a:114).
6. Singapore Department of Statistics (1993:32-34); and Leow (2001a:114).
7. Singapore Department of Statistics (1994:65). The figures are estimations. Data for 1990 cover the larger age cohort 60 and older. No detailed figures are given for those 80 years old or older. The 1990 census reported 246,800 persons in the age cohort 60 and older. Therefore, the 26,200 CPF contributors reported in this age group represent 10.6 per cent of that cohort. Figures for the age cohort 40-44 in 2000 are based on the total number of Singapore residents in that age cohort who were working, as reported in Leow (2001c:35).
8. Singapore Department of Statistics (1992:65); and Leow (2001b:57-59).

Two other related features of significance concern social security as represented by the Central Provident Fund (CPF) and the status of being naturalised as opposed to having been born in Singapore. About 58 per cent of seniors in the year 2030 and 75 per cent of seniors on 2040 would have been CPF contributors (or would enjoy some form of social security) compared to less than 10 per cent of the 1990 senior generation. Similarly, 81 per cent of seniors in 1990 were born outside Singapore but this proportion will drop to about 20 per cent in 2030 and 15 per cent in 2040. That is, the situation would be exactly the reverse of that in 1990. About eight of every ten seniors will be Singapore-born, that is, they will have only one cultural home.

A comparison of Singapore population over 50 years of age in 1980, 1990 and 1995 in terms of other indicators of quality of life such as hospitalisation days, physical mobility, and labour force participation, confirms a steady improvement in the quality of life and social involvement of senior cohorts.[22] According to the 1990 population census, 93.8 per cent of people aged 60 and over were ambulant, that is, able to walk and move about unassisted.[23] The proportion of people aged 60 and older who indicated in two national surveys of senior citizens that their health was "not good" or "poor" actually decreased from 33.6 per cent in 1983 to 16.6 per cent in 1995.[24] This positive picture of the health of our senior citizens is likely to remain or improve in the coming decades with further advances in medical knowledge and greater concern for healthy living habits in the population.

Another important finding of the 1980-1995 comparison of senior cohorts[25] (also illustrated by the projections in Table 4.1) is that the proportion of seniors with secondary school or university education increased noticeably. An expected outcome of improved educational qualifications of the senior citizens is their level of participation in the labour force and the kinds of occupations they have. The same study shows a significant increase in the proportion of men and women aged 50 to 59 who remain working. This increase is explained in part by the change in retirement age from 55 to 60 stipulated in the Retirement Age Act of 1993 that came into effect on 1 July the same year, but it is not the sole factor. Most or all employees at that time would have job contracts indicating the retirement age as 55. With the legal change in retirement age, "employees have the right to continue working up to 60 years, although their contracts of service or collective agreement provides for a lower retirement age."[26]

The Act increased the social 'space' for people to continue in active employment but it was a personal decision for the employee to take up that space and exercise his or her right to continue working beyond the age of 55. The participation rates for people aged 55 to 59 suggest that many took that option, particularly women. The proportion of employees increased accordingly from 52.5 in 1980 to 68.6 in 1995. On the other hand, there was a decrease in labour force participation from 1980 to 1995 among people aged 60 and older. A possible explanation may be found in the type of occupations held by seniors. The socioeconomic transformation of Singapore society over the past 25 years is reflected in its occupational structure: the major shift is the significant increase in professional and technical occupations and managerial positions and a definite decline in jobs related to agriculture. The same trends are evident among senior working people with some additional features. Although the most evident occupational change from 1970 to 1995 took place in jobs related to service and sales, this type of job was still the second most common occupation for people aged 50 and older. In the 1990s, the largest proportion of senior working people was in jobs related to industrial production. Two other important changes are the significant increases in the proportion of seniors in professional and technical jobs (from 4.9 in 1970 to 14.3 in 1995) and in managerial occupations (from 2.5 in 1970 to 15.6 in 1995).[27]

The policy plans that have been put in motion in Singapore are based on the 'greying' society assumption, that is, that the country will be burdened in the 21st century with an increasing number of frail, sick, and "dependent aged" (defined as people who are 60 or older). Such an assumption is inaccurate. The combined projected picture suggested by the preceding figures is one of an assertive, educated, independent, and articulate generation of seniors. Consequently, in contrast to the 1990 octogenarians (Table 4.1), the characteristics of Singaporeans over 50 years of age at the beginning of the 21st century suggest that future generations of seniors are likely to be healthier, more autonomous and more actively involved in their own family life as well as in their communities. A corollary of this trend is that the family and the society must adjust to the new needs, rights, and presence of older but *active* and *dynamic* generations of senior citizens.

Asian Trends

The transformation of the senior generation in Singapore is not unique as can be appreciated by the comparison of ten Asian countries (China, Hong Kong, South Korea, Japan, Indonesia, Malaysia, Singapore, the Philippines, Thailand, and Vietnam). One commonly used approach to assess the social impact of longer life expectancy is the Old-Age Dependency Ratio, the number of people aged 65 and older for every 100 persons aged 15 to 64 in the country. The Old-Age Dependency Ratio suggests the level of obligation of the population to care for their elderly and frail members (defined as people who are 65 and older). The Old-Age Dependency Ratio is the counterpart of the Youth Dependency Ratio (number of persons 0 to 14 per 100 persons aged 15-54 in the population). The latter denotes the level of responsibility of adults to care for dependent children.[28] Both demographic measures are based on the assumption that the youngest and oldest members of society are vulnerable and need to be looked after by the stronger and more adept members (defined as people 15 to 64). This principle is practically universal in human communities. The drawback is the conventional definition of 'old' that does not keep pace with changes in science, technology and other aspects of life. As countries develop, so do the nature of the senior generation, its impact on society and the meaning of 'old age'. William Strauss and Neil Howe conveyed this succinctly, "Generations come in cycles. Just as history produces generations, so too do generations produce history."[29]

The data in Chart 4.1 show that despite the great country to country variation that characterises Asia — in wealth creation, language, ethnicity, religion, cultural background, and political system, among other features — two visible changes took place in the span of 50 years across the region: people are having fewer children and living longer. A close-up picture of the situation of seniors is in Chart 4.2. By the year 2000, Japan was by far the country with the largest proportion (25.9) of seniors, defined in this discussion as people aged 65 and older (Chart 4.2). In a distant second place were Hong Kong (14.5) and Singapore (10.2). To ascertain the changing nature and impact of the senior generation in the ten countries, only two of their attributes are available for the cross-national comparison, their level of education (I use illiteracy rates as a proxy indicator) and their contribution to economic development (I use labour force participation rates as a proxy indicator).

CHART 4.1 OLD-AGE AND YOUTH DEPENDENCY RATIOS, 1950-2000

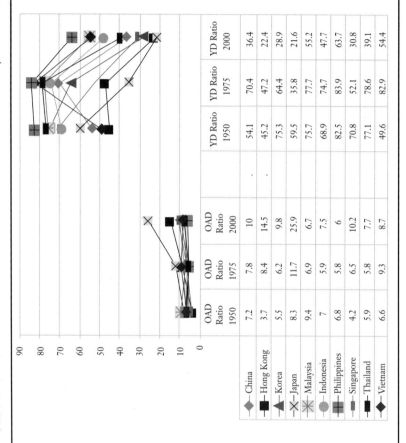

	OAD Ratio 1950	OAD Ratio 1975	OAD Ratio 2000		YD Ratio 1950	YD Ratio 1975	YD Ratio 2000
China	7.2	7.8	10	.	54.1	70.4	36.4
Hong Kong	3.7	8.4	14.5	.	45.2	47.2	22.4
Korea	5.5	6.2	9.8		75.3	64.4	28.9
Japan	8.3	11.7	25.9		59.5	35.8	21.6
Malaysia	9.4	6.9	6.7		75.7	77.7	55.2
Indonesia	7	5.9	7.5		68.9	74.7	47.7
Philippines	6.8	5.8	6		82.5	83.9	63.7
Singapore	4.2	6.5	10.2		70.8	52.1	30.8
Thailand	5.9	5.8	7.7		77.1	78.6	39.1
Vietnam	6.6	9.3	8.7		49.6	82.9	54.4

Source: Calculated from United Nations Populations Division (2002).

OAD Ratio: Old-Age Dependency Ratio is the number of persons 65 years old and older per 100 persons aged 15 to 64.

YD Ratio: Youth Dependency Ratio is the number of persons 0 to 14 years per 100 persons aged 15 to 64.

CHART 4.2   TRENDS IN OLD-AGE DEPENDENCY RATIO, 1950-2000

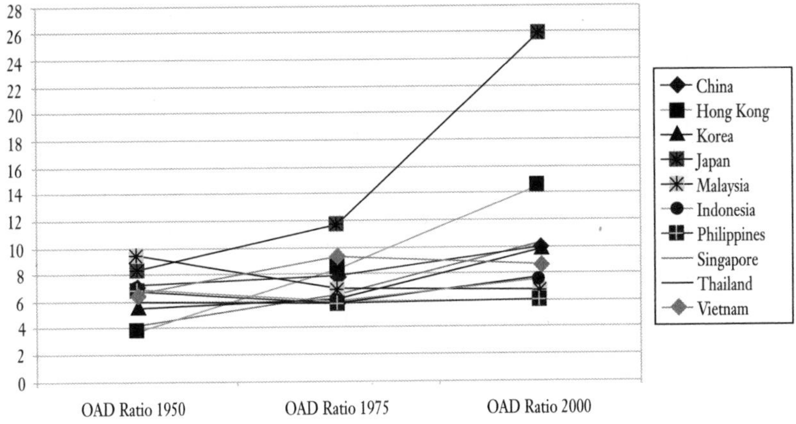

Source: Calculated from United Nations Population Division (2002).

(a) A Better Educated Senior Generation

There is a discernable trend across the ten countries towards a better educated generation of seniors (Chart 4.3). The illiteracy rate of an age cohort is the "proportion of persons in that age group who cannot read with understanding and cannot write a short simple statement on their everyday life."[30] The proportion of the illiterate among people aged 65 and above has dropped steadily in all ten countries over the two decades. The country with the lowest illiteracy rate among seniors (and with the best educated seniors) is Japan followed distantly by South Korea. The illiteracy figures for Japan are estimated based on studies of Japanese society documenting the high level of education of the population[31] and its deep-seated regard for education. It is common for Japanese to describe their society as "*gakureki shakai* (a society oriented inordinately to educational credentialism)."[32]

The common trend towards a better educated senior generation should not obscure the differences among the ten countries. Of the various factors explored in the search for explanations of the significant differences in illiteracy rates of the senior generation, one stands up: the country's overall socioeconomic progress ascertained by the Human Development Index. As indicated in Chapter 2, the HDI denotes a country's life

95

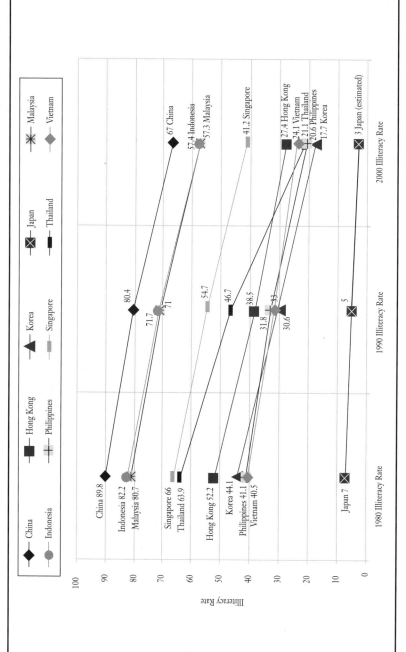

CHART 4.3   TRENDS IN ILLITERACY RATES OF PEOPLE AGED 70 AND OLDER, 1980–2000

Source: Calculated from United Nations Population Division (2002).

expectancy at birth, adult literacy rate, the combined gross enrolment ratio in primary, secondary, and tertiary education, and the Gross Domestic Product per capita in US dollars.[33] Chart 4.4 illustrates the strong inverse association between overall human development and the illiteracy rate of seniors (people aged 70 and older in this chart following the United Nations data) in the year 2000. This association is expected given that the HDI includes adult literacy rate. But the interesting message in this chart is that, contrary to the popular image of 'the elderly' as a generation left behind, the situation of the senior generation reflects the state of development of the total population.

CHART 4.4 ILLITERACY RATE OF PEOPLE AGED 70 OR OLDER AND HUMAN DEVELOPMENT INDEX, 2000

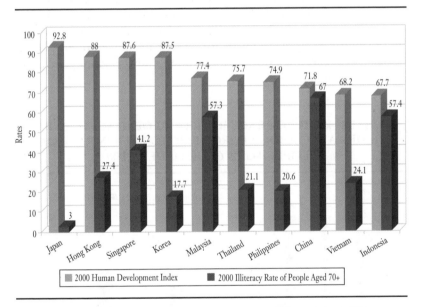

Source: Calculated from United Nations Population Division (2002); The Economist (2003).
Correlation: r = -.681; p = .043

(b) Decreasing Labour Force Participation

It would be reasonable to expect that the senior generation's contribution to the country's economy would expand in accordance with the steady increase in their level of education. This appears to be the case as suggested by the figures in Chart 4.5. However, the apparent trend is only an estimate as there are two age cohorts in this comparison, seniors aged 65 and over and seniors aged 70 and over.[34] A better perspective of the labour force participation of seniors is conveyed by Charts 4.6 to 4.9.

From a historical perspective, the contribution of the senior generation to the labour force has declined in all the ten countries over the past 50 years (Chart 4.6). More revealing, however, is that labour force participation of seniors is lowest in Singapore and Hong Kong which are among the wealthier countries (Chart 4.7) with the highest scores in Gender-related Development Index (Chart 4.8) and with the highest use of information technology (as indicated by the proportion of personal computers per 10,000 population in Chart 4.9). Hong Kong and Singapore are different from the other eight countries is another important respect: both are global cities, and Singapore is a city-state as well. This feature is significant because their economies are pinned to the ups and downs of the world economy more than that of the other eight countries. The latter have a substantial domestic economy and a significant agricultural sector, absent in Singapore and Hong Kong. Thus, there are more job opportunities for the senior generation in the other eight countries.

CHART 4.5 ILLITERACY RATE OF PEOPLE AGED 70 OR OLDER AND LABOUR FORCE PARTICIPATION RATE OF PEOPLE AGED 65 OR OLDER, 2000

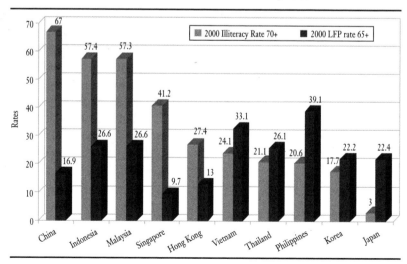

Source: Calculated from United Nations Population Division (2002).

CHART 4.6 LABOUR FORCE PARTICIPATION OF PEOPLE AGED 65 AND OLDER, 1950–2000

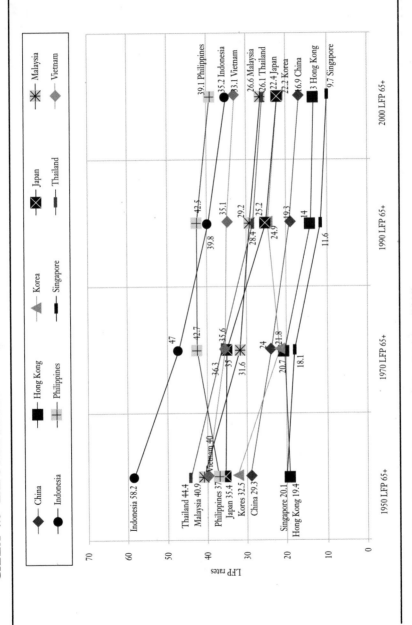

Source: Calculated from United Nations Population Division (2002).

CHART 4.7 TOTAL LABOUR FORCE PARTICIPATION RATE OF POPULATION AGED 65 AND OLDER IN 2000, AND 1997 GDP PER CAPITA AS PERCENTAGE OF JAPAN'S GDP

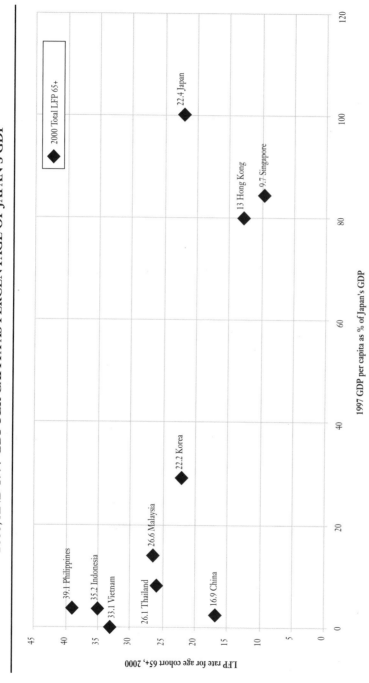

Sources: Figures on labour force participation are calculated from United Nations Population Division (2002); figures on GDP per capita from World Bank (2002) were used for the calculation taking Japan's 1997 GDP as 100. Correlation: r = -.676; p = .032.

CHART 4.8   TOTAL LABOUR FORCE PARTICIPATION RATE OF POPULATION AGED 65 AND OLDER IN 2000, AND GENDER-RELATED DEVELOPMENT INDEX 2002.

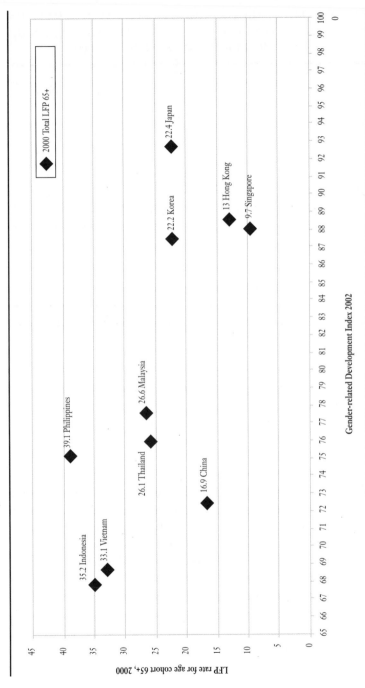

Sources: Figures on labour force participation are from United Nations Population Division (2002); figures for GDI are from United Nations Development Programme (2002: 222–225).

Correlation: r = -.661; p = .037.

CHART 4.9 TOTAL LABOUR FORCE PARTICIPATION RATE OF POPULATION AGED 65 AND OLDER IN 2000, AND PERSONAL COMPUTERS PER 10,000 PERSONS IN 2000.

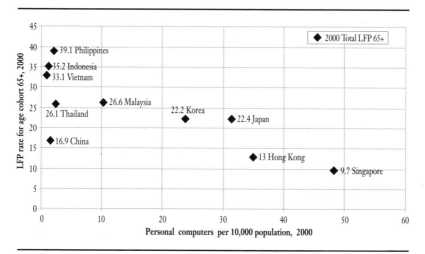

Sources: Figures on labour force participation are from United Nations Population Division (2002); figures on personal computers are from World Bank (2002). Correlation: r = -.770; p = .009.

To appreciate the situation of seniors we need to think in terms of social space, that is, the presence and range of opportunities or "life chances" (Weber's term) open to a person throughout his or her life trajectory to attain goals and independence. Sociologist Robert K. Merton referred to this phenomenon as "opportunity structure" that varies across a person's life-span.[35] Merton's concept is useful in conveying the power exerted by social arrangements and regulations (particularly those limiting access to areas of the country's socioeconomic or political activity), upon the life chances of individuals or groups. Two examples of the role of opportunity structure will suffice. The social space for seniors in the country's wealth production is drastically reduced when employment opportunities are limited by regulations on age. Structural arrangements that set mandatory retirement age in a country are the best example of the reduction or termination of social space for senior citizens. When companies give preference to job applicants below the age of 40, 50, or 60, they are effectively reducing employment opportunities for qualified and experienced but older applicants. Moreover, in addition to the loss

102

of income, the inability to continue earning a living because of compulsory retirement leads to a significant reduction in the social capital both ways: the company loses the employee's contribution, and the retiring employee suffers a reduction in social capital as he or she has to leave the informal network of friends and co-workers.

It appears that in response to the pressures of world economic competition demanding higher levels of technology and innovation, Hong Kong and Singapore are reducing the social space for seniors in the labour market. With an increasingly better educated senior generation, this attitude is myopic as it would be in detriment of their economies to continue curtailing the opportunity structure for a significant proportion of their populations, particularly considering that, as global cities without the benefit of natural resources, their only or main asset is their people.

HOME AND SOCIAL CAPITAL

A great deal of attention is paid by policy experts and social scientists to one dimension of social capital (defined as the network of intergenerational relationships characterised by mutual esteem), the relationship between parents and their children of all ages. Studies cover a wide range of aspects of this relationship including infant care, juvenile delinquency, and the support of aged parents by their adult children. All these and other aspects of the parent-child relationship are important. One of the reasons for highlighting the role of seniors as grandparents has to do with the considerable increase in life expectancy in Asia over the past 30 years. The implications of this demographic fact for families are exciting. Referring to the same trend (that began much earlier) in the United States, sociologists Andrew Cherlin and Frank Furstenberg wrote: "For the first time in history, most adults live long enough to get to know most of their grandchildren, and most children have the opportunity to know most of their grandparents."[36]

Social capital is first generated at home, in the privacy of the family. Evidently, the first contacts of a young child with people older than his or her parents usually take place in the family and may involve the larger or extended group of relatives. Among these early intergenerational contacts one of the most significant is that between children and their grandparents. What is not obvious to most people, however, is first, that children acquire their perception (whether positive, indifferent or negative) of their grandparents from what other adults in the family do and say; and second, that children usually extend that perception to the senior generation in general, not just to their grandparents.

Consequently, the benefits of an affectionate or positive relationship between these two generations (grandparents and grandchildren) are many, but two deserve special attention. One of these benefits is that grandparenting builds a bridge for the senior generation to become actively engaged in the present and to project themselves into the future. This benefit may be more or less prominent depending on the cultural values of different societies. The other benefit of this bond across generations is the enhancement of value transmission. The cultural roots of a community take many forms and may wither away if not for the conscious effort to pass them along to the young. Compared to busy working parents, grandparents today have more time[37] and knowledge on traditions to teach the young child folk songs and games and to narrate engaging stories of life in times past, where the heroes or heroines proudly displayed cherished values. Once children begin school and grow older, the time they spent at home with parents and grandparents is reduced. But the principles and values they absorbed from the older generations in early childhood tend to strengthen their sense of identity.

The time spent with grandparents is more than just play and folksongs. A team of Thai ethnographers studied a group of 12 families in a rice-farming village in Northeastern Thailand.[38] They found that children in the village have a close relationship with their grandparents on a daily basis. Boys sleep in the room with the grandfathers and girls in the same room with their grandmothers. As the children participate actively in farming work and other chores around the house from a very young age, they are taught the required skills by their parents and grandparents. Compared to the parents, grandparents on the whole interacted with the grandchildren in a more 'didactic' manner as they would typically answer a grandchild's question by demonstrating in a show-and-tell fashion. The same method was used when teaching the grandchildren how to do chores.[39] Grandparents also teach their grandchildren to pray and to be respectful of elders.[40]

A similar situation was observed by Myrna Blake in her study of seniors in Malay families in Singapore: grandparents impart valuable knowledge on the customs and regulations on marriage, weddings, and other important life events.[41] In terms of life transitions, "Becoming a grandparent is the one certain event which establishes the status" of a senior person.[42] Another important aspect of the life of senior Malays, both men and women, is that even in their 70s, many continue to work in part-time or casual jobs of a type permitted by their level of education. Men as "temporary clerks, security guards, sweepers, and labourers" and women more often in selling home-made food, or as cleaners, "seamstresses, masseuse and Quran teachers."[43]

In Japan, the proportion of seniors 65 years old and older living in three-generation households decreased from 78.3 per cent in 1975 to 52.8 per cent in 2001.[44] This proportion is lower than that of Singapore where 73.8 per cent of seniors aged 65 and above in the year 2000 were living with their children.[45] Yoshio Sugimoto, a Japanese sociologist, sees the fact that one of every two seniors live with their children and grandchildren as a good 'external' sign of the endurance of the extended family and "the survival of traditional family values."[46] Yet, referring to Japanese urban families, he adds, "In *ura* reality [the dark, concealed side] ... most [of these families] make this arrangement for pragmatic rather than altruistic reasons." On the other hand, he reports that rural family households show a stronger tendency to preserve the traditional extended family[47] thus giving grandparents and grandchildren greater opportunity to interact.

The family structure changes taking place in China over the past two decades as a result of the government's measures to control population growth are resulting in an interesting shift back to the extended family form. Zheng Yi reports that 18.3 per cent of all family household in the 1990 census were three-generation extended family household (grandparents, parents, and children). There was also a small proportion of two-generation family household that involved only grandparents and their grandchildren. Yi suggests that the "middle generation," the parents, were away working in another location to support the entire family financially and the grandparents looked after the grandchildren.[48] The return to the extended family form among a small but significant proportion of families in China, explains Yi, might be stimulated by two main factors. One is the economic reforms that permitted the presence of small family businesses which required the cooperation of family members. The other is that

In the cultural context of Chinese society ... [filial piety] (*xiao*) has been one of the cornerstones of Chinese society for thousands of years and is still highly valued. The philosophical ideas of ...

[filial piety] include not only respect for older generations but also the responsibility of children to take care of their parents.[49]

A similar emphasis is made by researchers of the Vietnamese family on the presence of traditional values supporting the extended family and filial piety. As Le Thi reports, "Old parents rarely live alone. Having many children, they often choose to live with the eldest or the youngest child." In the rural areas, is not unusual to see large extended families "sharing a common long house."[50]

The Filipino approach to childcare reveals the important role played by grandparents in the socialisation of their grandchildren. A study of childcare arrangements among working mothers found that grandmothers and grandfathers are the main sources of childcare for urban and rural working mothers.[51] The traditional extended family presided by the grandparents or the surviving grandparent, is still a very important source of social capital, even if the component nuclear families do not share the same residence.[52] This family type represents the modified extended family form I mentioned earlier.

One may assume that the small geographical size of Singapore offers the senior generation a greater opportunity for continuous contact with their grandchildren. As indicated earlier the overwhelming majority of seniors aged 65 and older were living with their families in 2000, and data from the 1990 census show that grandparents were the second most popular childcare givers after parents.[53] This three-generation family trend is strong: in 1983, 79 per cent of seniors aged 60 and older were living with their children and grandchildren, but this proportion increased to 84.4 per cent in 1995.[54] These figures confirm the finding from earlier studies that the senior generation from the Chinese, Malay, Indian and Eurasian communities in Singapore cherish the close contact with their children and grandchildren.[55]

The role of grandparents as childcare givers is, of course, not unique to Asian societies. Under certain conditions, the senior generation in industrialised nations may find themselves facing the responsibility of caring for their young grandchildren whether or not this duty was part of their retirement plans. For example, there has been an increase in this trend in the United States where "about 3.5 million U.S. children now live with a grandparent" as the result of an increase in disruption of marriages, the need of single parents to work, and an increase in the phenomenon of children raising children (teenage births), among other things.[56] But given the large size and complex composition of the American population, studies reporting attitudes (usually based on small groups) tend to produce inconsistent findings on what the American senior generation perceive as desirable. A detailed psychological study of a group of white middle-class American families across three generations found that "grandparenting ... seems to offer elders one of the most positive and vital involvements of old age" but the researchers found that "grandparents are often deprived of relationships with grandchildren."[57] On the other hand, two American observers suggest that under normal conditions, "white, middle-class American elders" if given a choice, would prefer "to live independently as long as possible, to enjoy their children and grandchildren from a distance (except for occasional visits) and [to pursue] their own interests and values."[58] It is possible that both types of attitudes on the significance of children and grandchildren are present among different groups of American senior citizens.

The relevant message of this comparison is that less developed countries must learn from the experiences of other nations that are some way ahead in economic development. The preceding data show that, in contrast to today's senior generation, the future generations of Asian seniors will be better educated and most probably career-oriented or inclined to remain economically active so as to preserve their financial independence among other reasons. Already in 1995, 40 per cent of Singapore seniors aged 60 and older stated that financial reasons led them to work after retirement, while 55 per cent declared that their main reason was "too lead an active life" and not to feel bored.[59] Consequently, compared to today's grandparents, the senior generations of the future will be even less likely to be available full-time at home and willing to take up the care of their grandchildren with the same dedication. This tentative scenario does not match the collective goal of preserving a strong three-generation family where grandparents are the main grandchild minders. The dilemma for the educated and healthy senior generation person will be how to reconcile the discrepant objectives of (a) preserving his or her residential and financial independence and self-reliance; and (b) enjoying fully the role of parent and grandparent in the midst of a three-generation family.

Furthermore, this is not only the dilemma of individuals. The changes in opportunities and choices open to individuals are shaped by developments affecting the larger society for example, economic growth, improvements in the educational system, higher levels of technology, better and more challenging opportunities in the job market, and the availability of housing.

CREATING SOCIAL SPACE FOR THE SENIOR GENERATION

Creating social space for a given group or category of people in a society is to open opportunities and to offer them the means by which they can attain optimum development. The creation of social space for the senior generation requires the society's willingness to encourage the active involvement of its senior citizens. It looks as if Japan's and Singapore's willingness is substantial. A great deal of effort has been invested in both countries (in Singapore mostly over during the past decade) to ascertain the economic and social situation of the senior generation, the community's views on the senior generation, and the latter's own attitudes and opinions.[60] These studies help to focus the public's attention on the situation of the senior generation and in providing necessary background information. But the creation of social space requires actual action both from the public and private sectors. Creating social space takes place when legislation or administrative regulations are introduced and implemented to set up facilities and procedures that give the senior generation actual avenues for their optimum development and integration into the mainstream of society. Singapore's policy-planners have enlisted the cooperation of the private sector in a joint effort to discuss concrete policy directions involving the senior generation. One recommendation implemented in 1993 was to increase the retirement age progressively. The Retirement Act of 1993 sets the minimum retirement age at 60 and it empowers the Singapore Minister for Labour "to raise this minimum retirement age up to a maximum of 67 years."[61] On its part, the Singapore Ministry of Health sent in August 1994 a four-member delegation of top officials to Japan to study the Japanese approach to provision of health care services for the senior generation including the setting up of two new rehabilitation centres.[62]

These are indications that public efforts to create social space for the senior generation are being made in Japan and Singapore. Besides measures to increase employment opportunities, numerous services, activities and further studies continue on the part of public sector, private sector and mixed sector groups. Yet, one unintended consequence of this positive trend is that the dilemma encountered by individual persons considering withdrawal or retirement from the labour force is also a *collective* dilemma for the society: how to combine successfully family life and work. In the case of people who are beyond the age of 65, the dilemma is how to integrate them as active participants in the labour force while preserving and supporting their close and continuous interaction with their children and grandchildren, ideally in a three-generation family.

The predicament involves, in particular, the healthy senior generation. The proportion of healthy senior generation will increase with the ability of medicine to prevent, control and manage the current typical afflictions of old age. Thus, as shown earlier, the number of healthy seniors is expected to increase steadily. It is this group that will be encouraged to remain in their jobs. The offer will be attractive to healthy seniors as it brings active involvement, it helps them to generate their own financial support, and it represents self-reliance, among other things. That is, the senior generation of the future would be financially and socially less dependent on others than the senior generation of today if the opportunities are open to them.

From a different perspective, the dilemma of combining family and work is compounded by the fact that both seemingly incompatible objectives, the working status of the senior generation and their active involvement in their families, are desirable collective goals in most Asian countries. Not only do grandparents play a very important role in the transmission of cultural values to the young but, in addition, working parents' preferences are clear. If working parents had a choice, they would prefer to leave their children under the trustworthy care of grandparents than under the supervision of childcare centres or maids. Yet, the grandparenting role is feasible only when healthy grandparents are inclined to perform it and when they do not have a full-time job (which is the reason working parents are unable to look after their children themselves).

The task of devising a collectively acceptable merger of family and work for the healthy senior generation must be included in the agendas of all relevant organisations in each country. The two most relevant aspects of this challenge are: housing and work schedules. On the matter of housing, there are three important and concurring trends. First, the three-generation family represents a home where children enjoy the care and attention of parents and grandparents. This is seen as the ideal arrangement in studies of people's attitudes on family and childcare. The second trend is that with the healthy senior generation becoming more financially independent in the future, more of them are likely to prefer keeping their own home, rather than moving in with the larger family. The third trend, suggested by several studies, is that having separate homes does not deter two-generation families from maintaining a close network of relationships through frequent visiting and exchanging of mutual aid (in kind, time, and cash) with their parents, other married siblings, their spouses and children, and other kin. This kinship network typically found in urban settings is the *modified extended family*.

Taken together, these three trends sketch a positive picture. On the one hand, the three-generation family is already an established ideal and people who can implement it have done so. This means that the value of family togetherness has not been lost and what is now needed is to continue inculcating it to the young, particularly at home and in the schools. On the other hand, families who cannot live under the same roof for various reasons keep the kinship network alive as modified extended families. Living near each other is the next best alternative as it minimises transportation and increases opportunities for personal contact. The location of their home near their adult children's would thus become a more popular choice than it is today.

While home proximity enhances family contact, flexible work schedules, or flexitime, help to diminish the dilemma of combining family and work. Basically, flexitime allows a full-time worker to meet his or her contractual weekly hours (for example, a 44-hour working week) by selecting among a range of alternative work schedules. For the healthy senior generation who prefer to continue full-time in the workforce but who do not want to miss their grandchildren's childhood, flexible work schedules will help them, if they so choose, to coordinate their free hours with those of their married children. More young children will have either a parent or grandparent looking after them most of the time. Flexitime brings many other advantages to the workers, including increased control over their work and leisure. The latter is a very important aspect for all workers but it is crucial for older employees. Regrettably, the obvious advantages of flexitime are seen as one-sided by some organisations. It is often argued that companies and employers do not benefit from flexitime as much as employees because flexitime is unsuitable for certain kinds of work or industrial production. Nevertheless, some experts point out that flexible work schedules and similar arrangements that give greater control over one's time increase job satisfaction, productivity, and the overall quality of life.[63] The controversy goes on. Flexitime deserves careful consideration and study because of its advantages as one way of facilitating the combination of family and work.

CONCLUSION

To summarise, the network of close intergenerational relations forms the social capital of a community across time. The three-generation family and the modified extended family represent that network where the senior generation of today — including retirees and homemakers with the time and wish to look after their grandchildren — figure prominently and affectionately. However, future trends shaped by sustained economic and social development will transform the senior generation into an active and autonomous generation. In a certain way the future is here. Measures have already been taken in some countries (notably Japan and Singapore) to create social space for the aged. The retirement age has been extended and efforts are made to persuade the healthy senior generation to postpone retirement. Most adults, irrespective of age and gender, will be in the work force in the next decades. This is in line with sustained economic development but there could be a corresponding decline in the time workers have for their children and grandchildren. Just as economic development is an important social goal, so is family life, the bullion of social capital. This is the dilemma of combining work and family, two aspects of our lives that are seen popularly as incompatible.

Are the formation of social capital and economic capital truly incompatible? The qualified answer is no, providing that measures are taken to minimise contradictions and to harmonise these two goals. Finding solutions to the dilemma is a complex task. Still, we may begin by adjusting our values to accept the principle of respect for the autonomy of the senior generation:

> To respect an autonomous [person] is, first, to recognize that person's capacities and perspective, including his or her right to hold views, to make choices, and to take actions based on personal values and beliefs. But respect ... [also] involves treating [persons]

so as to allow or enable them to act autonomously. That is, true respect includes acting to respect, not the mere adoption of certain attitude.[64]

Endorsing this principle is a precondition to proceed with the two pragmatic first steps suggested earlier. One is enhancing opportunities for the formation of modified extended families. The other is to study carefully the application of flexible work schedules and its connection with productivity and job satisfaction in different sectors of the economy.

Finally, to meet the challenge of integrating family life (social capital) and work (economic capital) two factors should be evident. First, the principle of respect for autonomy does not conflict with community-oriented attitudes when the latter are part of the values and beliefs of the members of that community. Second, this principle and the two initial approaches towards the solution of the family-work dilemma (home proximity to other members of the family and the option to select one's work schedule), would benefit citizens of all ages, not just the senior citizens.

ENDNOTES

1. See Beauchamp and Childress (1989:67-119).
2. The latter was the predominant collective image of the senior generation in the 1980s found in a study of Singaporeans' attitudes towards old age. See Advisory Council on the Aged (1988a) and (1988b).
3. See Jowett and Loomis (1941:223).
4. See Coleman (1990).
5. See Putnam (2000:19, 351-5).
6. See Coleman (1990:304-306).
7. Examples of the impact of Coleman's concept of social capital are found in Clark (1996); Stone and Hughes (2002); and Putnam (2002:5-6). See also Fischer (1982) for an earlier analysis of the basic idea of social networks.
8. See Putnam (2000:19).
9. See Putnam (2000:21-22).
10. See Putnam (2000:21).
11. See Weber (1978:387-390).
12. See Putnam (2000) and (2002); Stone and Hughes (2002).
13. See Putnam (2000).
14. See Putnam (2002).
15. See Stone and Hughes (2002:3).
16. See Stone and Hughes (2002:2).

17. See Stone and Hughes (2002:12).
18. See Inoguchi (2002:371-2).
19. See Inoguchi (2002:389-390).
20. See Bott (1971); and Fischer (1982).
21. See for example Ditch, Barnes and Bradshaw (1996); Borgatta and McCluskey (1980); Kohli, Rein, Guillemard and van Gunsteeren (1991); and Cherlin and Furstenberg (1992).
22. See Quah (1998:205).
23. See Shantakumar (1994:156).
24. See Singapore Ministry of Health (1996:41).
25. See Quah (1998).
26. See NTUC (1996:31).
27. See Quah (1998:207).
28. The trend towards smaller families is discussed in Chapter 3.
29. See Strauss and Howe (1991:35).
30. See United Nations Population Division (2002:41).
31. See Asahi Shimbun (2003:228).
32. See Sugimoto (2003:36).
33. For a detailed explanation of the HDI calculation see United Nations Development Programme (2002:253).
34. As presented by the data source, the available figures on illiteracy rates cover the age cohort 70 and over while the data on labour force participation refer to the age cohort 65 and over. See United Nations Population Division (2002).
35. See Merton (1973:548-549); and Stompka (1996). Merton's concept 'opportunity structure' is discussed further in Chapter 5 of this volume.
36. See Cherlin and Furstenberg (1992: 25).
37. Population census figures for 1990 indicate that 38.6 per cent of people aged 60 and older have 40 hours or more per week of leisure time compared to 12.5 per cent or less of younger adults. See Lau (1994:144).
38. See Amornvivat et al (1990).
39. See Amornvivat et al (1990:56).
40. See Amornvivat et al (1990:111).
41. See Blake (1992:10).
42. See Blake (1992:12).
43. See Blake (1992:18-19).
44. See Asahi Shimbun (2003:32).
45. See Leow (2001b:131).
46. See Sugimoto (2003:175-176).
47. See Sugimoto (2003:176).
48. See Yi (2002:20); and Irving (2002:71) on the same situation in Hong Kong.

49. See Yi (2002:32).
50. See Thi (1999:64-65).
51. See Alcantara (1995:86-91).
52. See Medina (1991:17).
53. See Quah (1998:67).
54. See Singapore Ministry of Health (1996:15-16).
55. See Blake (1992:119); Jernigan and Jernigan (1992); Tham (1989).
56. See Institute of Social Research (1994:8).
57. See Erikson, Erikson, and Kivnick (1986:306).
58. See Jernigan and Jernigan (1992:100).
59. See Singapore Ministry of Health (1996:37).
60. See Chen and Chang (1982); Tham (1989); Chen and Cheung (1988); Kua, Ang, and Merriman (1986); Phua (1987); Blake (1992); Shantakumar (1994); Sugimoto (2003:72-81).
61. See NTUC (1996:31).
62. See Singapore Ministry of Health (1995:25, 55).
63. See Moore-Ede (1993); Mado-sha (1990).
64. See Beauchamp and Childress (1989:71).

CHAPTER **5**

From 'His Family, Her Duty' to 'Their Family': The Gender Issue

With the implied premise that family matters cannot be discussed in a gender vacuum, the preceding chapters on marriage, parenthood, and social capital in families, have paved the way to this direct deliberation on the gender issue. I address in this chapter the problems faced by Asian women and men in their striving to attain a coherent social life whereby the joys and benefits of marriage and parenthood may be successfully combined with their developing as intelligent, efficient, hard-working, and thriving income earners, if they so wish. The context is contemporary Asia, or more specifically, four East Asian (China, Hong Kong, Japan, and South Korea) and six Southeast Asian (Indonesia, Malaysia, the Philippines, Singapore, Thailand, and Vietnam) countries. The struggle for coherence of their gender norms is a relatively new phenomenon in these countries compared to Western countries. It may be traced back to about five decades ago — although developing at a different pace in each country and more so in urban than in rural areas — and it has increased in intensity due to the improvement in women's education and the mounting social pressures on them to succeed on both fronts, their homes and their non-family occupations. With men's and women's gender roles being closely intertwined, any changes in one necessarily affect the other. This preoccupation is manifest in this discussion despite the dearth of direct information of men's attitudes and actions on gender matters compared to the attention that women's position in society has received from social scientists.

For anyone acquainted with recent social science research findings, this problem of opposite demands on women is not new and it is not unique to Asia. Then what, if anything, is characteristically Asian? I identify and discuss in this chapter the interesting and perhaps uniquely Asian combination of three factors or contradictory signals — and the

115

way in which women try to make sense of them and organise their lives around them. These three factors are: the traditional value on the different roles of women and men; the exigencies of an industrial economy that encourages and rewards the joint participation of men and women in the labour force; and the modern value of gender equality. I examined these factors earlier in the case of Singapore[1] and, as far as the available data permit I expand their analysis here to the ten Asian countries. By making a cross-national comparison, I hope to emphasise the importance of macro-sociological differences across countries in the context of similarities afforded by some common traditions that transcend political boundaries. After outlining the relevant sociological ideas guiding the analysis, the second section deals with the main factors or contradictory signals, and the third section discusses the struggle for coherence.

PERTINENT SOCIOLOGICAL IDEAS

Two central concepts provide the basis for this discussion on gender and family: (a) Max Weber's ideas of 'life chances' and social status; and (b) Robert K. Merton's concept of opportunity structure. These concepts provide the groundwork for my analysis of everyday life conditions of men and women together with the notions of gender-role stereotypes and Jessie Bernard's typology of gender-role ideologies.

Drawing sociological principles on human behaviour from his analysis of the formation of social classes and the differential allocation of status in society both of which affect people's "life chances,"[2] Max Weber proposed that "stratification by status goes hand in hand with a monopolization of ideal and material goods and opportunities."[3] He defined status as "an effective claim to social esteem in terms of positive or negative privileges typically founded on life style"[4] and other characteristics of the person such as religion and ethnicity. Weber called attention to the fact that life chances and opportunities are differentially available to or unreachable by a person depending on his or her status in society.

Weber's ideas were developed by Robert K. Merton who highlighted in his theory of social structure[5] the allocation of differential status positions to individuals playing multiple roles in society as members of interconnected social networks. In Merton's view, social status operates through two types of structures: normative structures and opportunity structures. Normative structures are "the patterned set of expectations regarding the socially defined, appropriate behaviour for an incumbent of that status."[6] On opportunity structures, he explained:

> […] each social status has an opportunity aspect that includes both the set of life chances (Weber's term), options, resources, and facilities differentially accessible to the incumbent and the correlative opportunity structure which distributes and redistributes the probabilities of such differential access. … Together, normative structures and opportunity structures exert constraining and facilitating influences on behaviors, beliefs, attitudes, and motivations of persons located in them. And the behaviors they induce have consequences that often reshape social institutions.[7]

His notion that a person's social status directly affects his or her "differential access to opportunities" in society helps to elucidate the connection between individual and society or, as he put it "the interplay between structural context and individual action" whereby

> (1) the (variously changing) arrays of opportunities represent objective *conditions* confronting acting individuals — *agents*, as they are now often described — who (2) are constrained or aided in gaining access to diverse types of opportunities by their positions in the social structure, which (3) locate individuals in terms of their status-sets (i.e., the array of their social attributes such as class, sex, race, ethnicity, age, religion, etc.).[8]

It is necessary to let Merton speak directly on his analysis of social status and structures of opportunity because of the clarity of his ideas and the particular relevance that the analysis of normative structures and structures of opportunity have to the scrutiny of the social position of people in society in terms of their gender, as women and men of the 21st century.

Based on evidence that most societies today have a normative structure that dictates clearly different norms for men and women, I argue that by virtue of their gender, women are restricted to or attributed a socially-assigned status-set that severely limits their life chances or opportunities for goal attainment. This is because, in a similar fashion that it affects the senior generation (discussed in Chapter 4), and in contrast to the situation of men, the opportunity structure open to women offers narrower social spaces both at home and outside the home, in the realm of non-family structures and social networks (for example in educational, employment, and political participation opportunities). As an Asian woman awakes to the realisation that she could challenge the restricted socially-constructed opportunity structure within which she is expected to operate, she begins to confront resistance from the community's norms. Resistance is expected because the normative structure of Asian communities is founded on ancient traditions that form the cornerstone of the Asian ethos and — as Weber and Merton suggest — are used by people to validate different structures of opportunity for women and men. The differential opportunities given or denied to women and men are said to be dictated by an all encompassing religious and/or philosophical cosmology.

MAIN CONTRADICTORY SIGNALS

In reference to Merton's normative structure, three trends that affect the social definition of gender roles may be identified in some Asian countries namely, the permanence of traditional values, the exigencies of a modern economy leading to the state's intervention in encouraging further female participation in the labour force, and the concept of gender equality promoted through universal education and modernisation. These three trends may operate concurrently in the more economically developed countries in Asia and, particularly, in large Asian cities, and create incongruous demands in the lives of men and women. Let us look into each of these trends individually.

Traditional Values

Advances in science, technology, international trade, and the incomparable expansion and sophistication of mass media over the second half of the 20th century led some observers to declare the fading of cultural barriers and the advent of a world culture that would turn us all into world citizens. Some of this is happening through the undeniable close economic interdependence of regions and continents. Yet, the pervasiveness of cultural idiosyncrasies has been recognised all along.[9] Moreover, the past decade has witnessed an unexpected revival of ethnic sentiment and a sense of urgency in bringing back community's traditions and identity to their pride of place. China, for example, is experiencing a more open expression of cultural traditions aided by the political and economic reforms of the past decade. This process is seen in the subtle leaning towards the extended family in the form of three-generation households and in the emergence of small family businesses.[10] In Hong Kong, the combination of tradition and modernity is captured in many aspects of life including family norms.[11]

Japan presents a dramatic illustration of the co-existence of the old with the new because of its leading position in Asia in modernisation and economic development. Considering the sharp decline in fertility rate in Japan, one of the most evident expressions of the permanence of tradition in modern Japan is, surprisingly, in the aspect of motherhood. Following traditional values, mothers are expected to dedicate themselves unreservedly to child upbringing. Sociologist Muriel Jolivet suggests that this high social expectation of the mother's role is nearly impossible to attain, frightens young Japanese women, and may be one of the main reasons for their apparent reluctance to have children.[12] Women who work part-time are another example of the strain of combining traditional Japanese norms on female domesticity with the necessity to earn a living in the market economy. Their image at the workplace as well as in the community is one of domesticity: "housewives who work part-time are still housewives."[13] In his analysis of stratification in contemporary Japan, Yoshio Sugimoto asserts that the ancient patriarchal traditions are responsible for the subjecting of Japanese women to "a Japan-specific system of gender control."[14] The government supports traditional values that encourage reliance on family and kin, particularly for the care of parents by their adult children. Emiko Ochiai graphically describes the double burden of child and elderly care that Japanese women are expected to bear when referring to policy-makers' position on welfare costs: "Japan is expected to become an aged society, so you housewives had better get your act together."[15]

The Japanese policy-makers' principle that families should look after their own, is very similar to the position of the Singapore government. Singaporeans receive continuous exhortations from their political leaders on the importance of cultural traditions. The message that one must never forget one's roots[16] is underscored for all Singaporeans, whether their cultural tradition is Malay, Indian, Chinese, or any other. The majority of the Singapore population is Chinese (76.8 per cent) and the two main minorities are Malays (13.9 per cent) and Indians (7.9 per cent).[17]   Cultural traditions involve mores, beliefs, and values on what is right and wrong including the prescription for correct or proper behaviour of individuals as men and women in the community, as well as their obligations and rights in their association with one another. Among the influences that shape the social meaning of gender roles in Singapore, these cultural beliefs and values are important and surprisingly similar. As we have seen in Chapter 3 and as will be elaborated later, women, whether Chinese, Malay, or Indian, are inclined to see marriage and motherhood as two of the crucial goals in their lives. However, the present official encouragement to Singaporeans to strengthen their cultural traditions has introduced a contentious dimension to the already controversial social definition of women's roles. For the Singaporean Chinese, that dimension is the legacy of Confucius. This legacy is found not only in China, Hong Kong, and Taiwan, but also in the cultural traditions of Japan, South Korea, and Vietnam.

It is beyond the scope of this discussion to dwell on the cosmology of Chinese thought. But, it is relevant to identify the definition of the social roles of men and women in the writings of Confucius given that Confucius is considered as the key exponent of the cultural legacy of the Chinese more so than the Taoist or any other Chinese tradition. In the search for the Confucian position on the status and roles of men and women in society, one finds that a predominant feature of his teachings is that they were addressed primarily or almost exclusively to men. Three decades ago, in his comparative analysis of Socrates, Buddha, Confucius, and Jesus, the "paradigmatic individuals" in history, philosopher Karl Jaspers protested:

> One is struck by Confucius' indifference towards women. He has nothing to say of conduct in matrimony, speaks disparagingly of women [...] and frequently remarks that nothing is so hard to handle as a woman. The atmosphere around him is distinctly masculine.[18]

Jaspers' point is readily verified by a review of Confucius' texts.[19] This explains why the same comment is found in many other analyses of Confucian thought.[20] For example, in their comparative study of Asian religions, George Fry and his colleagues[21] conclude that "Confucius taught a philosophy of male domination. While the husband was to be 'righteous' to his wife, she was to be 'obedient' to her husband"; these authors also point out that "while Confucius speaks of the father-son relationship, he has nothing to say about the function of the mother"; they note that, overall, "female figures are notoriously absent from the Confucianist tradition," Confucius made some references to women, for example in Book I.13, Book III.22, Book IV.18, Book IV.19, and Book V.1 of the Analects. Yet, A. H. Black[22] points out, "when women are casually mentioned in these texts, it is generally in terms of kinship or marriage ties." I agree with Black that "if there is anything on which Confucian texts are clear it is that the male should be dominant."[23]

While most analysts agree on this central feature of Confucius' teachings, there is no clear consensus on the explanations given for the Confucian directive on the subjugated role of women vis-à-vis men. Black feels that Confucius neglected this aspect as his "reasons for female submission to male are frequently unstated."[24] Others differ. It is possible to assume that no explicit explanations were considered necessary by Confucius if he was referring to the prevalent values of his time. Indeed, some argue that Confucius' teachings are simply a forceful reminder of fundamental values in Chinese society. Jaspers[25] argues that Confucius, as any other philosopher, "does not advance his ideas as his own" but, rather, brings forth ideas from a superior source; Confucius was "the voice of antiquity" advocating "not imitation of the past but repetition of the eternally true."

Following the same line of explanation, Creel[26] states that, as far as family relations are concerned, "Confucius seems to have added little that was new" considering that the value of subordination to authority was already evident in the works of earlier writers. In the same vein, Chung[27] suggests that subordination was a crucial and required manifestation of loyalty and obedience, which Confucianism deemed as "virtues central to all human relations." These virtues were expressed in the "subordination of the son to the father, the wife to the husband, and the subjects to the rulers." Chung feels that this emphasis on subordination is expected given that the fundamental aspect of Confucius' doctrine "was to maintain the immutable harmony...and equilibrium underlying both the universe and human society."

Furthermore, as the strong voice of cultural tradition, Confucius has personified Chineseness across time. His philosophy "dominated the schools of China for almost twenty-five hundred years" wrote Fry and his colleagues,[28] adding that "in one sense, Confucius was China,

China was Confucius." It is precisely this aspect of Confucianism that is most relevant in the context of the present discussion on the impact of traditional values upon the social roles of women in Singapore, Hong Kong, and China. The teachings of Confucius, as I indicated earlier, are promoted by some Chinese community leaders in Singapore as embodying the quintessence of traditional Chinese culture and, thus, as the traditional values that all Chinese should follow. As the discussion proceeds, it will become apparent that for women in Singapore who are of Chinese descent, this message is one of the contradictory social signals they receive. The same may be said of Malaysians of Chinese descent and of women in Hong Kong and China, all of whom may be presented with the teachings of Confucius as the embodiment of Chinese cultural traditions.

Naturally, traditional values also shape the roles of men and women among the other two main ethnic minorities in Singapore, the Malay and the Indian communities. Among the Malay population in Malaysia, the people of Indonesia and the Malay community in Singapore, religion is the main driving force. In Singapore, Islamic law principles apply to regulations on marriage, marital relations, and divorce, among other family aspects. Some of these regulations vary slightly from those applied in other Muslim countries. In fact, variations in Islamic family law are also found among the states in the Federation of Malaysia. Under the Muslim Law Act in Singapore, Islamic principles on the equality between women and men are manifested in matters such as the consent of the bride as a requirement for the legal registration of the marriage;[29] the wife's right to retain her own property after marriage,[30] and her right to "maintain a suit in her own name" and to be sued "as if she was unmarried."[31]

While gender equality is upheld by the above regulations, Muslim law contains some other provisions that reflect a differential perception of the status of men and women. The two most common examples of this differential treatment are found in the regulations on the capacity to marry and on divorce. Concerning the capacity to marry, Muslim law stipulates that "a woman who is already married is not allowed to marry again while the marriage is subsisting" but it is possible for a man "to marry more than one wife up a maximum of four, provided he is able to treat his wives with equity."[32] As Ahmad clarifies, this flexibility for men "has been restricted" in Singapore by requiring that the Kathi (Registrar of Muslim marriages) holds "an inquiry to satisfy himself that there is no lawful obstacle to the marriage according to Muslim Law and the Administration of Muslim Law Act."[33]

This principle of wider options allowed to Muslim men in marriage is found in divorce legislation as well. International research findings indicate that in general, divorce has a connotation of failure, either in the minds of the couple involved, in the public sphere, or both. This connotation tends to persist regardless of ethnic or religious differences.[34] It is thus not surprising that among the Muslim community, "although divorce is permitted, it is not encouraged and, in religious theory...it is frowned upon." Nevertheless, the husband may divorce his wife "by pronouncing a *talak* or repudiation against her."[35] But a wife wishing to divorce her husband needs to follow a more complicated process. She could apply for divorce on grounds of: (a) "failure of condition" or *cerai taalik* (husband's failure to maintain her for more than three months or her husband's assaulting her) but she has to present evidence to prove the charges; or (b) annulment of marriage or *fasakh*; or (c) by *kholo'*, that is by obtaining the husband's agreement upon payment of compensation to him. More importantly, Ahmad indicates that "While the *talak* can be the unilateral act of the husband, it is necessary for the woman to apply to a Kathi or a court for a degree of *cerai taalik*, *kholo'* or *fasakh*."[36] Considering the above manifestations of gender equality and gender differentiation in the pronouncements of Muslim law, it is evident that the two fundamental events in family life, marriage and divorce, are more affected by segregating regulations than by those regulations enforcing equality. In his comparative study of four Muslim countries, sociologist Riaz Hassan explains that "the improvement of the status of women and children" was an integral part of the earliest phase of the Islamic movement, but as it has happened in other religions, "the religion later was hijacked by men, who interpreted the sacred texts in a way that was inimical to Muslim women."[37]

In the case of the Indian community in Singapore, its high internal diversity prevents easy generalisations. There are numerous ethnic subdivisions and religious groups in the Indian community.[38] This feature justifies the assumption that the Indian community is guided by both secular and religious traditions. It appears that the same general characterisation may be made of the Indian community in Malaysia. One interesting example of the secular Indian traditions is The Laws of Manu. It deals with custom and convention and is a work of the

"Epic period" of Indian philosophy originating around the sixth century B.C. While the section on the "Status and Duties of Women" contains numerous verses honouring women, there are explicit precepts on the behaviour of men and women. The following verses are the most relevant:

> [2] Day and night women must be kept in dependence by the males of their families, and, if they attach themselves to sensual enjoyments, they must be kept under one's control... [3] Her father protects her in childhood, her husband protects her in youth, and her sons protect her in old age; a woman is never fit for independence... [147] By a girl, by a young woman, or even by an aged one, nothing must be done independently, even in her own house... [154] Though destitute of virtue, or seeking pleasure elsewhere, or devoid of good qualities, yet a husband must be constantly worshipped as a god by a faithful wife.[39]

A common principle across the long history of ancient Indian philosophy is the subjugation of women and the dominance of men.[40] The Laws of Manu represent the most explicit but by no means the only work stressing female subjugation. Discussing the contemporary situation of marriage and caste rules among Singaporeans of Indian descent, Mani[41] suggested that Indians were becoming more flexible in expressing their dissenting views on traditional rules of marriage but they do still adhere to them in practice.[42] As far as legal procedures affecting family life transitions such as the registration of births and marriages as well as divorce proceedings, Non-Muslim Indians in Singapore are covered by the secular Common Law of the country just as the rest of the non-Muslim population. Indonesia has also a secular legal framework following its "strict separation of religion and the state."[43]

Gender segregation among the Singaporean Chinese is mostly dictated by a secular tradition, Confucianism (if one agrees that it is a philosophy, not a religion).[44] In contrast, the most influential tradition dictating gender segregation among Singaporean Malays is religious rather than secular; 99.6 per cent of the Malays in Singapore are Muslim according to the 2000 Population Census. However, in the case of Singapore Indians, both secular and religious influences are found. Indeed, in addition to the Indian secular traditions mentioned above, Singaporean Indians may also be influenced by their religious beliefs (Hindu, Muslim, Christian, Sikh or any other religion as the case may be)[45] when defining their beliefs on the appropriate roles of men and women in their community.

Nevertheless, the influence of traditional precepts, whether religious or secular, upon one's everyday life, is neither dominant nor constant. It is normal for people of all religious faiths and cultural traditions to interpret, adapt, and transform their religion's precepts in their daily lives just as they adapt their cultural traditions and borrow from other cultures in their attempt to maintain control over their own lives. This latter process or pragmatic acculturation[46] combined with the inclination to adapt and interpret religious canons represents one of the methods used by women in their striving for coherence, as it will be explained later.

The Exigencies of a Modern Economy

In addition to the influence of traditional values, the second main trend affecting the social definition of gender roles in Asian countries is represented in the exigencies of a modern economy. As I indicate in Chapter 7 of this volume, Japan started its fast pace economic development way ahead of the rest of Asia and joined the ranks of the wealthy countries. Following Japan, four other Asian countries, Singapore, Hong Kong, South Korea, and Taiwan surprised the global community by springing from obscurity to economic prominence within the relatively short span of two decades. These four "little dragons" distinguished themselves in the 1980s and 1990s by their fast pace of economic development and their sustained efforts to compete successfully in international markets. Along their path to development, all these countries had to make adjustments and changes of various kinds in their traditional ways of thinking and doing things. But the change in attitudes is not widespread and has not kept pace with the economy.

Let us take Singapore as an example. Singapore recognised at the outset the need for a change in the traditional prescriptions defining the role of women if economic development plans were to be effective. Accordingly, two steps were taken by the government in the early 1960s concerning family and labour. On the aspect of family, the Women's Charter 1961 established the equality of women in marriage, divorce, and rights and duties regarding property and financial matters.[47] The Charter represents the State's attempt to release women from their traditionally sanctioned subordination to men in so far as it was needed to encourage women to participate in the labour force. The following year female civil servants received a salary increase from 80 per cent of their male counterparts' to equal pay and entitlement of pension "even if they are married."[48] Notwithstanding the positive significance of this early government move towards gender equality, it is interesting to note that the principle of equal pay for equal work has not yet been incorporated into the labour legislation. That is to say, this principle is applied to the civil service but it is not obligatory for the private sector. The government's position on this point has been to take the lead and hope that private sector employers will follow. But further improvements in labour legislation were enacted later including maternity leave. In fact, in 1998 maternity leave benefits paying 100 per cent of wages during the covered period were already operating in China, South Korea, Malaysia, Indonesia, the Philippines, Singapore, Thailand, and Vietnam; in Japan only 60 per cent of the wages are paid.[49]

In the context of Asia these are changes in the right direction. However, other nations' legislations are more advanced, for example Sweden's.[50] Sweden has a distinguished record of legislation in this regard with maternity benefits sanctioned by the Swedish Parliament in 1937. More significantly, parental leave after the birth of the child for both father and mother was passed in 1974 and extended to 270 days in 1978.[51] The move from *maternity* leave to *parental* leave for all workers is a fundamental step towards gender equality not only in the area of employment but also in the family: it represents the institutionalised recognition of the privilege and obligation of both parents to look after their children. Thus, when the corresponding changes in labour legislation are not made, the State sends mixed signals by treating women as the primary [or only] childcare givers and discounting the role of men as fathers.

Asian countries facing the dilemma of preserving traditional women's status while responding to the demands of economic development are compelled to modify conservatively their traditional values and norms — their normative structure, to borrow Merton's term — and to make the transition from the One-Role ideology to the Two-Role ideology. These role ideologies were formulated by sociologist Jessie Bernard.[52] Norms and values of the One-Role ideology assign the traditional roles of childbearing, childrearing and housekeeping services as the exclusive domain of women. In contrast, the *Two-Role* ideology stresses the importance of devising "adjustments that would render it easier for women to combine motherhood and the care of a home with outside activities," that is, with paid employment outside the home.[53] Bernard proposed a third notion, the *Shared-Role* ideology, whereby "childrearing and socialisation" are deemed to be "far too important to entrust to one sex alone; both parents should participate" and both "should have the option of part-time participation in the labor force."[54] Bernard identified as the first formal manifestations of the *Two-Role* ideology at the policy-making level two policy initiatives, the report from the Royal Commission on Population in the United Kingdom in 1949, and the establishment of the Commission on the Status of Women by President J. F. Kennedy in the United States in 1961. For policy-makers in both countries, the central argument was that women's participation in the labour force was an essential requirement for the nation's economic development and defence.[55] This ideological change in the perception of gender roles, from the *One-Role* to the *Two-Role* ideology, took place in industrialised countries in mid-20th century. Some optimistic observers believe that this ideological change — affecting the normative structure, using Merton's concept — is now geared to move away from the *Two-Role* ideology and towards the *Shared- Role* ideology. After some five decades of the *two-role* ideology, no definite signs of such a fundamental change are evident in Western nations.

In Asian countries, the historical transition from the *One-Role* ideology to the *Two-Role* ideology has been evolving slowly and at different pace in different countries. Still, my observations suggest that two trends are discernable in the ten Asian countries in this study: (a) the *Two-Role* ideology encompasses the social acceptance of women holding two types of roles, the domestic role and the non-domestic income-earning role and thus, married women who are income-earners are still perceived as primarily responsible for the family's well-being at home; and (b) if for whatever circumstances there is need to choose between home and paid job, the married woman and mother is expected to give preference to her domestic role.

We need to remind ourselves of an important qualification at this juncture. The term 'income-earning' in this context refers to officially recorded paid wages for work performed. But the transition from the *One-Role* to the *Two-Role* ideology does not mean that women did not work before, under the *One-Role* ideology. This qualification is very important when discussing women's work. Historical and archeological records indicate that from ancient times and practically everywhere, women have laboured, alone or alongside men, for the economic security of their families. Yet, the social norms of traditional societies prescribe that a woman's labour — even income-earning labour — is an integral part of her one and only duty, attending to the needs of her family and home. This is the *One-Role* ideology. Contemporary life in rural communities that have withstood the passage of time in Africa, Latin America, and Asia,[56] confirm the active involvement of women in the tilling of the fields, planting seed, tending to the crops, cottage industries, and practically any other income-earning activity needed to support the rural household. A Japanese female farmer put it starkly: "I used to nurse a baby sitting on the ridge between the rice paddies and that was the only time I got to rest."[57] When a peasant nursing mother is getting ready for the day's chores in a Latin American village, she ensures that her shawl is tied well to keep her baby securely strapped to her back while she works in the field.

In full realisation that women have always worked, it is important to present a comparative picture of the changes in women's paid work over the past decades. To accomplish this I have to use official figures on rates of economic activity which international organisations and census bureaus in all countries defined by convention as "the proportion of women in the total female population aged 15 and over who are working or actively looking for work." These figures do not capture work that is unpaid, and most work done by women as family members not officially employed is unpaid. Notwithstanding these limitations of the data, the female economic activity rate is a common indicator of women's participation in the labour market and thus of their contribution to wealth creation. Thus, an increase in this rate suggests a change in norms on the status of women and women's move away from the *One-Role* ideology and into the *Two-Role* ideology. The historical trend as it occurred from 1950 to 2000 in the ten Asian countries is presented in Chart 5.1.

CHART 5.1 TOTAL FEMALE ECONOMIC ACTIVITY RATES, 1950-2000

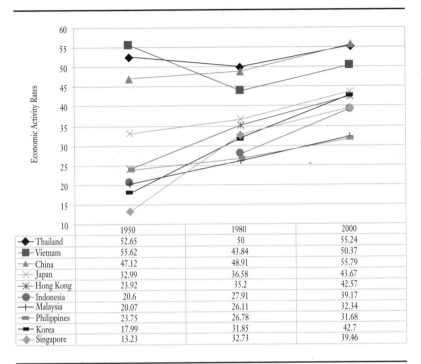

	1950	1980	2000
Thailand	52.65	50	55.24
Vietnam	55.62	43.84	50.37
China	47.12	48.91	55.79
Japan	32.99	36.58	43.67
Hong Kong	23.92	35.2	42.57
Indonesia	20.6	27.91	39.17
Malaysia	20.07	26.11	32.34
Philippines	23.75	26.78	31.68
Korea	17.99	31.85	42.7
Singapore	13.23	32.73	39.46

Source: Calculated from International Labour Organisation (2002). Female economic activity rate is the proportion of women in the total female population aged 15 and over, who are working or actively looking for work.

Their political regimes differ, and with the exception of Thailand, all the other nine countries have experienced colonisation and the destruction of war either directly or indirectly during the course of the 20th century. These features must be kept in mind when trying to explain the three important changes in attitudes and behaviour suggested by the figures in Chart 5.1. The first and clearest change over the past 50 years is that women in all ten countries have increased their active participation in their nations' economies since 1980 and thus may be said to fall within the two-role ideology. Second, the political ideological overhaul that China first, and later Vietnam, experienced with the establishment of the Communist regime seem to explain their position among the top three countries in terms of women's involvement in the formal economy. The transition in Vietnam was understandably uneven due to the war years. A corollary of this situation is that democracy cannot compete with the speed at which behavioural change in gender roles is induced by communist regimes. The change in women's participation in economic activity began about two decades later in Singapore, South Korea, the Philippines, Malaysia, and Indonesia.

The third notable point is the case of Thailand. Compared to their counterparts in the other countries, Thai women had the highest rate of economic activity in 1950 and 1980 and a rate very close to that of China in 2000. Thailand is generally considered a democratic country and has never experienced colonisation or suffered the effects of war directly. Thailand's case is difficult to explain with the available demographic data. Let us turn to another kind of data. In her study of the values and norms of Thai people, Suntaree Komin confirmed the popular belief that Thai men and women received clearly different socialisation in their childhood based on gender-specific roles. She found that the three most important life concerns of Thai women were the happiness and security of their family, self-esteem, and success in life, in that order. They placed a very low value on equality and freedom (seen as political values) and other "issues of broader societal concern." In contrast, Komin reports that the three most important life concerns of Thai men were national security, political equality, and freedom (that is, political values). They placed self-esteem and life success at a lower level of priority. Thus "Thai men in general are not as concerned with family as are women, leaving the maintenance and responsibility to the women, who seek and cling to it as the central, if not the only concern of their life."[58] Komin's study was based on data from two surveys, a national survey conducted in 1978, and a national rural sample survey completed in 1981.[59] Any extrapolation of her findings must be done cautiously considering that it is highly likely that some changes have occurred in the values of Thai people over the past 20 years. Carefully, therefore, we may use Komin's data to interpret the figures in Chart 5.1: Thai women could be seen as the archetypal representation of the two-role ideology. Both the domestic and the financial spheres of their families fall under their purview. They are energetically involved in economic activity as an expression of their felt responsibility for their families' welfare. It appears that although more women in all the ten countries are working now in paid jobs, Thai women have held that responsibility for a longer time and perceive it as part of their cultural norms.

The comparison of economic activity rates for different age cohorts provides additional information on the transition towards the two-role ideology. Charts 5.2 to 5.4 present the trends in economic activity for the cohort of women 25-29 who are of marriageable age or have married recently (see discussion of marriage age in Chapter 2 of this volume); the cohort of women 35-39 most of whom are at the stage of raising children; and the cohort 45-49 most of whom are mothers of adolescents or young adults and thus would have less urgent domestic demands on their time on a daily basis. With the notable exception of Thailand, China, and Vietnam, the situation of women aged 25 to 29 has gone through a substantial change in the span of five decades: from dedication to home in 1950, to employment in the year 2000 (Chart 5.2). In contrast, the cohort of young women (aged 25-29) in China, Vietnam and Thailand have consistently been busy earning a living for themselves and their families and this pattern has not changed much over the past 50 years.

CHART 5.2   ECONOMIC ACTIVITY RATES OF FEMALES AGED 25-29, 1950-2000

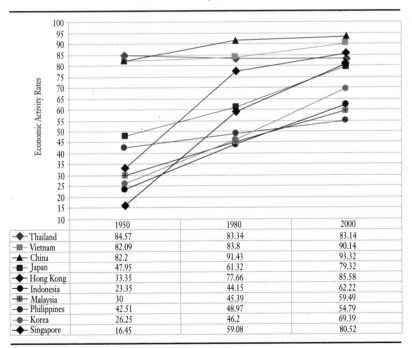

	1950	1980	2000
Thailand	84.57	83.34	83.14
Vietnam	82.09	83.8	90.14
China	82.2	91.43	93.32
Japan	47.95	61.32	79.32
Hong Kong	33.35	77.66	85.58
Indonesia	23.35	44.15	62.22
Malaysia	30	45.39	59.49
Philippines	42.51	48.97	54.79
Korea	26.25	46.2	69.39
Singapore	16.45	59.08	80.52

Source: Calculated from International Labour Organisation (2002). Female economic activity rate is the proportion of women in the female population aged 25-29, who are working or actively looking for work.

CHART 5.3   ECONOMIC ACTIVITY RATES OF FEMALES AGED 35–39, 1950–2000

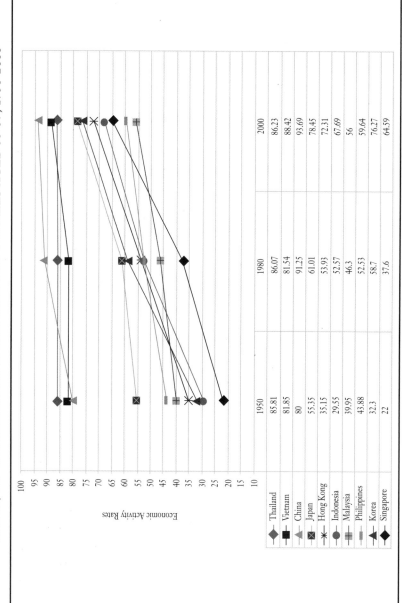

	1950	1980	2000
Thailand	85.81	86.07	86.23
Vietnam	81.85	81.54	88.42
China	80	91.25	93.69
Japan	55.35	61.01	78.45
Hong Kong	35.15	53.93	72.31
Indonesia	29.55	52.57	67.69
Malaysia	39.95	46.3	56
Philippines	43.88	52.53	59.64
Korea	32.3	58.7	76.27
Singapore	22	37.6	64.59

Economic Activity Rates

Source: Calculated from International Labour Organisation (2002). Female 35–39 economic activity rate is the proportion of women in the female population aged 35–39, who are working or actively looking for work.

CHART 5.4 ECONOMIC ACTIVITY RATES OF FEMALES AGED 45-49, 1950-2000

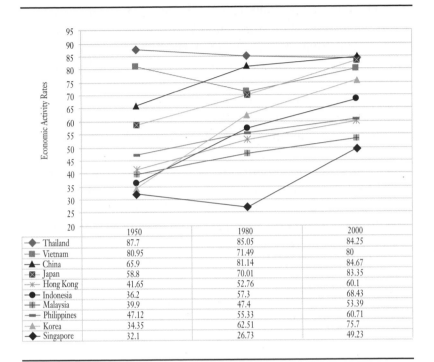

	1950	1980	2000
◆ Thailand	87.7	85.05	84.25
■ Vietnam	80.95	71.49	80
▲ China	65.9	81.14	84.67
▣ Japan	58.8	70.01	83.35
✳ Hong Kong	41.65	52.76	60.1
● Indonesia	36.2	57.3	68.43
✚ Malaysia	39.9	47.4	53.39
▬ Philippines	47.12	55.33	60.71
▲ Korea	34.35	62.51	75.7
◆ Singapore	32.1	26.73	49.23

Source: Calculated from International Labour Organisation (2002). Female 45-49 economic activity rate is the proportion of women in the female population aged 45-49, who are working or actively looking for work.

The presence of children does not seem to interrupt the income-earning activities of Chinese, Vietnamese and Thai women aged 35 to 39 (Chart 5.3). If we follow Komin's findings[60] on the values of Thai women, we would not be surprised as their responsibility for the security and happiness of their homes increases with the presence of children. For women in the other seven countries, their involvement in the labour force that started in their 20s continues into their 30s. Historically, their economic activity has increased steadily since 1950. On the whole, the presence of women aged 40 to 45 in the labour force has increase in the past five decades in a relatively steady fashion for all countries except Vietnam and Singapore (Chart 5.4). Both countries saw a decline of working women in this age cohort in 1980. A speculative explanation could be the early signs of the economic recession that led to retrenchment of older female workers.

The situation in 2000 (Chart 5.5) shows important variations across countries. While large numbers of Thai women continue to earn a living from their 20s to their 50s, the other two countries with high rates of female economic activity, China and Vietnam, see a moderate decrease of working women in the age cohort 45-49. Malaysian women also tend to withdraw from economic activity at about the same age, while South Korean, Indonesian and Filipino women tend to continue working into their late 40s. In sharp contrast, Hong Kong and particularly Singapore women, join the labour force in large proportions in their 20s but their resolve to tackle both home and job commitments (the two-role ideology) falters and they begin withdrawing steadily from the labour force after marriage or after the arrival of their first child due to the burden of family obligations.[61]

The extent of women's participation in the economy is further illustrated by the comparison with that of men. Chart 5.6 presents the total economic activity rates of females in three age cohorts in 2000 together with the total female rate as a percentage of the total male economic activity rate for the same year. Chinese, Vietnamese, and Thai women work in paid jobs almost at the same rate as that of their male counterparts. The female rates of economic activity in the other countries are lower than the male rates but still substantial.

In sum, the analysis of the exigencies of a modern economy points to two features that distinguish the case of Asian nations from that of industrialised nations. One feature is the current emphasis on the *Two-Role* ideology. Such an emphasis is confirmed by the data in Charts 5.1 to 5.5. The other feature is the manner in which the change from the *One-Role* to the *Two-Role* ideology was secured. In this regard, three paths may be tentatively identified. Some countries made the change as an integral part of a revolutionary change in their political regime (China and Vietnam); some countries followed the "active society" approach of guided change without a regime overhaul (Japan, Singapore, South Korea); and other countries let the market forces and civil society shape the playing field more or less freely (Thailand, Indonesia, Malaysia, the Philippines).

CHART 5.5   FEMALE ECONOMIC ACTIVITY RATES IN THREE AGE COHORTS, 2000

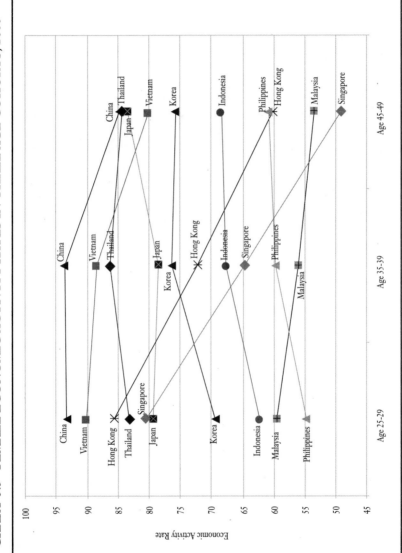

Source: Calculated from International Labour Organisation (2002). Female economic activity rate is the proportion of women in the female population in each age cohort, who are working or actively looking for work.

**CHART 5.6   FEMALE ECONOMIC ACTIVITY RATES IN THREE
AGE COHORTS, AND TOTAL FEMALE RATE AS A
PERCENTAGE OF TOTAL MALE RATE, 2000.**

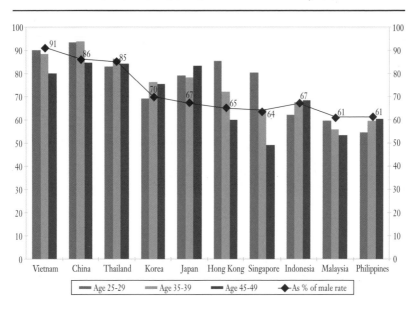

Source: Calculated from International Labour Organisation (2002) and United
Nations Development Programme (2002). Female economic activity rate is the
proportion of women in the female population in each age cohort, who are
working or actively looking for work.

The Value of Gender Equality

We have seen how two of the contradictory trends operate. On the one
hand, traditional values define the social roles of men and women in
terms of dominance and subordination. On the other hand, the practical
necessity of utilising all available human resources to attain higher
economic development motivates the political leadership to promote
some aspects of equality to help and encourage women to participate
actively in the labour force in addition to looking after their families.
The third factor in this equation is the value of gender equality.

Let us understand by gender equality the situation whereby women
and men are considered equal in all spheres of life, that is, in terms of
their rights and obligations as citizens of a nation, as individuals in a

democratic society, as members of the labour force, and as partners in marriage and parenthood. It is clear from the preceding pages that the value of equality between men and women is not indigenous to secular Asia.[62] It may be more accurate to say that the idea of gender equality has been 'imported' from other cultures, particularly from Europe and the United States.

The history of gender equality is analogous to the history of the women's movement. Originally, the women's movement was focused on the public struggle of women "to win an effective recognition" of their equality with men as citizens but, by definition, it also covered "the rights of women in all areas of social life."[63] The origins of this struggle may be traced back to the second half of the 19th century.[64] But some scholars, pointing to the lives of outstanding women in history, suggest that there were already signs of female assertiveness in the late Middle Ages in Europe and the beginnings of a women's movement in the early 19th century in the United States and Europe.[65]

Perhaps more importantly, historical analyses have found a correlation between the dawning of the women's movement and the onset of industrialisation in Europe and the United States.[66] Technological and social changes in the nature and style of economic production in a society have considerable effect upon the lives of its members. As new definitions of work, leisure, task responsibility, and task difficulty are created and accepted, these definitions tend to affect also people's values and attitudes towards interpersonal relations. In Western societies, women have responded to these influences earlier than men. In his voluminous study of the "rise of women" in the United States, Russia, Sweden, and Italy, Meyer[67] documents the incipient women's movement in these countries as initiated by women themselves who usually were successful in enlisting the cooperation of a few members of the all-male establishment. In the eyes of the establishment, these men, acting as brokers, would typically add credibility to the women's lobbying for access to education, voting rights, jobs and other demands. Nevertheless, there is no evidence that the few male supporters of the women's movement were essential in securing its success.

Lest a misconception of social consensus among women is created, there is another aspect of the women's movement towards gender equality in Europe and the United States that needs to be taken into consideration. That aspect is the increasingly vocal reaction or counter-movement to what Ronald Fletcher[68] calls "an apparently widespread casualness and irresponsibility in attitudes and behaviour in both sexual relations and marriage alike." In her argument on women's liberation as a "myth," S. A. Hewlett describes the current situation thus:

> While the right-wingers have been urging women to stay at home when the vast majority of American women cannot afford to do so, even if they wanted to, the modern feminist movement has told them to get out into the workplace and take what is rightfully theirs. Caught in the middle are the 'displaced homemakers', whose sense of security in the home has been swept from under them [...].[69]

Put differently, after more than a century of debate, women in Western countries have not reached a consensus on the most appropriate and desirable definition of their social roles. Having abandoned the *One-Role* ideology that restricted the female role to the home, Western women have realised the hardships involved in the *Two-Role* ideology — the incorporation of a job or career to the role of sole homemaker. The ideal is, as Bernard suggested, the *Shared-Role* ideology. Although the sharing of all roles by men and women would be the ultimate testimony of gender equality, there is no indication that such a situation has been reached in the West. Reviewing the accomplishments of the women's movement, an American feminist lamented "for all the pioneering that brave and ambitious women have done, the female majority remains outside, earning 70¢ to the man's $1 in stereotypically female jobs."[70] The situation is no better in Europe. Comparing the average female earnings as a percentage of average male earnings in the 14 Member States of the European Union in 1995, it was found that women's earnings ranged from a lowest 55 per cent of male earnings in the United Kingdom, to the highest 91 per cent in Luxembourg. Luxembourg was an exceptional case. In none of the other 14 European countries did female earnings reach 85 per cent of male earnings; seven were below 75 per cent, and in the other seven female earnings were between 75 to 84 per cent of male earnings.[71]

Asian countries show some similarities and some differences with the above processes of gender equality in Europe and the United States. In terms of similarities, one may observe that the pace and degree of changes undergone in Asian countries, particularly Japan, Hong Kong, Singapore, and South Korea, in their transition from an underdeveloped economy to an industrial economy have affected people's values and attitudes by raising their awareness of the importance of universal education, the need for a skilled labour force and the need to tap all available talent, both male and female, to boost economic development.

Yet, these countries show a significantly different implementation of those new perspectives. Whatever the improvements in labour legislation enacted in the ten Asian countries, the groundwork has been typically the effort of either large organisations such as labour unions, or of policy planners convinced that it is profitable to increase the proportion of female workers at certain cycles of the economy. In Singapore, for example, it was the political establishment, spearheaded by its male political leaders, not a women's movement, that began promoting some basic principles of gender equality in Singapore and created the 'social space' for women's participation in the political process.[72] In most countries the scope of the gender equality principles promoted by the state are usually limited because the state's aim is not to make radical changes in the social definitions of male and female roles but, rather, to create the basic necessary conditions to bring women into the labour force without altering their traditional roles of wife and mother.

As the most economically advanced Asian nation, the case of Japan is informative. It suggests that the weight of tradition in Asia may successfully counteract or delay the pull towards equality of gender roles, that is, towards the *Shared-Role* ideology. There is a strong corporate emphasis on the subordinate role of women in Japan. This feature has been marked as one of the "shortcomings of Japanese-style personnel management" as it leads to a gross under-utilisation of female talent and to a situation where "the principle of egalitarianism is applied only to male employees."[73] Indeed, some prominent Japanese women deplore that, despite the 1985 law banning sex discrimination and the fact that Japanese women are "among the best educated women in the world," Japanese women are, "by Western standards, second-class citizens in their own country."[74]

To sum up, a brief look at the three main contradictory signals received by Asian women indicates the presence of a conflicting situation. Traditional values praise the dominant position of men and the virtue of female subordination. The exigencies of a modern economy have led the political leadership to promote the need for women to join the labour force and, as an incentive, to legislate the equality of women in some aspects of family and working life in order to facilitate their managing of two roles. But it may be unrealistic to expect that the drive for comprehensive gender equality be promoted by the state unless it becomes clear to the establishment that such a change is not in detriment of men, who enjoy open structures of opportunity but, rather, profitable for everyone.

With the main normative values in Asia supporting gender role distinctions and allocating a superior status and thus better structures of opportunity to men, it is unlikely that the drive for change be initiated by the majority in the civic society. It is probably a minority of women with a particular sensitivity for political participation who could begin working towards that end. Over the past few decades a few mostly educated women have worked, sometimes jointly, sometimes individually, towards the organisation of active groups to represent and voice the needs, and aspirations of women. Some Japanese women believe the women's movement in Japan has been unsuccessful although it had its active days in the 1970s and 1980s.[75] This opinion may not be shared by all women and the case of Japan may not necessarily represent other countries. Women's determination to and involvement in changing the normative structure in their own societies deserves detailed attention. But that analysis is beyond the scope of this discussion.

In addition to the presence of women's organisations, the idea of gender equality in any society may be promoted or discouraged by the formal educational system at the primary and secondary levels. Higher education, on the contrary, is decisively encouraging and one of the most effective vehicles for the transmission of gender equality values.[76] Textbooks used in primary school often have serious gender biases that some countries have tried to overcome.[77] Nevertheless, gender equality may be said to be implemented in the educational system to the extent that it offers equal opportunities of entry and treatment to male and female students. The proportion of female students who proceed to university in Japan has been steadily increasing from 2.5 per cent in 1960 to 32.7 per cent in 2001.[78] An increase in university-educated women is also reported in Singapore[79] and Thailand.[80]

A more comprehensive regional perspective of the advances in women's tertiary education — and thus their possible exposure to the idea of gender equality — is obtained from the ten countries' scores on the Gender-related Development Index (GDI). The GDI is a composite index of "the inequalities between men and women" in life expectancy at birth, estimated earned income, and education. Education is ascertained by two measures: adult literacy and the combined primary, secondary, and tertiary gross enrolment ratio.[81] The GDI ranges technically from 0.1 (complete inequality) to 1.0 (complete equality). In 2000, the country with the highest score was Norway (GDI = 0.941) and the lowest score was obtained by Niger, in Africa (GDI = 0.263).[82] As expected, economic development and GDI scores go hand in hand.

The four most economically developed and industrialised[83] countries, Japan, Singapore, Hong Kong and South Korea, also display a widespread level of technology as indicated by the proportion of personal computers per 10,000 persons in the population (Charts 5.7 and 5.8 respectively). These four countries have the highest GDI scores. Compared to women in the other six countries, women in Japan, Singapore, Hong Kong, and South Korea enjoy, overall, a higher level of equality by virtue of their improved life expectancy, income, and education. It is reasonable to expect that, with more women in tertiary education, these countries would be more exposed to a wider range of arguments on gender equality.

CHART 5.7 INDUSTRIALISATION AND GENDER-RELATED DEVELOPMENT INDEX, 1999-2000

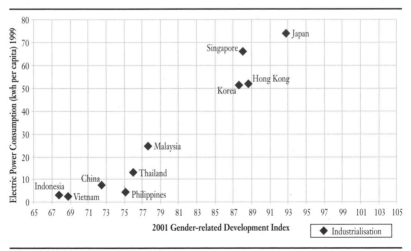

Source: Figures on electric power consumption are from World Bank (2002); Gender-related Development Index scores from United Nations Development Programme (2002). Correlation: r = .901; p = .0001.

CHART 5.8 TECHNOLOGY AND GENDER-RELATED DEVELOPMENT INDEX, 2001

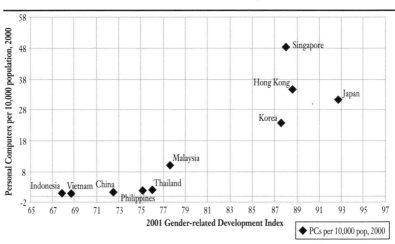

Sources: Figures on personal computers are from World Bank (2002); Gender-related Development Index scores from United Nations Development Programme (2002). Correlation: r = .900; p = .0001.

Why, then, with the presence of women's organisations, good economic development and a reasonably educated female population, there are still no signs of a collective female will to gain comprehensive gender equality in Japan, Singapore, Hong Kong and South Korea? In addition to the fact that this is a generic, not just an Asian problem (witness the absence of comprehensive gender equality in most countries around the world), it appears that there is another important reason particular to Asia. Asian women exposed to the idea of gender equality find themselves struggling for congruity among three contradictory ideologies: the *Shared-Role* ideology implied by the idea of equality; the *One-Role* ideology promoted by traditional values on female subordination; and the *Two-Role* ideology justified by the exigencies of economy development.

STRUGGLE FOR COHERENCE

How are Asian women responding to the unenviable challenge of reconciling these opposite social expectations? There is no simple answer but in some countries it appears as if compartmentalising

142

spheres of activity and separating attitudes from behaviour may be two of the most common approaches towards a pragmatic solution to the conflict. Compartmentalising one's spheres of activity, that is, separating one's role obligations in terms of time, space, or both, helps to minimise the strain caused when those roles are incompatible.[84]

Compartmentalising is discernible when examining the rates of economic activity in 2000 by age group (Chart 5.5). Women in Singapore and Hong Kong tend to enter the labour force in their early 20s and stay on until about the time of marriage or the arrival of their first child. For most women in both countries, these life transitions happen between their late 20s and early 30s. Then they leave their paid jobs to give full attention to their families. In Japan, the compartmentalising is less pronounced and goes the opposite way: more women become economically active after their children are older. A move in the same direction as Japan's is seen in South Korea where women with young children attend to family first and by their late 30s, once their children are in school, they may take a paid job. Among the less economically developed countries, Malaysian women tend to follow the Hong Kong and Singapore pattern of compartmentalising, while the trend among Indonesian and Filipino women resembles more that of Japan and South Korea.

As the actual and ideal age for marriage and parenthood changes, the pattern of compartmentalisation of roles will also change. It is possible, for example, that the future will see a trend towards combining both home and paid job obligations throughout their working life trajectories. This is already evident among some university-educated women involved in career-track jobs in Asia, and it has become the pattern in Northern European countries and the United States.[85]

While the participation of women in the labour force is a sign of their moving away from the sole role of homemakers, the types of occupations they hold in the labour market reflect the extent to which women have advanced in traditionally male-dominated occupations. It appears that most women's occupations in Asian countries are stereotypical female jobs such as operators in processed food manufacturing, textiles production, and electronics, and occupations such as teachers, nurses, secretaries, and clerks. The robust drive towards computerisation and information technology in Japan, Singapore, Hong Kong, and South Korea, is leading to the upgrading of clerical workers' skills and will probably open more space for women as a natural

143

transition from clerical work and data management. These projections are intuitive given the dearth of comparative data on specific occupations held by women in the ten countries.

One approximation to a regional comparison in the type of occupations held by women is their presence in the upper echelons of decision-making in their countries. Chart 5.9 shows that in accordance to their political ideology supporting gender equality, Vietnam and China have the largest proportion of parliament seats occupied by women. Yet, that proportion is not 50 per cent (following the proportion of women in the total population) but only 26 per cent in Vietnam and 21.8 per cent in China. With no declared political ideology supporting gender equality, it is not surprising that the other eight countries have an even lower proportion of women in parliament. More importantly, their presence in their countries' top legislative body is not commensurate with their participation in the economy. Anecdotal information indicates that women consider political office as being a highly engrossing duty that would not permit them to meet their family obligations in the manner they believe is appropriate. As mentioned earlier, Komin found that Thai women and men see political matters as being in the realm of male activity. But that perception may be changing among younger women.

Hence, we find that working women are participating in larger numbers in their countries' economy but they have not made inroads into the labour force significantly enough to attain a similar distribution of male and female workers along the full spectrum of occupations. A related and relevant feature of the actual situation of women in the labour force is their income. Data from Singapore, for example, show that irrespective of the prestige of an occupation, most jobs are better paid when performed by men than by women.[86] But the Singapore data may not be directly comparable to data from other countries and cannot reach 100 per cent gender equity because of the national service increment, a unique Singaporean phenomenon.[87] Still, in general the differential earning power between men and women has been present for many decades and is by no means peculiar of Singapore. As mentioned earlier, analysts point to the same problem in industrialised countries.[88]

Taking into consideration all other economic and social arrangements that might explain gender differences in wages, the lower wages of women may still be interpreted as a further indication of the

**CHART 5.9   PERCENT PARLIAMENT SEATS OCCUPIED BY
WOMEN AND TOTAL FEMALE ECONOMIC ACTIVITY RATE AS
A PERCENTAGE OF TOTAL MALE RATE, 2000**

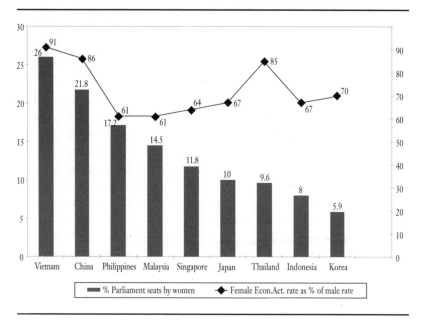

Source: Calculated from United Nations Development Programme (2002).
Female economic activity rate is the proportion of women in the female
population in each age cohort, who are working or actively looking for work.

prevalence of the *Two-Role* ideology and thus of the narrower structures
of opportunity open to women. This state of affairs was explained three
decades ago by Erik Gronseth in terms of the social values held at the
time in the United States whereby men's jobs in general — and husbands'
jobs in particular — were deemed to be more important than the jobs of
women — or of working wives — given the social perception of men and
husbands as the family's principal economic providers.[89] Most signs point
to the conclusion that the higher status given to the husband as the
principal economic provider has not changed much in the past three
decades, at least not in Asia.

In addition to behaviour, the realm of attitudes and opinions also
needs to be explored to identify to what extent a separation of attitudes
and behaviour is used by women in their struggle for coherence. That

145

is, women may find it possible to reconcile conflicting social pressures when they think *liberal* but act *conservative*. For example, Singaporean women, particularly the better educated, are inclined towards liberal or modern attitudes concerning hard work, education, lifestyle options other than marriage, a non-traditional definition of marriage as companionship, and the feasibility of preserving a certain level of independence after marriage and of combining both career and family.[90] Yet, being influenced by both traditional and modern values, the Singaporean working mother faces contradictions in her everyday life. Two of the most serious contradictions are a pervasive feeling of inadequacy as a mother and the strain of shouldering the burden of home management in addition to her paid job responsibilities. In accordance with the *Two-Role* ideology, the husband is more likely to be the sole or main provider — responsible for supporting the family financially — as well as for what is traditionally defined as 'male' responsibilities at home such as doing minor repairs (72.1 per cent of a national representative sample of married persons said the husband is in charge of this); paying bills (69.1 per cent); and filling income tax forms (60.6 per cent). The most common home duties people saw as "female" responsibilities were cooking (77.8 per cent); doing the laundry (75.4 per cent); cleaning the home (69 per cent); and caring for a sick family member (68.1 per cent).[91] The same trend was documented in studies conducted in the 1980s.[92]

THE FUTURE: MORE OF THE SAME?

This chapter demonstrates that Asian women are confronted with a conflicting situation to which they feel they have to adapt. The conflict is created by the presence of three contradictory social trends namely, the emphasis on traditional values that shape the social status of women and restrict their opportunities to attain personal goals; the exigencies of a modern and fast growing economy; and the value of gender equality received mostly through higher education. As women see it, despite their deficiencies, each of these forces has positive aspects. Traditional values promote family stability and a sense of social order; the need to maintain a fast pace in economic development and to provide the best for their families requires women's contribution as much men's; and the principle of gender equality fits well with the value of meritocracy and the respect for hard work and educational qualifications. The Asian woman accepts these separate positive postulates but has to face the inevitable conflict that they produce. Her solution is, in my view, not satisfactory but it is a way of coping.

Discussing women's struggle for coherence, I have referred in the preceding pages to research findings from ten Asian countries: Japan, South Korea, China, Hong Kong, Indonesia, Malaysia, Singapore, the Philippines, Thailand, and Vietnam. There are significant differences across these ten countries and generalisations need to be treated with caution. The emerging picture suggests that gender values continue to mould a person's status and life opportunities and create contradictory demands on women. The data suggest that women attempt to reconcile opposite demands and expectations in two ways. One approach used by most women is to compartmentalise, or separate, their two roles by allocating different segments of their life cycle to each one: they join the labour force only while they are single or childless; or after their children are older. This 'solution' is not good for women on a career track or women working due to financial necessity. Their other approach is to separate attitudes from behaviour by opting for being liberal in thought but traditional in action. The most clear indications of this separation are the following contrasts: women put their hard earned occupational skills to good use when they join the labour force and start a career, but they quit on the belief that good mothers must stay at home; women believe in hard work and education to attain success but they do not demand, as a collectivity, equality of treatment in the labour force; women believe in a marriage based on companionship and love rather than subordination, but they accept the traditional subordinated duty of housekeeper in addition to their job obligations as a corollary of the perceived unsuitability of men for these chores.

Looking into the future is always risky, particularly if one does not have solid bases for forecasting. Cautiously, then, I suggest that the three contradictory social trends are likely to continue in the foreseeable future. The main challenge for sociologists studying gender roles is to identify through further research the best possible avenues for both men and women to be able to attain their life and family goals at minimum cost and optimum gain. The *Shared-Role* ideology may be one of several possibilities. But there are many important questions that need to be explored. For example, can the *Shared-Role* ideology take root in different cultural soils? Would gender equality produce some 'side-effects' more undesirable than the problems it is meant to solve? On the other hand, can a modern society avoid the implementation of gender equality altogether? Can any society become enlightened — truly civilised — when half of its members regard the other half as inferior?

ENDNOTES

1. See Quah (1998:144-175).
2. See Weber (1978:929).
3. See Weber (1978:935).
4. See Weber (1978:305-306).
5. See Merton (1968).
6. See Sztompka (1996:12).
7. See Sztompka (1996:12-13).
8. See Sztompka (1996:154); and Merton (1995).
9. See Yi (2002:32); Mar and Richter (2003).
10. See for example Lewis (1999); Rosen et. al. (2000); and Elashmawi (2001).
11. See Ting and Chiu (2002).
12. See Jolivet (1997:77).
13. See Ochiai (1997:14); and Breadbent and Morris-Suzuki (2000).
14. See Sugimoto (2003:146).
15. See Ochiai (1997:69).
16. See *Straits Times* (1990a); Lee (1996).
17. See Leow (2001a).
18. See Jaspers (1957:47).
19. See for example, Waley (1938); Doeblin (1940); Ware (1955).
20. See, among others, Creel (1949) and (1962); Fung (1948); Chan (1963); Chai and Chai (1973); Lu (1983); Fry et. al. (1984); Tu (1984); Lincoln (1985); Li (1986); and Chung (1989).
21. See Fry et.al. (1984:106-7).
22. See Black (1986:169).
23. See Black (1986:170).
24. See Black (1986:170).
25. See Jaspers (1957:43-44).
26. See Creel (1949:125-127).
27. See Chung (1989:153).
28. See Fry et.al. (1984:88).
29. See Ahmad (1984:198).
30. See Ahmad (1984:218-219).
31. See Ahmad (1984:215).
32. See Ahmad (1984:206).

33. See Ahmad (1984:206).
34. See Wallerstein and Kelly (1980); Wong and Kuo (1983); O'Leary (1987); Steinmetz (1988); Wallerstein and Blakeslee (1990).
35. See Ahmad (1984:220).
36. See Ahmad (1984:221); Sharifah (1986:186-7).
37. See Hassan (2002:169). The four countries in his study are Indonesia, Pakistan, Egypt, and Kazakhstan.
38. See Ryan (1971); Mani (1979); Ling (1989); Sandhu and Mani (1993).
39. See Radhakrishnan and Moore (1957:190-191).
40. See Radhakrishnan and Moore (1957).
41. See Mani (1979).
42. See Sandhu and Mani (1993).
43. See Hassan (2002:24).
44. According to the 2000 Population Census, 16.5 per cent of the Singaporean Chinese were Christians; 18.6 per cent did not identify themselves with any religion; and 64.4 per cent were Buddhists or Taoists. The latter two are religious groups who basically accept the canons of behaviour taught by Confucius concerning the roles of men and women. See Leow (2001a:xiv).
45. Singaporean Indians have a wider variety of religions than their Chinese or Malay counterparts. The three largest religious groups among Indians in 2000 are Hindus (55.4 per cent), Muslims (25.6 per cent) and Christians (12.1 per cent). See Leow (2001a:xiv).
46. See Quah (1989:5-8).
47. See Quah (1981:36-37).
48. See Rahim Ishak (1979:73).
49. See Republic of Singapore, (1981:42); Singapore Ministry of Labour (1987:36-39); Chua and Theyvendram (1990:44-49); NTUC (1996:22-23); and World Bank (2001).
50. See Ditch, Barnes, and Bradshaw (1996).
51. Quah (1990:14-16); Moen (2003).
52. See Bernard (1972:236).
53. See Bernard (1972:236-237).
54. See Bernard (1972:243 and 1974:339-341).
55. See Bernard (1972:237).
56. See Liao (1998:144).
57. As quoted by Ochiai (1997:16).
58. See Komin (1991:40-42).
59. See Komin (1991:240-242).
60. See Komin (1991). See also Chi (1991:64-65) on the co-ownership of crops by husband and wife who work together in rice farming.
61. See Quah (1998:128); Quah (1999).

62. For a detailed discussion of the principle of gender equality in Islam see Hassan (2002:167-187).

63. See Fletcher (1988a:88).

64. See Fletcher (1988a:88); and Meyer (1987).

65. See Doyle (1985:320-329).

66. See Meyer (1987).

67. See Meyer (1987).

68. See Fletcher (1988b:133).

69. See Hewlett (1987:272-273).

70. See Ehrenreich (1990).

71. See Ditch, Barnes and Bradshaw (1996:58).

72. See Quah (1998:158-159).

73. See Hasegawa (1986:65-66).

74. See Makihara (1990:35).

75. See Ochiai (1997:91-95).

76. See Kelly and Elliot (1982); Bloom (1987:106-107).

77. See Quah (1980).

78. See *Asahi Shimbun* (2003:228).

79. See Quah (1998:161).

80. See *Alpha Research* (1994:35-36).

81. For a detailed description of the GDI calculation see United Nations Development Programme (2002:255).

82. See United Nations Development Programme (2002:222-225).

83. Note that level of industrialisation is ascertained by electric power consumption (kwh per capita).

84. See Burr (1973:133); Burr, Leigh, Day and Constantine (1979:82-84).

85. See Moen (2003:333-337).

86. See Quah (1998:165).

87. The national service increment represents the social contract with all able-bodied males aged 18 to 40 whereby they are compensated for the two years that they must spend in compulsory full-time military training. See NTUC (1996:103-105).

88. See Ehrenreich (1990); Ditch, Barnes and Bradshaw (1996:58).

89. See Gronseth (1973).

90. See Quah (1998); and Quah (1999).

91. See Quah (1999:16).

92. See Ministry of Community Development (1987:25); and Singapore Council of Women's Organizations (1989:5).

6

Conflict, Divorce and the Family Court

The preceding chapters discuss family life from the perspectives of spouse selection, marriage, parenthood, and the gender divide. I pay special attention to attitudes and actions of ordinary people as portrayed by personal interviews and the accounting of their activities in censuses and other statistics. The objective of this chapter is different and two-fold: to inform on unresolved marital conflict in Asia and to discuss an institution set up to deal with marital breakdown. On the first objective, I introduce the most relevant features of the Asian setting and present the trends in marital breakdown using comparative divorce statistics from seven of the ten Asian countries discussed in previous chapters, three in East Asia (Japan, Hong Kong, South Korea) and four in Southeast Asia (Indonesia, the Philippines, Singapore and Thailand).[1] To meet the second objective I discuss the process of institution building by focusing on the family court as one institution dedicated to the management of family conflict. I discuss four aspects of the family court: the definition and history of the family court concept; its multidisciplinary nature; problems in the implementation of a family court blueprint for the solution or containment of family conflict; and an overview of the family court in Singapore. The Singapore experience may be useful to other countries in the region.

MARITAL BREAKDOWN

Divorce is not the same as marital conflict. Every couple encounters conflict along the marriage trajectory and, as we shall see, most couples manage to keep it within tolerable limits. But an increasing minority of couples is not successful at this. For them divorce is the final outcome of a long series of accumulated and unresolved grievances on the part of one or both spouses. Precisely what leads to the breaking point varies from one couple to the next and from culture to culture. The common link in all marriages that break down, however, is the realisation that there is no additional effort he, she, or both could possible make to save the marriage.

The Social Setting

Systematic studies examining the problem of divorce began in the United States in the 1900s[2] and often involved the examination of cultural differences through comparisons with immigrant families from various European countries. In their 60-year review of family research, Stephen Bahr and his colleagues found that the typical main reasons for divorce reported by those studies were differences in religious beliefs, values, or outlook of life; infidelity; drinking or other destructive habits; and personality differences.[3] American studies conducted in the 1930s already recognised that not all couples facing those types of difficulties get divorced. One of the studies published in 1938 reported that in contrast to other wives, women who sought divorce were financially more independent.[4]

Further research helped to clarify the nature of the problem and the factors conducive to divorce. By the end of the 1980s, studies[5] had confirmed that among the main factors conducive to divorce were differences in religion or values; infidelity; destructive habits including drug abuse, drinking and violent behaviour; personality differences; and young age at marriage. On the other hand, people in unhappy marriages faced major impediments to seeking divorce including the absence of alternative financial support (mostly for wives who were not working or had no marketable job skills), concern for the children, and religious beliefs emphasising marriage as a life-long commitment.

Are the American research findings from the first 60 years of the 20th century relevant to Asia today? Yes. Although the broken marriages examined are clearly from another time and place, the intriguing detail is that marriages in Asia appear to break down for very similar reasons, and people (especially women) in unhappy marriages tend to cite the same kind of grounds for not seeking divorce.

Describing the main reason for their divorce, 24 per cent of the 55 divorced people in a study of family life in Singapore[6] pointed to differences in values, ideals, goals or outlook in life; 20 per cent felt it was the difference in personality or character that lead to a "communication breakdown"; and another 20 per cent said it was infidelity that caused their marital problems. These answers coincide with the reasons for divorce given by Singaporean divorce petitioners in 2002. The Women's Charter — Singapore's legislation governing the non-Muslim population on family matters — stipulates a minimum of three years should have passed after the date of marriage, before a person is permitted to file for divorce, unless there is proven "exceptional hardship suffered by the petitioner" or "exceptional depravity on the part of the respondent." The sole legal ground for divorce is "that the marriage has irretrievably broken down" which means demonstrating to the court that "the petitioner finds it intolerable to live with the respondent" due to adultery; objectionable behaviour; or continuous desertion or living apart continuously for at least three years.[7] Of the 1,337 husbands who were granted divorce in 2002, 32.5 per cent indicated "unreasonable behaviour" as grounds for divorce and 60.3 per cent argued they were living apart for the required three years or more. Adultery was indicated by 2.8 per cent of them. In contrast, "unreasonable behaviour" was the grounds for divorce cited by 51.9 per cent of the 2,669 wives who were granted divorce in 2002; 44.2 per cent of wife-petitioners cited separation for three years; and 1.8 percent cited adultery.[8] Anecdotal information suggests that separation usually takes place due to either objectionable behaviour or adultery on the part of one of the spouses. However, the petitioner may prefer — or may be advised by his or her lawyer — to indicate separation as grounds for divorce in the divorce petition.

Family matters pertaining to marriage and divorce among the Muslim population in Singapore, Malaysia, and Indonesia are governed by the Syariah Court following the Shafii School of Islamic Law.[9] Men are permitted to take more than one wife provided they obtain the required permission from the Court and his current wife or wives.[10] In Singapore, population statistics on marriages and divorces are recorded separately, under the Women's Charter for non-Muslims, and under the Syariah Court for Muslims. Concerning the reasons for divorce, the figures on Muslim divorces in Singapore in 2002 show a trend among Muslims similar to that among non-Muslims: the two most common grounds for divorce were "personality differences" (given by 39.7 per cent of the petitioners) and infidelity (16.7 per cent).[11]

Talking about the circumstances surrounding the timing of their divorce, some divorced parents from Singapore, Japan, South Korea, and

Hong Kong mentioned to me the same reason: they prolonged a marital relationship that "was hopeless" until the children were "old enough" to take the bad news and to be independent. Most of them felt that when their youngest (or only) child completed secondary school, it was a signal that he or she was "old enough." There was a certain tacit agreement on this between the disaffected spouses. But other researchers found that some Japanese parents stay on together longer, "until the last child is married so as to avoid damaging their prospects"[12] and Filipino couples considering separation stay together "for the sake of the children" or "to maintain the family's good name."[13] In Singapore, South Korea, Hong Kong, the Philippines, and Thailand, wives whose marriages are breaking down are more likely to seek divorce if they have job skills and hold secure employment, compared to women who have always been housewives and have no paid job experience, even if they completed a degree before they got married. The years that homemakers spend looking after their families full-time create a serious knowledge gap that they cannot easily overcome, especially in countries with an advanced level of technology.

Having job security and education is also an important factor for women considering divorce in Japan.[14] But the cultural impediments may be severe. The family household registration system (*koseki*) covers all members of each household and records "each individual's gender, birthplace, date of birth, parents' names, position among siblings, marriage, and divorce" and these detailed records of "each individual *koseki* [...] are filed in the local municipal office."[15] According to Yoshio Sugimoto, the *koseki* system is an impediment to divorce for women because

> Divorce requires two separate family registers to be established and, if the couple have had children, each child must be shifted into one of the new registers, in most instances the mother's. Because copies of these papers are often required on such crucial occasions as employment and marriage, people can be stigmatized as the children of divorced parents through this public documentation. Fearful of a 'tarnish' being placed on their children's registers, many married couples, particularly women who are deeply involved emotionally in their children's well-being, vacillate over divorce even when the option is a sensible one.[16]

This peculiarity of the Japanese family system may explain the higher divorce rates among older couples. I will return to this feature later in connection with the latest divorce trends for the seven Asian countries.

In general, the cultural restraint is apparently working among younger couples. Moreover, while contemporary divorce statistics for Japan show an increase in divorce rates, Japanese social scientists are not alarmed. They take a long view by comparing divorce rates over a period of more than one hundred years. Sugimoto sums up: "The highest recorded divorce rate (divorces per one thousand persons) was 3.4 in 1883, while the postwar peak was 2.3 in 2001 [...] and is among the lowest recorded in industrially advanced nations."[17]

Japanese divorce legislation originated from the Meiji Civil Code of 1898. It was modified into the Civil Code of 1947. According to the provisions of the 1947 Civil Code, a person seeking divorce could opt for one of four alternatives. The most common option is "divorce by agreement of both parties" (*kyogi rikon*) in which case no legal counsel is necessary. A second option is "divorce by arbitration" (*chotel rikon*) with the Family Court as mediator; this option is followed when "divorce by mutual agreement cannot be reached." The third approach is "divorce by judgment" of the Family Court (*shimpan rikon*) that takes place "when divorce cannot be established by mediation." The fourth option is "divorce by judicial decision" at a district court (*saiban rikon*) and it is followed when the divorce "cannot be established by the family court."[18] Masahito Sasaki and Terry Wilson report that the traditional Japanese aversion to litigation is diminishing and the number of divorces through the courts is increasing accordingly.[19]

Following a historical pattern, Filipino women facing marital problems are more likely to search for ways of coping rather than to accept the breakdown of the marriage but this may be changing. Belen Medina reports that in a study of civil court cases from 1986 to 1990, the majority were filed by the wives: "62.5 per cent of the annulment cases, 79.55 per cent of the legal separation cases, and 93.88 per cent of the support cases had the wife as the petitioner."[20] Divorce regulations making divorce final for Filipino Muslims are provided by the "Muslim Code of Personal Laws" that basically follows the Syariah Court's provisions for Muslims in other Southeast Asian countries.

But the secular legislation dealing with family matters for non-Muslims in the Philippines is the New Family Code which allows only legal separation or annulment. The latter provision stipulates that annulment of a marriage is granted "if one of the contracting parties is psychologically incapacitated to perform the essential marital obligations, even if this incapacity surfaces only after the marriage is contracted." Evidence of psychological incapacity must be presented, thus the procedure requires legal counsel and expert evaluation by psychiatrists both of which are expensive.[21] Legal separation, on the other hand, does not permit the separated spouses to marry someone else and it is granted on grounds of physical violence, moral pressure on the spouse "to change religious or political affiliation"; corrupt behaviour such as inducing the petitioner or a child "to engage in prostitution"; imprisonment for more than six years; drug addiction or alcoholism; bigamy; infidelity; "attempt by the respondent against the life of the petitioner"; or abandonment "without justifiable reason for more than one year."[22] Nevertheless, according to Medina, three alternatives are used by people who wish to dissolve marriage ties: conversion to Islam as they are able to divorce and marry again if they are Muslims; obtain a divorce in another country; or get an annulment by the Church.[23]

Current Vietnamese family norms have been influenced by the drastic political and socioeconomic upheavals the country has endured over the past century. Add to these influences the rich variety of indigenous ethnic minorities and religious traditions that include Confucianism, Buddhism, Islam, and Brahmanism.[24] Running through these pieces of the mosaic is a common element: the importance of family and village. Sociologist Rita Liljestrom points to the war as a time when the deep significance of family shone through: "we have seen the role blood relationships and family affinities played for national liberation and class struggle. For the sake of their family honour, people were ready to die." But, like many other social scientists have indicated, Liljestrom sees the dark side of this emphasis on family and village as being "conducive to patriarchy, regionalism, and factionalism, thus standing in the way to democratization" and gender equality.[25]

It is thus easy to appreciate that the reasons that keep married couples together or break them apart in Vietnam are perhaps more complex than in other Asian countries. This complexity is one of the reasons for the dearth of divorce studies in Vietnam, according to Vietnamese sociologist T. H. Khuat. He identifies four main reasons for divorce. The first is "Consequences of feudalistic marriage and family system" that may allude to a clash between the 'new' communist principle of gender equality and the ancient principle of male superiority dictated by Confucian and other traditional values dominating the realm of family relations. This problem of contradictory values is faced by most men and women in Asia as discussed in Chapter 5 of this volume. The second reason for divorce in Vietnam is "differences in character of the couples." The third reason is conflicts with in-laws, "especially the wife and her mother-in-law." And the fourth reason is adultery. Khuat reports that the first two reasons are the most common.[26] With the exception of conflicts with in-laws, these main grounds for divorce are rather similar to those argued by divorce petitioners in other Asian countries. Another trend similar to that in all the countries studied is that the majority of divorce petitioners are wives.

Divorce Trends

The most reliable figures available for a comparison across countries are the percentages of divorced people in different age cohorts. Seven countries with complete figures at two points in time within a five-year interval (1990/91 and 1995/96) are included in this comparison: Japan, Hong Kong, South Korea, Indonesia, Singapore, the Philippines, and Thailand.

The first interesting trend is on the differences across countries on the timing of divorce along a person's life trajectory. Most divorces tend to occur after the age of 30. Comparing the proportion of divorced men in three age cohorts, men aged 30 to 34, 40 to 44, and 50 to 54, in 1990/91 (Chart 6.1), we can detect different patterns across countries. Thailand and Philippines have low proportions of divorced men in all three age cohorts and the proportions are similar in all three age groups. South Korean men are more likely to divorce in their early 40s and the probability of divorce diminishes among older men. The trend in Hong Kong and Singapore in 1990/91 was rather similar: a marked increase in divorce among men in their 40s and 50s compared to younger men. In contrast to all the other countries, Japan had the highest proportion of divorced men in all three age groups and a significantly higher proportion among older men. Reflecting the general steady increase in divorce rates, the proportion of divorced men in 1995/96 was higher in all three age groups for all countries except among older men in Indonesia and Thailand. Again, just like five years earlier, in 1995/96 Japan had by far the largest proportion of divorced men in the age groups 40 to 44 and 50 to 54, followed by Singapore, Hong Kong, and South Korea.

The figures on the proportion of divorced women in the same three age cohorts (30-34, 40-44, and 50-54) indicate some important differences with men as well as differences across countries (Chart 6.2). The rates of divorce for women are also increasing in all countries and this increase comes out clearly in the comparison of figures from 1990/ 91 and 1995/96 for all countries, except Indonesia. The reasons for the drastic drop in proportions of divorced men and women in Indonesia are not evident as yet, particularly in contrast to the increasing trend in the rest of the region. Other studies have also documented significant variation across ten year periods in Indonesia.[27] As in the case of men, Japan and Singapore have the highest proportion of divorced women aged 40 and older. The trend in South Korea remained the same from 1990/91 to 1995/96, with the highest proportion of divorced women in the age group 40-44.

Of the various factors explored as possible explanations of the differential timing of divorce across the seven countries (trends in Charts 6.1 and 6.2) three related factors came across unmistakably: level of economic development, level of general human development, and gender-related development. Two examples will suffice to illustrate the situation. First, compared to economically less developed countries, the timing of divorce tends to be at an older age in countries with higher levels of economic development, and this trend is the same for men and women (Charts 6.3 and 6.4). With the highest Gross Domestic Product (GDP) per capita in Asia, Japan is the best example of this trend, followed at a distance by Singapore and Hong Kong. As I pointed out earlier, the Japanese culture reinforces the postponement of divorce among couples whose marriages are under strain, to a time after the children are grown-up and settled in their own marriages. There is a very strong correlation between GDP per capita and the proportion of divorced men and women in the age groups 40-44 and 50-55. The charts show selected cohorts for the sake of brevity.

An illustration of the reverse side of the link between the overall economic development and divorce timing is offered by the countries' Human Development Index scores[28] (Chart 6.5). Divorces are more likely to occur at a younger age in countries with low levels of economic development. Chart 6.5 shows the proportion of divorced women in the age cohort 20-24 in 1995/96 according to the country's HDI.

CHART 6.1 DIVORCE TRENDS FOR MEN AGED 30-54 IN 1990/1991 AND 1995/1996

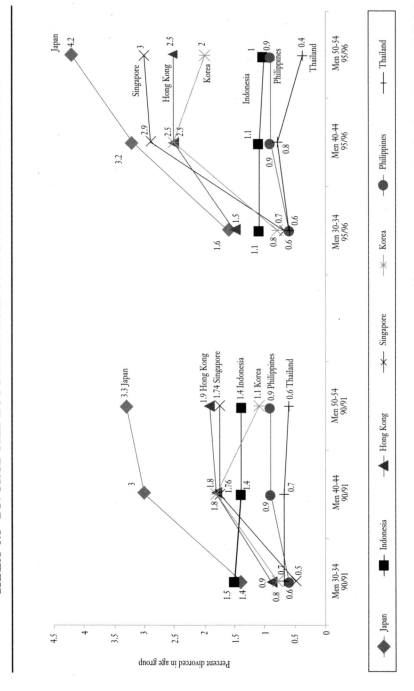

Source: Calculated from United Nations Statistics Division (2002); Lau (1992) and Leow (2001b).

CHART 6.2   DIVORCE TRENDS FOR WOMEN AGE 30-54 IN 1990/1991 AND 1995/1996

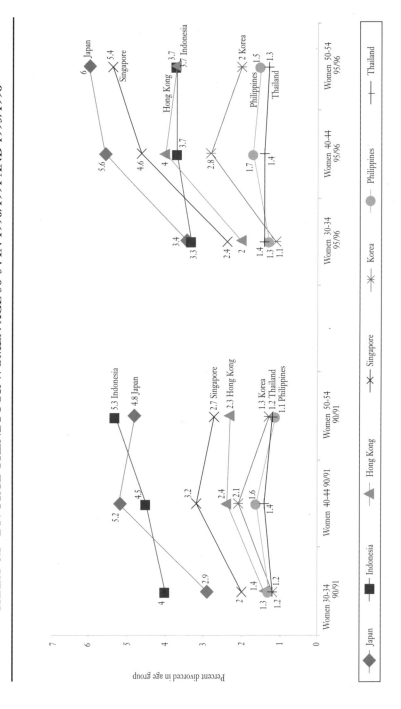

Source: Calculated from United Nations Statistics Division (2002); Lau (1992) and Leow (2001b).

Indonesia had the lowest HDI score and the highest rate of divorce among women aged 20-24, followed by Thailand and the Philippines. As seen in Chapter 2, of the seven countries in this comparison, Indonesia has the lowest age at marriage; and marrying young has been associated with a shorter length of marriage in numerous studies around the world. It is relevant to recall that in contrast to non-Muslims in the region, Muslim marriages tend to occur at a younger age, and the rates of divorce tend to be higher.[29]

As a way of summing up the influence of socioeconomic development, the contrast between early and late divorces is presented in Chart 6.6. The first section on the social setting of divorce conveyed the importance of cultural values and social arrangements that facilitate or retard the process of marital dissolution. Those factors are less tangible and require separate and closer analysis in Asia but are beyond the scope of this book. We may turn now to the notion of the family court as a potentially valuable institutional arrangement to deal with family conflict.

CHART 6.3   DIVORCE TRENDS AMONG WOMEN AGED 40-44 IN 1995/1996 AND ECONOMIC DEVELOPMENT

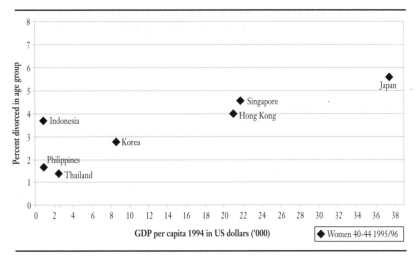

Sources: Calculated from World Bank (2002); and United Nations Statistics Division (2002).
Correlation: r = .861; p = .013

CHART 6.4   DIVORCE TRENDS AMONG MEN AGED 50-54 IN 1995/1996 AND ECONOMIC DEVELOPMENT

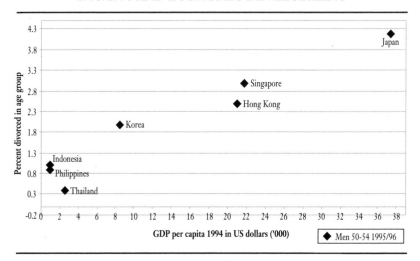

Sources: Calculated from World Bank (2002); and United Nations Statistics Division (2002).
Correlation: r = .968; p = .0001.

CHART 6.5   DIVORCE TRENDS AMONG WOMEN AGED 20-24 IN 1995/1996 AND HUMAN DEVELOPMENT INDEX

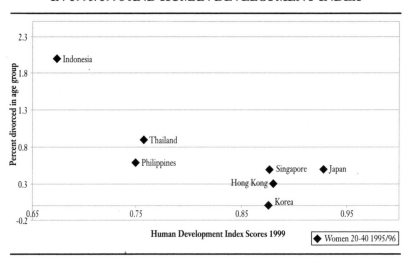

Sources: Calculated from United Nations (2002); and ESCAP (2002).
Correlation: r = -.813; p = .026.

162

CHART 6.6 DIVORCE TRENDS FOR WOMEN 20-24 AND MEN 50-54 IN 1995/1996

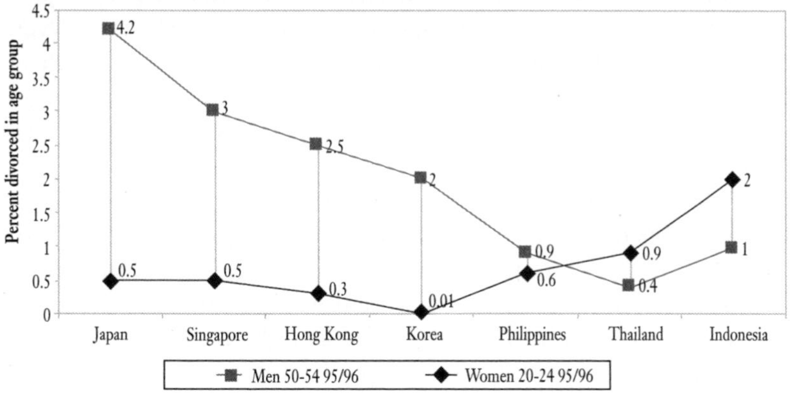

Source: Calculated from United Nations Statistics Division (2002); Lau (1992) and Leow (2001b).

WHAT IS THE FAMILY COURT?[30]

Several definitions of the family court have been proposed and tried out over the years by legal experts in various countries. But, in spite of the variation in wording, the essential accepted meaning of the family court as a judicial institution in the current legal literature is still the "classical" definition first used in 1925 in Toledo, Ohio, when the Family Court of Toledo was set up. Following the Toledo definition, a family court is

> an integrated and unified jurisdiction in a single court with competence over all aspects of family stress ... [for example] juvenile delinquency ... divorce, nullity and separation ... guardianship and custody disputes; maintenance; matrimonial property disputes; domestic assaults; child neglect and cruelty; adoption; affiliation. Instead of jurisdiction over such matters being fragmented between several courts, it is consolidated in a single court, although there may need to be specialized divisions or sections within that one court.[31]

It is apparent then that the idea of the family court as a unified judicial institution has been around for eight decades, and that the concept of a family court originated in the United States. In his analysis of the

163

legal background of the family court, Neville L. Brown[32] traced the origins of the idea of a family court to the second part of the 19th century when the authorities in the United States and England became preoccupied with the handling of juvenile delinquency. Brown, a British lawyer, conceded that "the Americans had a short lead" over the British in establishing juvenile courts: the first juvenile court was set up in Chicago in 1899, and the British followed the movement with the passing of the *Children Act* in 1908.[33]

The ineffectiveness of the juvenile court in handling a variety of family problems of juvenile delinquents awakened in the minds of concerned officials and professionals the urgent need to improve the courts' institutional system and structure. Thus, the juvenile court served as a predecessor of the family court in both the United States and Britain. But interest in the concept of family courts grew faster in the United States, where a second historical event — after the Toledo Family Court was set up in 1925 — was, according to Brown, the in-depth study conducted by the New York Bar in 1954 on "Children and Families in the Courts of New York City." This study was crucial in the formulation of the American family court legislation in 1961. In contrast, the idea of family courts made an impact in Britain only in the 1960s.[34] The family court concept has been discussed in depth and tried out in various countries, particularly the United States, Canada, the United Kingdom and Australia. The concept captured the attention of policy-makers in Asia. It appears that with the establishment of its family court on 1 January 1949, Japan was the first Asian country with a family court system. By 2003, family courts had been established in Hong Kong, South Korea, Singapore, and Thailand. The notion is under debate in Malaysia, where legal experts have called for the prompt establishment of the family court to deal with family conflict among the non-Muslim population in a comprehensive and efficient manner.[35] The Muslim population in Malaysia have the Syariah Court for the application of Islamic Law to family-related matters.[36] Public debate on the family court concept is never smooth, however. An illustration close to home is Australia's experience where the family court was established in 1976.[37] It is common also to find intermediary arrangements made before a country decides to implement family courts. In England, for example, the Family Division of the High Court has been the historical bridge between the 19th century's juvenile court and the contemporary family court.[38]

Professional Collaboration

One characteristic of the family court is its multi-disciplinary nature. It is an institution that, as it will become evident, must be steered by at least two types of skills, legal and social science expertise. The family court presupposes the collaboration of legal professionals and social scientists in the conceptual analyses of social behaviour, justice, law, and order, as well as in the designing and running of a practical institution that serves individuals and families in conflict. At the institutional level, this requirement on collaboration across disciplines constitutes a major challenge to traditional procedures guiding a country's judicial system which recruits senior staff exclusively from the legal profession. At the level of daily practice, a certain measure of collaboration has been accepted for many decades. It is not uncommon to find in the judicial literature and in lawyers' publications, references to findings and concepts from the social sciences. Psychologists, social workers and other social scientists are also called from time to time as expert witnesses in judicial procedures. These macro- and micro-trends are framed within a larger historical picture tracing back the collaboration to end of the 19th century. In the 1880s American legal experts grew dissatisfied with classical jurisprudence. They lost "confidence in natural law theories" and became more inclined "to view law as a means of establishing social policy." Hence, among the legal profession, "the classical belief that the application of logic could determine a single, correct solution for every case gave way to the view that the answer to legal problems varies according to the social context."[39]

All things considered, in the case of the family court today, collaboration between legal professionals and social scientists is further supported by the necessity to improve the institutional response to family conflict. Just as it occurred in the United States, Britain, and Australia, concerned professionals in other nations are becoming increasingly critical of the problems created by the fragmentation of work among several courts dealing with family matters and the negative consequences of such problems for the individuals and families involved.[40] Besides the contradictions and frequent instances of "overlapping jurisdiction" created by the plethora of courts involved in a given case, the most frequently mentioned problems are the high costs to citizens in terms of legal fees payable to several courts, time spent going from one court to another in different locations and the inconveniences of dealing with different officials and legal personnel that have only a partial — and thus distorted or incomplete — view of the person's legal case and cannot appreciate the long-term consequences of their fractional solutions for his or her personal and family life. As summarised by the Law Reform Commission of Canada, the fragmentation of legal work on family conflicts causes "despair, confusion and frustration" and "As far as the general public is concerned there appears to be no reason why all legal matters arising from a matrimonial or family dispute should not be dealt with by a single court."[41]

These are clearly social problems. Yet, the voices raised in support of a judicial reform that would establish family courts come overwhelmingly from the legal profession rather than from social scientists (with the exception of some professional social workers with vast job experience with the judiciary system). The explanation may be that social scientists' concern tends to be more on social policy rather than on judicial reform *per se*. This difference in focus is, of course, derived from the difference in areas of expertise. In contrast to lawyers, social scientists are more inclined to approach family stress and conflict from a micro-perspective by looking into the social-psychological nature of internal relations among family members.[42] Or they may use a macro-perspective by analysing the country's social policies in the context of the social, political and economic frameworks under which such policies are formulated and implemented.[43] Some social scientists apply a combination of micro- and macro-perspectives.[44]

While the need for a unified family court has been perceived and promoted mostly by members of the legal profession, there are three main arguments that have influenced — positively or negatively — their collaboration with social scientists in the design and management of that institution. The first argument is that social scientists are the experts on family conflict. Most legal professionals involved in family law recognise the contributions made by the social sciences in the study of the family as a social unit and have expressed this recognition explicitly and implicitly by incorporating social science findings and concepts in their work.[45] Indeed, social science research over the past five decades has demonstrated the internal dynamics of the family as a social group including, among other aspects, evidence on the inter-dependence of family members and the negative consequences of personal crises for the individual's family life.[46] These findings are highly relevant to the judicial approach to divorce, child custody and other matters in family law.[47]

The second main argument on collaboration between legal professionals and social scientists is the dual role of the family court promoted by its supporters. This dual role of "adjudication and welfare" was put in the clearest terms by the Committee on One-Parent Families in England, otherwise known as the Finer Report. In their 1974 report, the committee recognised the uniqueness of the family court concept by asserting that the family court as a "judicial institution" seeks "*to do good as well as to do right*" even though "to promote welfare is an unusual function for a court of law."[48] In 1966 Neville Brown pointed to the same dual purpose of family courts when summarising the lessons learned from juvenile courts:

> the juvenile court demonstrated how legal institutions, with the help of the social sciences, could successfully resolve social problems in an intelligent and constructive way; that is, that courts and the law may serve people in trouble, as well as to vindicate rights, redress wrongs and mete out punishment [...] In every case it [the family court] would seek to diagnose and cure the underlying cause of the family disorder. Thus, in divorce it would think first of marriage-mending before marriage-ending. For this remedial function it would need to be buttressed with adequate expert assistance ... Where, however, cure proved impossible, the family court would perform its legal operation ... with the least traumatic effect on the personalities involved.[49]

Although legal professionals who advocate the family court tend to agree on its dual role of adjudication and welfare, there is no consensus on how far the family court should go in "*doing good*." The Finer Report emphasised that, of the two roles, the fundamental obligation of the family court is adjudication. It stressed that the goal of "achieving welfare must not be permitted to weaken or short cut the normal safeguards of the judicial process." and it warned that the persons approaching the family court should not be seen as "clients" or "patients" seeking "treatment." Instead, "the individual in the family court must ... remain the subject of rights, not the object of assistance."[50] Legal professionals opposing the family court concept as a multi-disciplinary institution reject its dual role. For them, adjudication should be the sole objective of the family court which they see as another type of subordinate court in the larger judicial structure.

This brings us to the third main argument on law and social science cooperation. This argument rests on the question: should the family court procedures be inquisitorial or adversary? The search for an answer to this question has moved legal professionals to further their dialogue with social scientists although the former do not fully agree yet on what is the right answer. In adversary or accusatorial proceedings, the parties decide on the issues of the dispute and on what evidence to present in court. In inquisitorial proceedings, the court may collect evidence directly.[51] Some legal experts believe that a combination of both inquisitorial and adversary proceedings is the best solution. Others disagree.

The combined proceedings position is inspired by social science research findings on the family as a dynamic social unit, and presumes close collaboration with social scientists. This position is best represented in the paper on the Family Court by the Law Reform Commission of Canada.[52] The Commission stated that "the resolution of family conflicts require some modification of the traditional adversary process. To leave reconciliation and settlement of issues exclusively in the hands of the lawyers is inadequate."[53] In contrast, the British Committee on One-Parent Families was more conservative. The British Committee felt that while the two types of procedure are not "mutually exclusive," and both are applied in divorce and child custody cases,

> To the extent that the court requires assistance by way of investigation or expert assessment of circumstances which it considers material, this function should be discharged by ancillary services which are attached to or can be called upon by the court, but whose personnel are not themselves members of the court. The bench of the family court is to consist only of judges [...].[54]

The position represented by the British Committee in the Finer Report is that collaboration with social scientists is encouraged, and that the family court bench "should, in every aspect of its jurisdiction, be able to call upon the aid of a competent person to make social and welfare enquiries and reports." But, at the same time, the committee insisted that priority must be given to the due process of law over the social scientists' input.

A similar reservation about collaboration with social scientists — in this case with social workers or psychologists acting as marriage counsellors or conciliation officers — was reported in a study of the

Bristol Courts Family Conciliation Service.[55] The study found that some divorce lawyers in private practice "were uneasy about the effect of a conciliation service on the solicitors/client relationship ... the clients might feel abandoned if referred to another agency." The legal profession's ambivalence on the collaboration with social scientists surfaced again. The author reported that there was "a general awareness" among solicitors "of the shortcomings of the adversarial system" in divorce proceedings. Solicitors interviewed felt that this problem and the absence "of legal aid from decree proceedings in undefended divorce" persuaded them "to find a separate conciliation service broadly acceptable."[56] In sum, three main arguments influence the level of collaboration of the legal profession with social scientists in the designing and implementation of the family court: their recognition of the social sciences' contribution to the study of family behaviour; their awareness of the importance of combining the concepts of adjudication and welfare in the family court though there is no agreement on how that combination would be determined; and their acknowledgment of the limitations of adversarial proceedings in family law.

As revealed by a review of published material (research reports, court cases, legal papers and articles in professional journals and books), an expected outcome of the combination of these three arguments is that collaboration between law and the social sciences takes usually two forms. On the one hand, lawyers tend to apply in their writings and legal practice what they learn from social sciences studies about social and family behaviour. This is particularly frequent among legal practitioners involved in family law. On the other hand, lawyers in family courts have now more opportunities to work with social scientists — primarily social workers and psychologists — in the handling of specific cases that require the latter's expertise as consultants, counselors, or conciliation officers.

The Challenge of Implementation

As suggested in the preceding pages, although most family law practitioners tend to agree on the importance of the family court concept, there is no consensus yet within the legal profession on specific and crucial aspects of its implementation such as the extent to which welfare should be combined with adjudication; the manner in which inquisitorial proceedings should operate; and how close to the family court bench should social scientists function. Naturally, the structure and implementation of the family court are strengthened to the degree to which these questions are resolved. However, findings from social science studies not only support the family court concept but also suggest guidelines for its implementation. A few examples will suffice. Sociological research findings on family behaviour strongly suggest that efforts at family conflict resolution are more likely to succeed when the family is approached as a dynamic and adaptable unit of interdependent individuals.[57] It is thus important to strive towards coordination and continuity in the judicial and other institutional procedures set up to help families in conflict. The family court as defined by Brown[58] is a very promising institution in this respect.

As mentioned earlier, the goal "to do good as well as to do right" was proposed by the Finer Report[59] as one of the top objectives of the family court. Social science findings confirm that when informal support networks fail or cannot fully provide help to families facing conflict, formal support institutions play a crucial role in assisting those families.[60] The family court is the best example of a formal support institution that individuals and their families can rely upon to suggest or provide equitable solutions as well as assistance to overcome hardship. But an important requirement of this dual goal is that a mediating structure should form part of the concept of the family court, preferably as the institutional partner of the family court rather than as one of its internal components.

Similarly, the introduction of inquisitive proceedings and the lessening of adversarial proceedings is an approach supported by social science studies. Relevant research findings show that the probabilities of successful conflict resolution increase when blame is avoided or reduced and when negotiation and bargaining are, correspondingly, emphasised in conflict management.[61] As Lisa Parkinson[62] rightly suggested the "gladiatorial divorce advocate" should not be a part of the institutional setting offered by the family court to help families in conflict.

In contrast to the active discussion of the family court concept in many countries, its implementation has been laggard. The lack of consensus on the answers to the last two questions (how to do good while doing right, and how to de-emphasise the accusatorial approach), is a major obstacle slowing down the implementation of the family court in some countries. Besides these difficulties there is, of course, another problem predicted and confirmed by social science research: resistance to change is a very common feature of human groups. Resistance to change is manifested in various ways. Among the most common arguments to delay or avoid a change that is otherwise supported, are financial costs and lack of physical space. In the mid-1970s, the British government argued that the delay in the setting up of family courts was due to the need for new buildings to house the family courts across England and that there were no available funds for this purpose. These arguments were strongly refuted by two bodies representing legal professionals supporting the implementation of the family court.[63] Other lawyers have reported that the family court occupies a very low position in the list of priorities of the legal system in many countries where the decision-makers attribute their delay to the fact that they are pressed by other more urgent matters such as a chronic backlog of unresolved court cases, an insufficient number of judges and other court personnel, or both.[64]

A Partner of the Family Court

Of all the possible reasons for the delay in implementation of the family court in some countries, the problem of combining welfare and adjudication is one of the most authentic and deserves special attention. As I mentioned earlier, the potential solution may be found in the concept of *mediation* presented in the form of a non-judicial institution or mediation service that I may call, tentatively, the Family Guidance Service.

The fundamental principle justifying the creation of the Family Guidance Service is that mediation efforts to save families from irretrievable marital breakdown should be offered to families as early as possible in the process of accumulating grievances that leads to the escalating deterioration of marital and family relations. The key issue here is how may the community assist the two spouses in saving their marriage. Mediation services are futile if they are offered only at the divorce court when, in the eyes of the spouses, their marriage has reached, or is very close to, the stage of irrevocable breakdown. In this respect, I agree with the position of the Law Commission[65] and the Finer Report[66] that it is too late trying to mend a marriage at the court stage. As Davis[67] emphasised, mediation should be "a first" and not "a last resort."

What is mediation? Basically, mediation is the community's effort to help the marriage partners — or family members — to reconcile their differences in an equitable and mutually respectful manner. Mediation may take the form of marital and family counselling, and should be accessible to any family in the community irrespective of the family's ability to pay for the service. A more elaborate yet useful definition of mediation was offered by I. Wolcott following the Australian experience. In her view, mediation means "To empower the parties to make informed decisions and agreements between themselves rather than ones imposed by outside parties through legislation."[68]

However, Wolcott's definition of mediation covers two separate processes, reconciliation, and conciliation. The definitions of these two processes offered by Finer[69] and Parkinson[70] are very relevant at this point. According to these authors, reconciliation is the mending up of disagreements and the resolution of serious conflict between the partners. It involves counselling with the objective of reuniting the spouses. In contrast, conciliation is best interpreted as a legal process that involves couples who are convinced that their marriages have broken down irretrievably. Conciliation refers to helping the couples to deal with the consequences of their decision to end the marriage and to settle the details of the divorce or separation including children's custody and other matters. As is true of reconciliation, one of the objectives of conciliation is reaching an agreement as amicably and fairly for both parties as possible.

As a partner of the Family Court, the Family Guidance Service would provide counselling and would have reconciliation as its *first* objective. For this purpose the Family Guidance Service must be staffed with professional counsellors, clinical psychologists specialised in family therapy, and social workers. A *second* objective of the Family Guidance Service will be to liaise with and to assist the Family Court at two levels: (a) to implement the Court's final attempt at reconciliation of couples seeking divorce; and (b) to work jointly with the Family Court's legal officers and case lawyers in helping the divorcing couples in the conciliation process.

This suggested division of labour between two partner institutions, the Family Guidance Service and the Family Court, seeks to settle the misgivings of legal professionals concerning the combination of welfare and adjudication as goals of the same institution. I concur with the Finer Report that the objective of community involvement in helping families in conflict should be a dual objective, that is, "to do good as well as to do right."[71] But in my opinion, the Family Court is not equipped to attain both objectives alone because it does not have the necessary expertise and because, as I said earlier, its intervention in providing help reaches the spouses too late. Unfortunately, the family court's correct location within the country's judicial system shapes its public image, and people tend to perceive it a legal and punitive forum to settle the affairs of a defunct marriage. Therefore my suggestion is to set up the Family Guidance Service as the mediating institution that will be a partner of the Family Court; will offer reconciliation services independently of the Family Court; will provide these services well before the marital problems lead one or both spouses to the decision to divorce; and will offer its counselling and mediation services to families in conflict whether or not divorce is involved.

At the same time, the expertise of the Family Guidance Service's professional staff will be utilised jointly with the legal expertise of the Family Court staff to help couples who, after counselling, have decided that they are beyond reconciliation. This will be the opportunity to combine adjudication and welfare. Moreover, the partnership between the Family Guidance Service and the Family Court will permit the latter to benefit from the professional expertise of the former in the use of inquisitorial proceedings that will elicit objective information and thus help the Family Court judges to arrive at just and equitable decisions.

A final objective of the Family Guidance Service is the efficient utilisation of professional expertise in order to increase the availability of family counselling to all members of the community. In most modern countries today, one finds an array of family experts from different disciplines, including psychology and social work. Most of these professionals may work in the private sector offering a variety of services both for a fee as well as free of charge through volunteer non-profit organisations. The Family Guidance Service should tap this pool of experts and services by taking the form of a *network* rather than becoming just another counselling service.

More specifically, the Family Guidance Service should have two levels: a main operating centre and a network of branches. The main operating centre or headquarters of the Family Guidance Service will offer basic family counselling services to the public and will function as the coordinating, research, and referral centre for family counselling. The branches will be constituted by a network of affiliated clinics and counselling services already available in the public and private sectors. In this manner, the existing public and private counselling clinics and services will be incorporated, if they request it, to the Family Guidance

173

Service. The link between these affiliated clinics and the operating centre should be kept strictly professional. The Family Guidance Service should not become a monopoly of services that may restrict the choices for the individual consumer of professional services.

I have discussed thus far the most important aspects of the family court concept and of its implementation from a global perspective. That is, I have identified common experiences in countries where the idea of a family court has been considered or attempted. To conclude this analysis I will review the family court concept and implementation in Singapore as an additional example of the persistence of institution-building features discussed in the preceding pages.

THE FAMILY COURT IN SINGAPORE

The Family Court was established in Singapore on 1 March 1995. It has evolved since then incorporating new features in response to local conditions and needs. The basic trend of collaboration between law and social sciences is not as advanced in Singapore as it is in some Western countries. But collaboration is taking place as illustrated by two of the three components of the Family Court organisation, the Family and Juvenile Justice Centre and the Family Court Support Group, where the social sciences are represented by the presence and contributions of psychologists and social workers. There is also a nascent trend towards the incorporation of social science findings into the published work of legal professionals.[72] Another feature that Singapore shares with other countries is that the concept of the family court was introduced locally by members of the legal profession rather than by social scientists. These lawyers[73] gave the same arguments in support of the family court that were originally introduced in the United States and the United Kingdom during the first half of the 20th century. A specific proposal to establish the Family Court in Singapore was submitted by the Singapore Association of Women Lawyers (SAWL) to the Attorney General's Chambers in the early 1990s. Interestingly, women's groups in Malaysia,[74] Japan,[75] and other countries have pursued the discussion of the family court concept, its implementation and improvement, and have made specific recommendations to legislative bodies in their own countries to that effect.

Singapore has faced similar hurdles to the design, approval, and implementation of the Family Court observed in the United Kingdom, the United States, Australia, and other countries. Just as their Western counterparts, our legal experts had to consider, among other aspects, the implications of combining welfare with adjudication; the particular advantages of inquisitorial over adversarial proceedings; the operation of inquisitorial proceedings; and the specific role of social scientists in the Family Court setting. On the other hand, resistance to change, which is one of the main obstacles faced by American and British proponents of the Family Court, does not constitute a major problem in Singapore. Change is a familiar situation for Singaporeans. Over the past two decades Singapore has been held as an international example of rapid change, whether economic, administrative, or social, including recent radical innovations geared towards the streamlining of the judiciary process.

Cultural Precedents

Singapore's history indicates that the ideas behind a Family Guidance Service and the Family Court, as well as their suggested partnership, are not entirely new to the various ethnic communities that have shared the island and the region known as the Straits Settlements as their home since Thomas Stamford Raffles founded Singapore in 1819. Historical records from those early years of the British colonial government in Singapore and Malaysia to the 'Malayanisation' scheme in the 1950s reveal two significant social features that may be seen as cultural precedents to the Family Court and the Family Guidance Service. These two social features were: the inclination of the Asian communities to request regulations from the British colonial authorities on matters pertaining family relations; and the creation of the Chinese Protectorate. Each of these features requires individual attention.

Let us deal first with the colonised population's trend to request the intervention of the colonial government. World history demonstrates that it is usual for colonised populations to manifest aversion to the interference of their colonial masters in matters pertaining to their private lives. Yet, contrary to expectations, there was a certain predisposition among the Chinese, Malay, and Indian Muslim communities to seek the intervention of the colonial government in establishing regulations that would provide security and order in their lives. This apparent contradiction is understandable if one considers the favourable attitude towards authority among the

Chinese, and the social situation of the immigrant population during the colonial era, particularly in the 19th century.

According to the analysis of Chinese law by Sidney Shapiro,[76] the Chinese accepted the moral and ethical principles justifying "a paternalistic authoritarian society" and thus "few Chinese questioned China's approach to law and order." But, Shapiro explains,

> What was questioned and reviled in bitter complaint, was the distortion and bypassing of the judicial system by cruel and corrupt officials, the ease with which the rich and powerful could escape punishment or buy favorable judgments, and the immense practical difficulties confronting persons of lower social status seeking a redress of grievances [...].[77]

Concerning the social conditions faced by most Chinese and Indian immigrants, life in colonial Singapore was characterised by a constant struggle to survive in an alien and often hostile social environment. Immigrant labourers were frequently at the mercy of secret society agents who "deceived and cheated" them[78] and it was common for these labourers to borrow the cost of their boat trip from China. This problem, as C.M. Turnbull suggests, led the labourers to a situation whereby "it was difficult to wipe out debt-bondage, and the hidden slavery of immigrant labour persisted for decades."[79] Those immigrants who did well enough to secure their survival had to persevere at making a living and working hard to save and to support the families they left behind in their motherland. A few immigrants would go beyond just saving to become powerful entrepreneurs and leaders of their communities. But with wave after wave of fresh immigrants, particularly from China, the struggle for survival was confronted by every new poor, often indebted, and uneducated labourer stepping out of a vessel at the Singapore harbour during the 19th century and in the early years of the 20th century.[80]

Female immigrants were not spared hardship. As the large majority of the immigrant labourers were males, either single or without spouses, the disparity in the sex ratio of the Chinese population was very large. Some historians assert that there were no Chinese female immigrants to Singapore before 1837.[81] Females made up only 14 per cent of the Chinese population in 1871, 16 per cent in 1881, and 18 per cent in 1891. One consequence of this imbalance was a high demand for prostitutes. Based on records kept by the colonial authorities,[82] it is estimated that 22 per cent of the Chinese women in 1871 were engaged in prostitution; this proportion fell to 14 per cent in 1881 and to 9 per cent in 1891.

Another consequence of the shortage of women was the introduction of the *mui tsai* system to Singapore. Under the *mui tsai* (literally "younger sister") system, poor parents gave their daughter to another family for a sum of money, ostensibly to give the girl a better home and for her to be treated as a member of her new family. The young girl could be expected to work as domestic servant in her new household and her employer "was obliged to provide her with board and lodging and to marry her off suitably" once she reached the "marriable age" of 18.[83] In practice, however, these girls would be "resold" to brothel "procuresses" and taken out of China. The colonial authorities in Singapore and Penang found that "the large numbers of [female] children ... brought down from China in almost every steamer ... to be trained for prostitution" were registered as "coming here to join their husbands, and the procuresses are described as being their mothers."[84] This was a thriving trade in the colony because of the high value of "the girl-child" or *mui-tsai* "as a potential wife and mother which she would not possess to the same degree in a country where females were in the majority."

The Indian and Malay communities in colonial Singapore shared with their Chinese counterparts a high probability of hardship and exploitation. Tamil immigrant labourers faced "a regularly organized system of kidnapping" and Tamil women would be "regularly recruited for prostitution in ... labour settlements" and subjected to "tragic" abuses.[86] The majority of Javanese immigrants were labourers who usually would come under "a notorious joint ... contract" whereby in exchange for an advanced sum of money to travel to Singapore, they had to promise that "If any of us should die or run away the persons who are left behind will be responsible for the payment of the said amount."[87]

This succinct look into the social conditions of the immigrant population helps to clarify the otherwise paradoxical records of petitions from the Asian communities in Singapore to the British colonial authorities to intervene and to introduce regulations on family matters. Some brief illustrations of these petitions will suffice.

The Legislative Council of the Straits Settlements were presented with a petition signed "in Malay and Tamil characters" by 143 Muslims on 30 January 1877, requesting "better means for recording marriages and divorces" to improve the existing informal or haphazard method of recording these important events; the official appointment of a Muslim Registrar under the purview of the Registrar-General of the Colony; and the licensing by the colonial government of "Imaums" who should solemnise marriages and divorces and who should be examined by the Registrar and Muslim experts concerning "their qualifications and integrity." The petitioners explained that if these regulations were not instituted, they

> fear that ... in future years their children may be without the means of providing the validity of their parents' marriages or their own legitimacy, and the title of property may be thereby greatly endangered.[88]

The Tamil Muslims or "Chuliahs," who arrived in 1786 preceding the Tamil Hindus, had already petitioned the Colonial authorities in November 1822 to appoint "a headman or Captain" to look after the interests of "the mercantile and labouring classes."[89]

Similarly, influential members of the Chinese community, or *towkays*, were well aware of the ordeals of the immigrant labourers and women. On 17 May 1871, they presented a petition to the Acting Governor requesting the appointment of "a trustworthy officer ... to superintend the *sinkhehs*" that is, the newly-arrived and indebted Chinese immigrant labourers, whom the *towkays* knew were "being deceived and cheated" by secret society agents.[90] A few years later, the Chinese community demanded the colonial government's intervention to contain or solve the negative consequences of gambling among "the lower class Chinese" namely, that "people who gamble and lose, sell their wives and children."[91]

From 1908 to the mid-1940s, the British colonial government faced recurrent informal pressure and formal petitions from the Straits-born Chinese and the English-educated Chinese to formalise marriage registration. Groups of China-born Chinese strongly opposed those efforts arguing that it was their duty and need to preserve their cultural traditions, including polygamy and concubinage. The British colonial authorities vacillated between action and inaction and finally approved the Civil Marriage Ordinance in 1940 presenting marriage registration as optional.[92]

The second major cultural precedent to the Family Court was the institution called the Chinese Protectorate. The appointment by the colonial government of a headman to lead and represent his colonised community was a well-known practice among European powers before the British Colonial government set up the Chinese Protectorate in 1877. The "Kapitan China system" as this procedure was popularly called, had already been instituted by the Spaniards in the Philippines, by the Portuguese in Malacca, by the Dutch in the East Indies, and by the French in Saigon and Phnom Penh.[93] Added to these practical examples from other colonial powers, the British colonial government was (as explained earlier) under pressure from the Asian communities in Singapore to modify their policy of "letting the Chinese rule the Chinese" and to set up some fundamental regulations to protect the most disadvantaged immigrants.

The proposed post of Protector of Chinese was defined as "an administrator who should be a thoroughly trustworthy European," should be able to speak and write the Chinese language, and should be available "at all times [to] the population requiring his assistance or advice."[94] More important for the purpose of this discussion, however, is the transformation of this institution over the years under the personal initiative and leadership of the first Protector of Chinese, W.A. Pickering. The initial duties of the Chinese Protectorate were to oversee and administer matters concerning the registration of immigrants and secret societies. The immigrant labourers felt an urgent need for a reliable authority to resolve grievances and internal disputes, and that could replace the treacherous alternative of arbitration by secret societies. Thus, when the Protector was finally appointed and began his work, "the coolies looked on him as a godsend, and thousands came to have their disputes settled in his office."[95]

The area of work of the Chinese Protectorate was soon expanded by Pickering based on his investigations of the social conditions of the immigrants. His concern with the protection of girls and women led him to set up a "Refuge" to house girls and women rescued from brothels. This Refuge was initially run by the Chinese Protectorate, but it latter developed into another institution, the *Po Leung Kuk* or "Office to Protect Virtue" managed by a committee of prominent *towkays* chaired by the Protector of Chinese. Based on historical records,[96] it was clear that for the women and girls who were born in brothels, or were living or working in brothels, or were in danger of abuse in their homes, the *Po Leung Kuk* was at once (in modern parlance) a refuge, a training centre in reading, writing, and household skills, a counselling centre, and a caring matrimonial agency.

As Protector of Chinese, Pickering created a style of intervention that suited well the community under his supervision. He "exercised his duties in a manner very similar to that of a village headman ... with one distinction ... he was generally incorrupt and accessible to everyone while the Mandarin in China was corrupt and could not be easily contacted by the villagers."[97] This approach and the pioneering roles of the Chinese Protectorate as an arbitrator and reconciliation agency in family matters increased its prestige among the Chinese community. Nevertheless, Pickering's success in combining 'quasi-judicial' activities and administrative duties was not viewed positively by the legal profession. In his 1878 Annual Report to the Straits Settlements Legislative Council he declared:

> [...] it has been alleged both by occupants of the bench and by certain sections of the public that the Protectorate of Chinese virtually usurps in many cases the functions of the Magistrates, besides interfering with the legitimate work of the local bar.[98]

Pickering recognised this problem of faint boundaries between the legal and judicial aspects of the Chinese Protectorate's work on the one hand, and his administrative role of arbitrator and counsellor in community and family disputes. This delicate issue of identifying and respecting the boundaries between various authority and expertise domains is an important part of the current discussion on the Family Court and the Family Guidance Service.

In sum, historical evidence from Singapore's colonial past show the need felt by the Asian communities for an institution that would provide equitable, prompt, and affordable arbitration in non-criminal matters including family relations and obligations such as marriage, adoption, inheritance, and divorce. The response of the colonial government to this need was hesitant. Still, they responded by providing some legislation (on immigration, secret societies, communicable diseases, and the protection of women and girls, among other aspects), and by setting up institutions such as the Chinese Protectorate, and the Refuge house for women and girls, and by encouraging the formation of a self-help institution, the *Po Leung Kuk*.

The Proceedings of the Straits Settlements Legislative Council which include the Annual Reports on the Chinese Protectorate do not have a specific classification of cases dealt with by the Chinese Protectorate. Thus, it is not possible to ascertain precisely the proportion of family or domestic cases brought to the attention of the Protector of Chinese. Notwithstanding the absence of precise figures, historians' analyses of other relevant documentation have led them to suggest that family-related cases occupied a considerable amount of the Protector's time.[99] Moreover, the nature of the Chinese Protectorate's work implies that it was the Colonial precursor of the Family Court in some respects, just as the work carried out by Pickering may be seen as resembling the idea of reconciliation and counselling activities of the proposed Family Guidance Service.

Main Features

After about a decade of analysis and discussion of the concept by local professionals — from law and sociology — in academic publications, the Family Court was officially opened in Singapore on 1 May 1995. Given the fast pace of economic and educational development, the conducive infrastructure and basic legal framework had been in place for some time. What was needed was the Government's political will to support the implementation of the family court concept. The presence of political will is a determining factor in the setting up of an institutional framework to assist families facing conflict, as exemplified by the situation in several Asian countries.

Perhaps circumstantially, public awareness of family issues gathered momentum in 1994 due to three developments: the international celebration of the Year of the Family; lengthy debates in Parliament on the filial obligation of children towards the support of their aged parents;[100] and the Prime Minister's appointment of the Inter-Ministerial Committee on Dysfunctional Families, Juvenile Delinquency and Drug Abuse. The public discourse on improving the national response to families in conflict continued in 1995 prompted further by the Report of the Inter-Ministerial Committee.

It has become a tradition in Singapore to study other countries' institutional responses to social problems and, if found useful, those institutions or procedures are selectively adapted — rather than adopted in full — to suit Singapore's needs.[101] It is then not surprising to see that the family court in Singapore does not follow entirely the distinguishing institutional features of family courts in other countries and exhibits features not typically associated with purely judicial institutions. The Family Court is one of the specialised Subordinate Courts in Singapore together with the Civil and Criminal courts, the Juvenile Court, and the Small Claims Tribunal. The Subordinate Courts represent the street level or access door to the three-tier judicial structure. Above them in the judicial hierarchy is the High Court and at the highest level is the Court of Appeal. The duties of the Family Court include dealing with divorce applications and proceedings, spouse and children maintenance, custody of children, adoption of children, protection of family members from domestic violence,[102] disputes over matrimonial property, and enforcement of Syariah Court orders.[103] Seven District Judges and one Magistrate were presiding in the Family Court in 2003.

The organisational structure of the Family Court comprises three elements: the Family Court properly, the Family and Juvenile Justice Centre (FJJC) and the Family Court Support Group. The FJJC is interdisciplinary and one of the latest additions to the Family Court. It was set up in March 2002 with a dual objective: to do research on "the criminogenic roots of offending behaviour" and on "familial intergenerational cycles of crime and disputes"; and to "provide a host of programmes and services to assist the court in making decisions, as well as to help families and individuals resolve their emotional (and hopefully, in the process, their legal) conflicts before, during and after the court process."[104]

Accessibility to the Family Court has been enhanced by educating the public on the available services and established procedure — mainly through the printed media, its Internet webpage and brochures — and keeping the fees relatively affordable. In 1995 the cost of filing a complaint was a token fee of S$1 to be paid at the Court Registry. The fees increased to a minimum fee of S$10 per affidavit in 2003. The divorce procedure in 1995 included "optional and free mediation service" with court mediators for the parties involved "prior to attending court" and again, if necessary, at a subsequent stage with the judge and court mediators; and the arrangement of mediation meetings in the evenings for the convenience of working couples.[105] By 2003, the Family Court had expanded the idea of mediation into three programmes, "Mediation and Counselling," "Project Heart," and "Maintenance Mediation." But in tandem with its philosophy that adjudication is "the primary duty" of the Family Court, the free mediation and counselling services are offered "to litigants as an alternative to litigation" in the process of arriving at a "harmonious resolution of family disputes" outside the court.[106.]

I have discussed in the preceding sections the fundamental features of the family court as an institution and expected implementation problems. That discussion helps us to identify two main and related questions on the Singapore version of the family court: what has been done about the limitations of adversarial proceedings in family conflict, and what is the response to the challenge of combining adjudication and welfare. The answer to the first question is clear and positive. The Singapore judiciary recognises the limitations of adversarial proceedings in family matters. The Chief Justice affirmed from the outset that "although the [Family] Court can try to mediate, it should not be the only one to do so" but "everything should be done to make mediation the mainstay of the Family Court."[107] Accordingly, mediation at the Family Court was publicised in the press from its inception as an opportunity to settle conflict amicably and as a better alternative to litigation.[108] The problem rests on the definition of mediation — and "successful" mediation — and the expertise of mediators. I return to this point later. These are aspects closely related to the question on adjudication and welfare.

That it is a challenge to combine successfully adjudication and welfare, and that this challenge is inherent in the family court as an institution, are problems that have been amply demonstrated by the long years of discussion on this matter in countries with family courts. The two seemingly opposite principles of "doing right" and "doing good" are advocated respectively by the legal profession and social scientists. These principles, of course, need not be mutually exclusive. Most people would hope for the ideal solution whereby they can apply both justice and welfare to solve family conflict. The developments since 1995 when the Family Court came into effect indicate that, as in other countries, Singapore faces the same challenge and is still working towards a solution.

There is an inclination to see adjudication and welfare as alternative rather than complementary approaches at the Family Court in Singapore. This inclination is evident in the pace of implementation of the family court concept, and in the character of the mediation structure. Let us look first at the pace of implementation of the Family Court. When it was established in March 1995, it included only matters related to adoption, spouse and children maintenance, and personal protection orders. The Family Court excluded divorce — one of the major aspects under the jurisdiction of family courts in other countries; it did not incorporate the juvenile court, a predecessor of the family court in the United States and England; and it did not cover the latest family conflict legislation represented in the Maintenance of Parents Bill. These omissions were highly unusual. The disregard for maintenance of one's aged parents, marital breakdown leading to divorce, and juvenile delinquency, are all essentially *family* conflicts entrenched in the nature of family relations, behaviour, and values. It would be natural for these three aspects to fall under the purview of the Family Court. However, uncertainty on the possible outcome of this new institution and hesitation to move beyond adjudication probably explain that the development of the Family Court is taking place in cautious, incremental steps.

The power to hear divorce cases and related matters was moved from the High Court to the Family Court on 1 April 1996, one year after the latter was set up. On 1 June 1996, a separate Tribunal was created at the Ministry of Community Development to administer the *Maintenance of Parents Act* approved by Parliament on 2 November 1995. Both the Tribunal for the Maintenance of Parents and the Juvenile Court remain separate from the Family Court. These three institutions represent three different levels of judicial intervention. Although the Tribunal has the same powers of a district court, it embodies the most benign level where priority is given — at least in principle — to the combination of justice, equity and welfare, that is, to doing right as well as doing good. This explains its location outside the Judiciary. At the opposite extreme is the Juvenile Court, a court of law where adjudication — "to do right" — is the main concern, and where the establishment of guilt or innocence by the rule of law is given uppermost consideration. The Family Court falls between these two extremes of judicial intervention because mediation — the opportunity for negotiation — is a potentially major element of its proceedings. In a typical Singaporean fashion, the Family Court concept and with it, the system's ability to combine adjudication and welfare, are being cautiously tested.

The second manifestation of the judicial system's inclination to treat adjudication and welfare as alternative rather than complementary approaches is found in the character of the mediation structure or, more specifically — as indicated earlier — in the definition of successful mediation and in the expertise of mediators. Let us review briefly what is offered before discussing the situation.

The stated objective of the "mediation and counselling" service "integrated into the case process" of the Family Court in 1997 was "to provide parties with a forum to settle their disputes amicably and to address the emotional issues present in cases which come before this Court".[109] Accordingly, a "Court Support Group" made up of "volunteers from welfare and religious organisations" to be "treated as court officials" was established concurrently with the Family Court with the purpose of "augmenting the pool of court mediators."[110] In 1995 the mediation service was provided "by court interpreters who receive training in mediation and 22 members of the court support group — social workers, counsellors, lawyers and psychologists who have volunteered their help."[111] The number of volunteer mediators increased to 37 the following year but their backgrounds continue to be mixed.[112] The mediation setting has improved from cubicles to better meeting rooms but an informal atmosphere continues with "no tables acting as a barrier between negotiating parties" encouraging the parties "to speak freely."[113]

We may recall that mediation may be applied to two distinct processes, conciliation and reconciliation.[114] Conciliation is the legal and amicable settlement of a dispute between two parties, normally with the impartial intervention of a third party or mediator. In cases of family conflict before the Family Court, conciliation takes place to determine the mutually agreeable terms of the termination of a relationship, usually a marital relationship. Aspects involved in the process of conciliation are financial, pragmatic, and tangible. Examples of these aspects are: division of property; payment of maintenance to spouse and/or children; and child visiting and child custody venues and schedules. At face value, the 'mechanics' of conciliation proceedings do not seem to differ substantially from court mediation sessions in civil cases dealing with disputes over property or the quantum of damages due to personal injury. Even if the contesting parties are not satisfied with the situation, they may still agree to a settlement for a wide variety of reasons including the high cost of a trial, inability to reach a better solution, expediency, convenience, fear of public disclosure of the problem, and the like. This occurs routinely in civil cases and may explain the judicial system's extension of its Court Mediation Centre's services to the Family Court. Conciliation normally takes place in cases where spouses are determined to seek divorce.

In contrast to conciliation, reconciliation is the emotional mending of serious disagreements or conflict among people who have shared their lives together, may wish to continue as a family, but do not know how to go about it. The prevalence of feelings over reason, the intense emotional involvement of the parties in the problem, the strong influence of each party's subjective perception of the situation upon his or her level of cooperation in mending the relationship, and their past inability to solve their problem in the privacy of their home, are all factors that require expert and sensitive analysis and treatment. Mediators need to be trained professionals. The good intentions of non-professional counsellors as volunteers even of they are lawyers, cannot replace professional training when dealing with serious marital and family conflict.[115]

It is crucial for governments establishing a family court to recognise that fundamental distinction between conciliation and reconciliation. This problem is in my view, more serious than the slow pace of implementation. As I expressed earlier, the important requirement for the Family Court to accomplish the dual goal proposed by the Finer Report[116] of doing good as well as doing right is the creation of a mediating structure that should function as partner of the Family Court. I tentatively labelled such a structure the Family Guidance Centre. Irrespective of the label given, the fundamental aspect of the mediating centre is the *expertise* it provides by virtue of the specialised training of its professional personnel such as clinical psychologists, family therapists, and social workers specialised in counselling families and individuals in conflict. No short training courses on mediation for court interpreters and other volunteers can replace the intense professional training received at university by qualified social scientists. A related serious weakness of a mediation service run by volunteers or court interpreters is that if they are not professional social scientists, they would function as mediators without the guidance of a professional code of ethics.

Moreover, running a mediation service exclusively or mainly on volunteer basis saves money but it is highly unsatisfactory as a permanent arrangement from the perspective of service quality. Experts who offer their services on a voluntary basis have full-time jobs and are overloading themselves with work. There is no doubt that their services are needed. An example of very important volunteer services is the free legal clinic and hospital referral service run by the Singapore Association of Women Lawyers [SAWL]. This service refers victims of domestic violence approaching the Family Court to one of eight hospitals in the scheme for immediate attention and the medical reports "forwarded to the court on an urgent basis." This volunteer service consumes a great deal of SAWL members' time and energies and, as its president declared, SAWL "agreed to run the clinic but had to decline the other request [by the Chief Justice of free legal representation for children] because it did not have enough resources." The clinic was then arranged tentatively for a year.[117]

The definition of *successful* mediation depends on whether the process is seen as conciliation or reconciliation. The system's preliminary self-assessment as well as press comments on the outcome of mediation signalled success in terms of proportion of cases settled out of court and the reductions in financial cost. From the perspective of numbers, about half of the disputes brought to the Family Court in the first few months after its inception were solved through mediation.[118] A positive assessment was given in Parliament in 1996: "At least 85 per cent of the 5,452 cases heard by the Family Court were resolved through mediation" and "in cases involving maintenance orders of wife and children, 87 per cent were settled through mediation" thus saving the expense and time of a court trial.[119] The Singapore Family Court reported in 2003 that "Since the introduction of mediation and counselling" in 1995, "mediation and counselling are now the norm rather than the exception" and "for contested divorce cases, less than 0.5 per cent of cases have proceed to trial. Litigation is therefore, in practice, used as a last resort after all attempts to settle the case amicably have failed."[120]

The financial cost of a trial is of course a major disincentive. In economic terms, avoiding a trial through mediation represents a considerable decrease in financial cost of divorce proceedings. The cost of legal procedures may be substantial as they could include, in addition to the "part-and-party costs" to be paid to the "winning party", the solicitor-and-client costs, court fees, and hearing fees.[121]

Financial costs, however, should not be the top consideration in the designing of the mediation structure or centre. From the perspective of people approaching the Family Court, money usually is not the major problem. Money problems are commonly one of the symptoms of family conflict, not the actual 'disease'. Social science research over the past 50 years has confirmed the indisputable importance of emotional and affectual aspects in the successful resolution of family conflict. A settlement through mediation by a third party may provide a solution to pragmatic problems. But if the mediator is not a professional counsellor, the process of mediation does not help the parties involved in resolving their emotional conflict and in mending their broken relationships.

In sum, although the Family Court is a very young institution in Singapore, it has already begun to demonstrate its usefulness as a sober and reliable avenue for family conflict resolution. However, the potential effectiveness of the institution has not been realised yet mainly because of the cautious and incremental pace of its development and the emphasis placed on cost reduction. Caution and economy are virtues commonly applied to Singapore's development plans and it is expected to find them in the design of its judicial institutions as well. Nevertheless, I reiterate two points: to succeed, the Family Court requires a parallel institution dedicated to reconciliation through a professional mediation service; and the need to improve the quality of the mediation service is sufficiently urgent to require immediate attention and to supersede cost considerations.

In conclusion, this chapter has demonstrated the pervasiveness of marital conflict and the steady increase in divorces in selected Asian countries. Although the overwhelming majority of marriages do not break down, marital conflict is part of marriage life and constitutes a burden to the entire family. The family court has been presented as an institutional framework that offers assistance to couples in the settling of their marital conflict in an equitable and just manner. But the Family Court is not a suitable service for couples in need of assistance to repair their broken or conflictive relationship as its purview is conciliation. Governments need to complement the Family Court with a partner institution focused on rescuing the marriage through counselling and mediation, and dedicated to assist with the process of reconciliation.

ENDNOTES

1. These were the countries with available divorce statistics for two time periods. China, Vietnam, and Malaysia, three of the ten countries covered in Chapters 2 to 5, were excluded because of the lack of comparable data at the time of writing this analysis.
2. See Bahr, Wang and Zhang (1991:1-2).
3. See Bahr (1991a).
4. See Bahr (1991b:4).
5. See Bahr (1991b:1-71).
6. See Quah (1999:61-63).
7. See Attorney-General Chambers (2003), Part X, Chapter 1 – Divorce, Article 94, Sections (1) and (2); and Article 95.

8. See Singapore Department of Statistics (2003:67).
9. See Ahmad Ibrahim (1984:9); Jones (1994:48); and Hassan (2002:23-24).
10. See Jones (1994:51-55).
11. See Singapore Department of Statistics (2003:82).
12. See Jolivet (1997:76).
13. See Medina (1991:182-183).
14. See Sasaki and Wilson (1997); and Sugimoto (2003:150).
15. See Sugimoto (2003:146).
16. See Sugimoto (2003:150).
17. See Sugimoto (2003:150); and Sasaki and Wilson (1997:131).
18. Sasaki and Wilson (1997:130-131); and Tokyo Metropolitan Government (2002).
19. See Sasaki and Wilson (1997:131).
20. See Medina (1991:177).
21. See Raquiza (2001).
22. See Medina (1991:180).
23. See Medina (1991:182).
24. See Liljetstrom (1991:16).
25. See Liljetstrom (1991:17).
26. See Khuat (1991:189-190).
27. See Jones (1994:169).
28. For a detailed explanation of the Human Development Index see United Nations Development Programme (2002:253).
29. See Jones (1994:218-267); and Jones (2001).
30. This section is an updated version of the family court analysis in Quah (1998:176-199).
31. See Hoggett and Pearl (1983:627).
32. See Brown (1966).
33. See Brown (1966); and Hoggett and Pearl (1983:627).
34. See Hoggett and Pearl (1983:627).
35. See Segaran (1999); and Lee (2000).
36. See Ahmad Ibrahim (1984) and Sharifah (1997).
37. See Star (1996).
38. See Hoggett and Pearl (1983:631); and Broomley (1981: 3, 663, 664).
39. See Monahan and Walker (1994:2).
40. See Lee (2000:11-12).
41. See Law Reform Commission of Canada (1974:7-8); Hoggett and Pearl (1983:626).
42. See for example, Olson et.al. (1989); and McCubbin, Sussman and Paterson (1983).

43. See Peden and Glahe (1986); Glazer (1988); Zimmerman (1988); Cherlin (1988).

44. See Kamerman and Kahn (1988); and Quah (1990b).

45. See Brown (1966); Parkinson (1982); Hoggett and Pearl (1983); Star (1996).

46. See for example, Pierce, Sarason, and Sarason (1996); Boss, Doherty, LaRossa, Schumm and Steinmetz (1993).

47. See Parkinson (1982); Star (1996).

48. See Finer (1974); Hoggett and Pearl (1983:630).

49. Quoted in Hoggett and Pearl (1983: 627, 629).

50. See Finer (1974); Hoggett and Pearl (1983:630).

51. See Finer (1974); Hoggett and Pearl (1983:632).

52. See Law Reform Commission of Canada (1974).

53. See Law Reform Commission of Canada (1974); Hoggett and Pearl (1983:632).

54. See Finer (1974); Hoggett and Pearl (1983: 632-33).

55. See Davis (1982).

56. See Davis (1982:12); Hoggett and Pearl (1983:649).

57. See for example Klein and Hill (1979); Hansen and Johnson (1979); McCubbin, Sussman and Patterson (1983); O'Leary (1987); Olson et.al. (1989); Boss (2002).

58. See Brown (1966).

59. See Finer (1974).

60. See Gottlieb (1981); Kamerman and Kahn (1988); Steinmetz (1988); Quah (1990d:10-13); Pierce, Sarason and Sarason (1996); Boss (2002).

61. See Sprey (1979); Wallerstein and Kelly (1980); McCubbin, Sussman and Patterson (1983); Olson et.al. (1989); Wallerstein and Blakeslee (1990); Blumel (1991); Irving (2002); Boss (2002).

62. See Parkinson (1982).

63. See Society of Conservative Lawyers (1979); Law Society (1979); Law Society (1982); Hoggett and Pearl (1983: 634-5).

64. See Murch (1980); Hoggett and Pearl (1983: 635).

65. See Law Commission (1966).

66. See Finer (1974); Hoggett and Pearl (1983:636-9).

67. See Davis (1982:11-13).

68. See Wolcott (1991:47).

69. See Finer (1974:4288).

70. See Parkinson (1982).

71. See Finer (1974).

72. Illustrations of this trend are the study on the development of law in Singapore by Andrew Phang (1990), and work on family law by Tan (1985), Lim, Ong and Mohan (1985a, 1985b); Cheang (1985); and Leong (1990).

73. See Cheang (1985); Lim, Ong, and Mohan, (1985a) and (1985b).

74. See Lee (2000).
75. See Ochiai (1997).
76. See Shapiro (1990).
77. See Shapiro (1990:212).
78. See Lee (1991:61).
79. See Turnbull (1989:23).
80. See Turnbull (1989); Lee (1991).
81. See Ng (1955); Buckley (1902:320).
82. See Lee (1991:86).
83. See Chu (1960:47); Purcell (1956).
84. See Pickering (1885).
85. See Chu (1960:51).
86. See Lee (1991:156).
87. See Lee (1991:162).
88. See Legislative Council of the Straits Settlements (1878).
89. See Lee (1991:159).
90. See Lee (1991:61).
91. See Lee (1991:119).
92. See Chu (1960:57-60).
93. See Lee (1991:63),
94. See Lee (1991:69-70).
95. See Lee (1991:85).
96. See Lee (1991:91-92); Chu (1960); Ng (1955); Wu (1959:7-8).
97. See Chu (1960).
98. See Lee (1991:85).
99. See Purcell (1956); Ng (1955); Chu (1960); Turnbull (1989); Lee (1991).
100. See for example Government of Singapore (1994a) and (1994b).
101. This is part of the process of pragmatic acculturation (selective culture-borrowing to satisfy specific needs) that may be observed in different areas of social policy in Singapore. For further discussion of pragmatic acculturation in policy formulation see Quah (1995).
102. See Singapore Supreme Court (1997:19).
103. Detailed information on the Family Court is provided at its website. URL address: http://www.familycourtofsingapore.gov.sg . See also Hong (1999) and Magnus (2000).
104. See *The Family Court of Singapore* website: http://www.familycourtofsingapore.gov.sg/profile/FJJC.htm
105. See *Straits Times* (1995b); Supreme Court (1997:23).
106. See http://www.familycourtofsingapore.gov.sg/programmes/mediation_counsel.htm
107. See *Straits Times* (1995a).

108. See *Straits Times* (1995b); and (1996a).

109. See Supreme Court (1997:19).

110. See *Straits Times* (1995a).

111. See *Straits Times* (1995b).

112. See *Sunday Times* (1996b).

113. See *Straits Times* (1995c). The same mixed background of untrained and trained volunteers continued in 2003.

114. See Wolcott (1991).

115. See Irving (2002).

116. See Finer (1974).

117. See Lee (1996).

118. See *Straits Times* (1995b).

119. See *Straits Times* (1996b); and *Sunday Times* (1996a).

120. See tofsingapore.gov.sg/programmes/mediation_counsel.htm" http://www.familycourtofsingapore.gov.sg/programmes/mediation_counsel.htm

121. See Singapore Supreme Court (1997:24-25).

CHAPTER 7

Home, Kin and the State in Social Change

The story of family and kin is rounded up in this concluding chapter with a look at the commotion outside the home. In the midst of two world wars and intensive conflict in the 20th century, people knew quietly in their hearts how precious their families were.[1] Yet, some observers argued that the family was collapsing under the pressure of the wealth pursuit. Has that happened? The search for clues in all the ten Asian countries studied in this book (China, Hong Kong, Japan, South Korea, Indonesia, Malaysia, Singapore, the Philippines, Thailand, and Vietnam) suggest that the answer would be "Yes" if we simply look into divorce trends and note that the wealthiest country, Japan, has the highest rate. On the other hand, the answer would be "No" if we consider carefully other aspects of family life such as marriage, parenthood and the kinship bond shown by the presence of grandparents. Marriage is a very important aspect in the lives of most people in these countries and they believe parenthood is a crucial event in one's life and want to give the best to their children; but what is changing radically is the perception of marriage, the perception of the ideal number of children, and the inclination of women to be income-earners by holding paid jobs or careers. The data collected suggest trends in those directions. Younger generations of married people prefer partnership in marriage and one or at the most two children. Three-generation homes and the close interaction with grandparents are common features in these countries as is the trend towards healthier, economically active, and better educated seniors. Women are more inclined to spend longer years in the labour force.

In other words, the preceding chapters demonstrate that Asian families are complex and resilient but findings also show that the impact — positive and negative — of external factors cannot be underestimated. Perhaps the most unrelenting external factors are economic development and political ideology (political system). Their presence is manifested most acutely in the friction between family and work in the homes of dual-income couples. A dual-income couple is one where both husband and wife have paid jobs or are looking for employment as both need to earn an income to support their family. The friction between family and work obligations faced by dual-income couples has been the object of intense study by social scientists in Western countries, particularly in the past two decades.[2] It is thus fitting that this final chapter deals with both factors: the impact of economic development in the form of a trend towards higher female participation in the labour force, and what state policies can do to assists dual-income couples in combining work and family life. In spite of the earnest search for a solution, a satisfactory combination of family and job obligations remains elusive for the vast majority of working people everywhere. Does this mean that job and family are irreconcilable dimensions of a person's life? No. Family and job are not easy to combine but they are not irreconcilable. On the contrary, social science research has shown that job performance and family life are closely interrelated and that a stable and happy family life exerts a positive influence on workers' job productivity.[3]

The combination of economic success with a satisfactory family life is a challenge that, while faced by individuals, needs to be met collectively as it involves the public and the private spheres of life. A collective effort to find better ways of doing things and to organise ourselves more equitably falls within the realm of social policy. Accordingly, I will discuss in this chapter the most relevant social policy ideas to help people in their efforts to excel in both family and work. The discussion will be divided in two main sections. I will bring together in the first section pertinent conceptual and social policy perspectives concerning family including some of the ideas introduced in previous chapters. In the second section I will apply those concepts and ideas to the identification and discussion of two critical family policy areas that require urgent attention in Asia, a region undergoing rapid economic development.

THE ROLE OF THE STATE

Some of the concepts discussed in previous chapters provide the context for this macro-level analysis of family and economic development. The first one is the concept of social policy defined as "the cluster of overall decisions relevant to the achievement of [society's] goals."[4] As indicated in Chapter 3, family policy refers to plans of action formulated to reflect those social values and to attain those social goals; and must provide the necessary conditions for the well-being of all families. A further clarification is in order: family policy is not social engineering. On the contrary, within a democratic system of government, family policy establishes "an opportunity structure which makes certain that society does not interfere or restrain the family's efforts to meet its collective needs."[5]

These definitions pave the way for the examination of three contentious beliefs at the core of family policy discussions. These beliefs are: the vision of government intervention as an undesirable intrusion in the privacy of the family; the apprehension that family policies might bring about value changes negative to revered traditions; and the strong belief in the ability of families to solve their own problems. Let us examine each of these beliefs.

To Intervene Or Not To Intervene

The first contentious belief on family policy is that the state should not intrude on family life. People who see government intervention as undesirable, believe that families should be left alone to solve their own problems. Should families be left alone or should the community intervene through the formulation and implementation of relevant policies? This is in part an ideological issue. However, the concept of social capital — discussed in Chapter 4 — will help us to establish a relatively objective point of reference. James Coleman[6] proposed that modern societies are composed of "a primordial structure based on, and derived from the family" and "corporate" structure "wholly independent of the family" and consisting of "economic organizations ... single-purpose voluntary associations, and governments."

While the corporate structure of a country focuses primarily on "human capital," the primordial or family structure is concerned with the nourishing of "social capital." Coleman argued that a country's loss in social capital is brought about by the changes undergone by the family in modern industrial societies. Coleman's idea points to the current imbalance between economic concerns (human capital) and family well-being (social capital). The single-minded emphasis on the growth of human capital leads the society's corporate structure to overwhelm working people with job commitments, absorbing their time and energies in the pursuit of economic development. While economic development is indisputably necessary, the nourishing and growth of the community's social capital represented in the family is fundamental for its complete progress.

Considering the improbability of regular individuals being capable of changing single-handedly the course of economic development, policy intervention may be an answer. Seen as collective agreement on the expansion of alternatives, social policy can give individuals more flexibility to design their own combination of job and family commitments. Another important argument in support of social policy is that legislation on the family in a democratic society is expected to have a three-fold feature: family policy expands rather than curtails individuals' choices; it identifies clearly its area of action addressing specific problems; and it has a built-in check delineating the limits of government intervention. The awareness that state intervention or policies may be abused led Berger and Berger[7] to recommend that family policy should focus on "the restoration of the private." These authors represent the moderate perspective on family policy as suggested in Chapter 3.

All told, the doubts of some observers on the contributions of family policy are often countered by the views of people who support the formulation of family policies. I propose that we consider seriously the following five basic issues on the feasibility and desirability of family policy, derived from the current expert discussion: (a) most countries have a multiplicity of family forms and family life patterns; (b) social policy is limited in what it can do to help families; (c) there is always the possibility of abuse of policies and thus there is a need for a system of checks and balances; (d) there is a high likelihood of negative unforeseen consequences of policies and thus it is imperative to exercise caution in policy planning and implementation; and (e) there are some types of family problems of such magnitude or nature that state intervention may be the only alternative.[8] The search for a satisfactory balance between the public and private spheres of life to accomplish job and family commitments is one of these problems.

Consequently, in recognition of these issues and based on the social policy experiences of developed countries, a basic family policy agenda should comprise the following objectives: (1) to provide the socioeconomic conditions required for the strengthening of family life and to help families in need; (2) to curtail excessive state intervention; (3) to discourage citizens' overdependence on the state; and (4) to encourage the participation of kinship, community, and other informal support networks in the provision of moral, social, material and other forms of help to families in need.

Apprehension About Value Changes

The second contentious belief on family policy is the apprehension that family policies might bring about value changes negative to revered traditions. Understandably, economic growth efforts have brought about a plethora of changes to Asian societies, some welcome, others not. Let us look into one of the controversial but most necessary value changes: the change in socially assigned gender roles. Chapter 5 illustrated how traditional beliefs on the appropriate roles of men (dominant) and women (subordinate) in society persist. In the traditional culture landscape, men take care of the public sphere of life involving corporate affairs and "human capital" while women attend to the private sphere of life, nurturing the young generation, and looking after the community's "social capital." Yet, the everyday obligations of working wives and mothers and their increasing level of education contradict those traditional beliefs.

Social policy initiatives addressed to facilitate the family-job combination for working couples encounter resistance because they require a change in the traditional division of labour between husband and wife. The experiences of post-industrial societies show that economic development has unsettled this traditional order of things. As the number and complexity of available jobs increase with economic development, the need to recruit workers opens job opportunities for women. With their higher educational attainment, career orientation, and easier access to paid jobs, women have begun to change their image of the ideal family, their conception of marriage and the value of a smaller number of children.

Moreover, an advanced level of economic development requires brain power irrespective of gender. Profit maximisation and productivity depend on recruiting the best person for the job. Thus, the social definition of the roles of men and women that is consistent with an advanced economy is that of gender equality. As explained in Chapter 5, gender equality is understood in this discussion as the situation whereby men and women are considered equal in terms of their rights and obligations as citizens of a country, as individuals in a democratic society, as members of the labour force, and as partners in marriage and parenthood. When a country struggling towards higher levels of economic development absorbs more women into the labour force but continues to expect from them a concurrent full-time concentration on their domestic family obligations, family well-being becomes a casualty rather than a beneficiary of wealth accumulation. Still, the emotional attachment to traditional gender roles is strong in most Asian societies and constitutes a major hurdle to the formulation and implementation of effective social policies to alleviate the burden of simultaneous family and job commitments.

Can Families Fend for Themselves?

The third contentious belief in the discussion of family policy is that families are autonomous and do not require external assistance to solve their problems. This belief requires qualification. One of the most relevant findings from social science research on the family during the past four decades is that stress is a normal part of family interaction but it varies in intensity and nature through the life cycle of family members. Some families are more successful than others in managing high levels of stress. Families that are unable to manage stress and are overwhelmed by crises usually have one or more family members who cannot perform their normal reciprocal roles such as nurturing, companionship, parenting, protection, and sustenance. The latter two roles are of particular importance for the well-being of the youngest and the most senior members of the family. Clearly, families in crisis who are unable to manage on their own are the type of families that may require external assistance from the state or from formal support networks, or both.

Studies on family stress[9] identify two stages families go through when afflicted by stress: the stress process which may or may not lead to a crisis; and the process of recovery, which may or may not be successful. The analysis of these two stages helps to identify the factors that hinder or assist the family's effort to deal with stress. In the first stage, the stress process, four components are most important. These components are: the problem or stressor; the family's resources to deal with the problem; the family's perception of the stressor; and the level of stress generated by the problem or stressor.

The first component of the stress process is the *stressor* (the problem, situation, or event that causes the stress) which may affect one or more family members. Stressors vary in terms of their source, type, duration, and density.[10] In terms of their duration, stressors may be *acute* or *chronic*. An acute stressor is a "one-time event" that has a brief duration. In contrast, chronic stressors are *situations* (not events) that represent the accumulation of grievances, conflict, and stress over time. An acute stressor may signal the beginning of a chronic stressor or may increase the conflict faced by a family under chronic stress. Regarding the type of stressor, stressor events may be *normative, developmental and predictable* events in the life cycle such as marriage, childbirth, school graduation and other rites of passage, or they may be *catastrophic, situational and unexpected* events. Considering their source, stressors may be *external* when they originate outside the family (i.e., famine, natural disasters, political upheaval) or *internal* when they are problems initiated within the family (i.e., alcoholism, child abuse, spouse battering). In terms of their density, stressors may be *cumulative* events, that is, events or situations that in the words of Pauline Boss "pile up, one after another" giving "no time to cope before the next stressor occurs." Or they could be *isolated* when it is just "one event that occurs with no other stressors."[11]

The second component of the stress process refers to the resources that the family normally has to deal with problems or stressors. Family resources may be of various kinds including the personality of family members, the level of family cohesion, the presence of a kinship network and network of close friends, financial resources, and knowledge on how to solve the problem or stressor. A family is unable to manage stress and to perform its usual roles when the stressors it encounters are greater than the family's resources to manage them.

The third component of the stress process is the family's subjective perception of the stressor. It is important to note two principles of subjective perception. On the one hand, a person's or family's subjective perception of a situation or event may or may not correspond to the actual situation as perceived by an impartial observer. On the other hand, the family's acknowledgement of the presence of the stressor is a necessary condition for the family's eventual recovery. This principle applies also if only one or a few family members perceive an event or situation as a stressor. This lack of agreement among family members on the presence or seriousness of a stressor impedes or delays the family's process of recovery. Lack of agreement is likely when the stressor itself is ambiguous. Ambiguity occurs in many situations, for example, illness

199

of a family member when diagnosis or prognosis is uncertain; lost of a family member through kidnapping or disappearance in war or armed conflict situations; and the more common situation of children of divorced and remarried parents. These children face the problem of "boundary ambiguity."[12]

The fourth main component of the stress process is the level or degree of stress experienced by the family. In general, and not discounting other factors, the level of stress experienced by a family is the outcome of the first three components: (a) the stressor — including its source, type, duration, and density; (b) the family's resources to deal with the stressor; and (c) the family's subjective perception of the stressor. Risking oversimplification, we may assume that a family is most likely to be unable to cope with stress when the stressor is a prolonged situation, is unpredictable, cumulative, and it is caused by someone or something within the family; when the stressor exhausts the family resources; and when the family perceives the stressor as unsolvable or ambiguous. Although families vary widely in their capacity to deal with stress, it is crucial to recognise that there will always be families who are unable to cope on their own. These families in crisis typically become unable "to perform usual roles and tasks"; "to make decisions and solve problems"; "to care for each other in the usual way"; and as the stressor intensifies, they are likely to shift their focus "from family to individual survival."[13]

Having endured the stress, families go through the second stage, the *process of recovery*. The four most important factors that may help or hinder a family's ability to recover from a crisis or stress are: the level of family cohesion; the willingness of the family to seek outside help from strangers or institutions (that is, the family's perception of the costs and benefits of seeking external assistance); the presence of kinship and other informal support networks; and the availability of formal community support networks which could be preventive or remedial. Some families can mobilise their own resources, including their extended kinship network, to cope successfully with stressors. Other families, however, fail in their attempts because the problems they face are greater than the family's ability or resources to manage them. These families in crisis are found in every country and constitute the families that only the state may be able to help.

Family policy represents the community's assistance to families facing conflict and stress. Considering that families go through these two processes, the stress process and the process of recovery, family policy must encompass the creation of preventive as well as remedial support networks. I will return to this point later on.

CRITICAL SOCIAL POLICY AREAS

We may appreciate that while most families may be able to muddle through their conflicts and stress on their own, there are families that need help. Some stressors affecting families may be created by the social arrangements a community or country sets in place for other purposes for example labour policies, childcare and education, and social security. Let us review some actual trends in the ten Asian countries covered in this study (China, Hong Kong, Japan, South Korea, Indonesia, Malaysia, the Philippines, Singapore, Thailand, and Vietnam) before focusing on specific policy areas.

Actual Trends

A profile of the ten Asian countries is presented in Table 7.1. The great variation in socioeconomic development among these ten countries is a fair indication of the complexity of the East and Southeast Asian region. Generalisations must be made with caution given the remarkable contrasts the ten countries display in their linguistic, ethnic and religious communities, urban-rural divide, size of population, political systems, and levels of wealth, among other things. Nevertheless, as seen in the preceding chapters, some important trends begin to emerge when cross-country comparisons of family life are made. The most relevant aspects of marriage, parenthood, gender, and family conflict have been covered in Chapters 2 to 6. At this juncture I wish to highlight the relevance of socioeconomic development as the context within which families live and grow.

The sharp country-to-country variation in stage of development across the region is evident not only in terms of the level of wealth alone but also in terms of social conditions conveyed by the Human Development Index (Chart 7.1). The HDI attempts to capture a country's "achievement" in three "basic dimensions of human development" namely, "a long and healthy life, measured by life expectancy at birth"; "Knowledge" ascertained by "adult literacy rate" and "the combined primary, secondary and tertiary gross enrolment ratio"; and "a decent standard of living as measured by GDP per capita (PPP US$)."[14] The

TABLE 7.1   PROFILE OF THE TEN ASIAN COUNTRIES IN THE STUDY

Characteristics	China	Hong Kong	Japan	South Korea	Indonesia	Malaysia	Philippines	Singapore	Thailand	Vietnam
Total area (1000 sq. km) 1998[1]	9,597.0	1.1	377.8	99.3	1,904.6	329.8	300.0	0.6	513.1	331.7
Total population (millions) 2001[2]	1,271.9	6.9	127.1	47.6	213	23.8	77.0	4.1	61.2	79.5
Average annual percentage population growth, 1990–2001[2]	1.0	1.7	0.3	1.0	1.6	2.4	2.1	2.7	0.9	1.7
Density (persons per sq. km), 2001[3]	136	6,909	349	483	118	72	258	6,726	120	244
Life expectancy at birth (years), 2000[4]	70.5	79.5	81	74.9	66.2	72.5	69.3	77.6	70.2	68.2
Total fertility rate (per woman), 1995–2000[4]	1.8	1.2	1.4	1.5	2.6	3.3	3.6	1.6	2.1	2.5
Urban population as a percentage of total in 2000.[5]	35.8	100.0	78.8	81.9	41.0	57.4	58.6	100.0	19.8	24.1
GDP per capita (PPP US$), 2001[4]	3,976	25,153	26,755	17,380	3,043	9,068	3,971	23,356	6,402	1,996
Human Development Index 2000[4]	0.726	0.888	0.933	0.882	0.684	0.782	0.754	0.885	0.762	0.688

1. Asian Development Bank (2000) *Key Indicators of Development in Asian and Pacific Countries*. Volume XXXI. Manila: Oxford University Press; Asahi Shimbun (2003) *Japan Almanac 2003*. Tokyo: Asahi Shimbun.
2. World Bank (2003) *World Development Report 2003*. Washington DC: Oxford University Press.
3. World Bank (2003) *World Development Report 2003*. Washington DC: Oxford University Press; Asian Development Bank (2000) *Key Indicators of Development in Asian and Pacific Countries*. Volume XXXI. Manila: Oxford University Press. Hong Kong's density figure is for 1999.
4. United Nations Development Programme (2002) *Human Development Report 2002*. New York: Oxford University Press.
5. United Nations Development Programme (2002) *Human Development Report 2002*. New York: Oxford University Press. UNDP indicates that figures are based on each country's definition of city and metropolitan area and must be compared with caution.

well-known impact of wealth on other aspects of a country's development comes across clearly in Chart 7.1: countries with the highest level of wealth (Japan, Hong Kong, Singapore, and South Korea) have the highest HDI scores as they are able to afford higher investments on their educational and health systems, and infrastructure to provide the population with better living conditions. On the other hand, let us not forget that these countries began their struggle up the ladder from the bottom. Their climb has not been smooth but it has been consistent, through determination and political will. Chart 7.1 also indicates that the gap in socioeconomic development between Japan and the other countries was nearly closed in the ten-year period 1990-2000 by Hong Kong, Singapore, and South Korea.[15] The development policies of these four countries are far from perfect but they deserve close study by their neighbours in the region to improve their own learning curve and prevent or minimise costly policy blunders.

CHART 7.1   SOCIOECONOMIC DEVELOPMENT 1990-2001

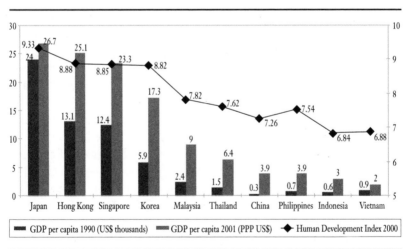

Sources: United Nations (2000) and United Nations Development Programme (2002). Definitions: GDP: Gross domestic product; GDP per capita (PPP US$) is the GDP converted into international dollars using purchasing power parity (PPP) conversion factors (World Bank, 2003: 245).

The process of urbanisation (Chart 7.2) is another policy-relevant feature of the ten countries. The proportion of the total population living in cities and metropolitan areas (as defined by each country) increased across the region from 1990 to 2000. The urban-rural divide signal different environments for families in the region and different policy challenges. Three distinct types of countries are clearly outlined by their proportion of urban population in Chart 7.2: the two global cities of Hong Kong and Singapore (a city-state); South Korea and Japan with a fairly high number of large cities; and the other six countries (the Philippines, Malaysia, Indonesia, China, Vietnam, and Thailand) with a substantial proportion of their population living in rural areas. These three types of countries face rather different challenges when it comes to assisting families in general and dual-income couples in particular. Farming work differs substantially from typical urban jobs in many respects including the types of stressors the workers and their families face, and the easiness with which you can mix your paid job with home duties. The notion of dual-income couples is usually associated with city jobs and urban workers. But in reality, a considerable proportion of Asian families are rural families. Separate policy strategies would be required to raise the standard of living of dual-income farming couples, and to help them deal with the demands of home and work. One of the most likely policy obstacles is the age-old belief that peasant women can accomplish both tasks by themselves "naturally" as they "have always lived that way."

Infant and maternal mortality rates reflect the health and well-being of families and, as it is well-known and confirmed in Chart 7.3, a country's level of wealth is highly influential in this regard (Pearson's correlation $r = -.907$ and $r = -.615$ respectively). I pointed out in Chapter 2 that the level of socioeconomic development is influential in another family life aspect: the timing of marriage. This link is confirmed in Chart 7.4 using national income (gross domestic product per capita). The level of socioeconomic development creates favourable conditions for higher educational and skills training of young people; it is usually (but not always) accompanied by the opening of educational institutions to women; and it increases the job market in range and level of sophistication of paid jobs. All these developments lead young people to postpone marriage while they get higher educational training or employment.

CHART 7.2   PACE OF URBANISATION

Source: United Nations (2000); United Nations Development Programme (2002).

CHART 7.3   INFANT AND MATERNAL MORTALITY AND NATIONAL INCOME

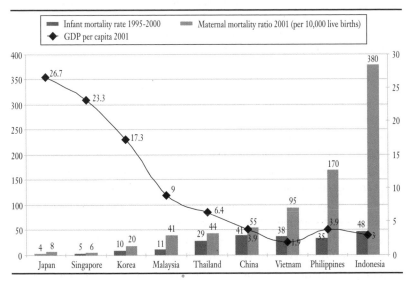

Sources: UNICEF (2002); United Nations Development Programme (2002).
definitions: Infant mortality rate 2000: probability of dying between birth and 1 year of age expressed per 10,000 live births. Maternal mortality ratio 2001: number of female deaths from pregnancy-related causes per 10,000 live births. GDP: Gross Domestic Product per capita (US$). Correlation of Infant mortality rate with GDP per capita: r = -.907; p = .0001. Correlation of maternal mortality rate with GDP per capita: r = -.615; p = .058.

CHART 7.4 TIMING OF MARRIAGE AND NATIONAL INCOME

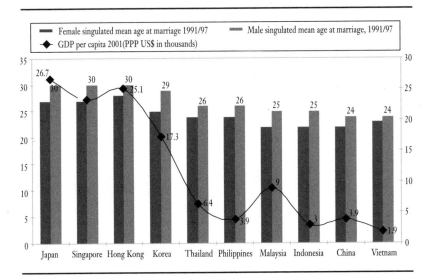

- ▬ Female singulated mean age at marriage 1991/97
- ▬ Male singulated mean age at marriage, 1991/97
- ◆ GDP per capita 2001(PPP US$ in thousands)

Sources: United Nations Statistics Division (2002); and United Nations Development Programme (2002). Correlation of GDP per capita with Female Singulated Age at Marriage: r = .913; p = .0001. Correlation of GDP per capita with Male singulated Age at Marriage: r = .972; p = .0001.

Level of wealth or national income influences family life in another way: poorer countries offer less educational facilities and opportunities for young people so their illiteracy level is high (Chart 7.5) and they tend to get married earlier (Chart 7.6). It is not surprising that as part of the social conditions typical of low income communities, female youth illiteracy is associated with high infant mortality rates (Chart 7.7).

In sum, all the above figures and the data examined in the preceding chapters support the assumption that the link between family and economic development in the ten Asian countries is following the same general path taken earlier by industrialised countries in Europe and North America. Higher levels of economic development are accompanied by higher participation of women in the labour force, higher educational attainment for women, later age at first marriage, and a smaller family size. Hence the significance of the three social policy perspectives discussed earlier: (1) policy intervention is required as it represents the collective effort to adjust and coordinate the society's goal to increase economic development (human capital) and families' need to protect and

206

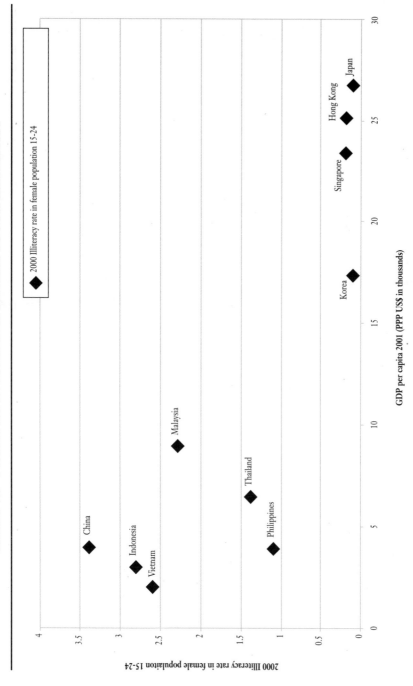

CHART 7.5   NATIONAL INCOME AND FEMALE YOUTH ILLITERACY

Sources: United Nations Development Programme (2002); and UNESCO (1999). Illiteracy rates for Japan and South Korea are estimations. Correlation: r = -.854; p = .002.

CHART 7.6 FEMALE YOUTH ILLITERACY AND TIMING OF MARRIAGE

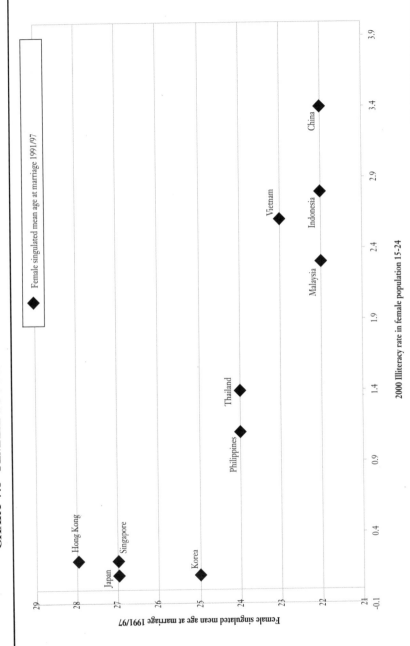

Sources: United Nations Statistics Division (2002); and UNESCO (1999). Illiteracy rates for Japan and South Korea are estimations.
Correlation: r = -.899; p = .0001.

CHART 7.7   FEMALE YOUTH ILLITERACY AND INFANT MORTALITY RATE

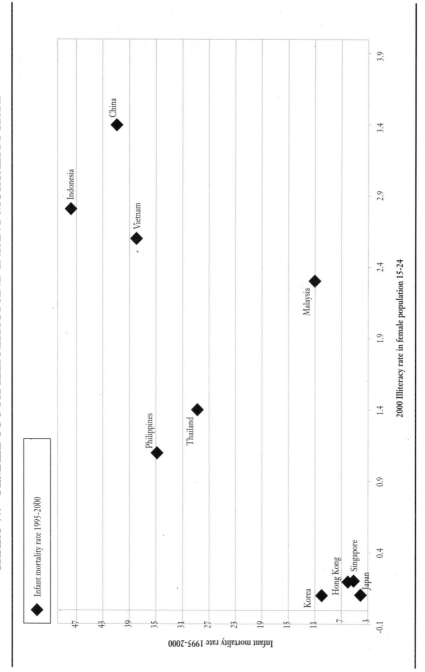

Sources: United Nations Statistics Division (2002); and UNESCO (1999). Illiteracy rates for Japan and South Korea are estimations.
Correlation: r = 0.808; p = .005.

nurture social capital; (2) the modification or change in the traditional values that define the role of women — from absolute domesticity to equality — is an inevitable challenge and prerequisite of further economic development; and (3) the increased complexity of the job market, of required marketable skills, and of job-family obligations involving both spouses, escalate the probability of family stress and conflict and consequently the necessity to give a helping hand to families whose resources are insufficient to recover from emotional and economic stress.

I suggest that the two main policy areas of high priority in Asian countries undergoing the painful cycles of economic recession and growth, are the needs of families under stress and the needs of dual-income couples and their families. While these two types of families — dual-income families and families under stress — may or may not overlap, studies suggest that dual-income families are likely to undergo stress affecting the marital relationship and the parent-child relationship. One of the objectives of social policy is precisely to offer families the opportunity and services to manage conflict and stress. Although the specific dimensions of the problems and their possible solutions vary across countries, these policy areas are needed in all countries undergoing rapid economic development. I will discuss separately the policy considerations concerning families under stress and dual career families.

Main Policy Areas: Families Under Stress

Given that conflict is a normal part of everyday life, and that the community is expected to set the norms and the facilities to assist families to cope with conflict and stress, family policies need to address the creation of both preventive and remedial support networks. Preventive support networks address normal or regular families through educational programmes (for example on marriage preparation, parenting, and family communication skills) as well as families at risk. The latter are families who are already dealing effectively with stressors on their own but may benefit from more knowledge and practical and expert assistance (for example individuals caring for a chronically ill or dying family members, single working parents, and children of single parents) in the form of information and training facilities, counselling, telephone help lines, day-care services, meals-on-wheels, and low-interest financial loans, among other services. Remedial support networks are those services and procedures provided by the society to help families seriously affected by high levels of stress and unable to manage and recover on their own. The discussion of remedial support networks involves two key questions: (1) Should remedial support services be provided? and (2) What kind of remedial support services are needed?

On the first question, an important consideration determining the society's willingness to provide and finance remedial support services is the *public image* of the stressors affecting families in need of external help. The public image of a stressor comprises the social acceptability of the stressor and the public's perception of its scope. Concerning social acceptability, if the stressor is perceived by the society as the consequence of improper or deviant behaviour, there would be a collective reluctance or opposition to the provision of remedial services to families or individuals affected. For example, many communities were reluctant to help AIDS patients and their families in the early years of the worldwide epidemic because of the belief that the disease was 'punishment' for deviant conduct. Another illustration is the current neglect of, or hostility against rape victims in some communities because of the belief that victims "asked for it."

In addition to the public image of the stressor, the provision of remedial support networks is decided on the basis of the perceived scope of the stressor by the society and its policy-makers. Perceived scope means *when the problem begins and when it ends and who is or are involved* and it is derived from idea of "community's punctuation of an event."[16] To illustrate: if the problem of drug addiction is defined as involving only the individual drug addict and it is officially deemed to be terminated when the person completes treatment at a drug rehabilitation centre, then there will be no services designed to assist the "ex-addict" to reintegrate in the community and the addict's family (parents, spouse, children) will not be defined as being in need of remedial support networks. Another example is the perceived scope of the problem of wife-battering: if the husband is prosecuted, the official perception tends to be that the solution is punishment of the aggressor and that the problem is resolved when he completes his prison sentence. Consequently, no remedial support services are available for the following individuals and time periods outside the "scope of vision" of the official definition of the problem: the aggressor's need of help in rehabilitation and re-adaptation, and his wife's and children's need to deal with the court case trauma, with the husband/father's absence, and with his eventual return to the family.

It is useful to complement this question on whether the society should provide support services with three other conditions (accountability, duty, and competence) proposed by D. Reiss and M.E. Oliveri in their study of the community's perspective of family stress.[17] They suggest that the community would be more inclined to render support services to families under stress when the community and its decision-makers view families as not being accountable for the problem; when families are deemed to have the duty of requesting outside help; and when families are defined as lacking the competence to solve the problem affecting them. Correspondingly, the community would be less inclined to set up remedial support networks if families under stress are defined collectively as accountable for their predicament, having the duty of managing the problem by themselves, and being competent enough to find a solution.

What kind of support services are needed to help families affected by high levels of stress but unable to solve their problems with their own resources? Once a country has the political will, the financial resources and the legal mandate to set up remedial support services, the array of services seems to be only limited by the creativeness and resourcefulness of its decision-makers and private initiative. The array of support services available in countries across the world is enormous and modern nations tend to learn from each other's experiences. Thus, instead of listing an arbitrary and incomplete list of specific services, I will indicate some important requirements of remedial support networks and the most important areas of family stress that need urgent attention by policy-makers deciding on the establishment of such networks.

Six requirements are, in my opinion, crucial in securing the accessibility of remedial support services to all citizens in need and their families. Remedial support services must strive to fulfill these requirements: (a) Services should follow a total family approach rather than dealing only with the individual. Valuable insights from family therapy demonstrate that even if the stressor appears to affect only one family member, the collective cooperation and support of his or her family are necessary for a successful resolution of the problem. (b) As far as possible, services must provide reliable support over time. Abrupt changes in counsellor or therapist and short-term assistance are detrimental to the family's progress in stressor management and resolution. (c) Confidentiality must be guaranteed by service providers. The protection of the family's privacy should be assured by designing appropriate procedures for conducting counselling and therapy sessions, recording data and handling documentation. The anxiety about breaches in confidentiality is one of the most serious barriers to the utilisation of support services by individuals and families in crisis. (d) The cost of the service should not become an impediment for its utilisation by indigent families. If fees are unavoidable to cover the provision of the service, they should be charged based on the person's or guardian's income tax returns and should be waived for people who do not qualify to pay income taxes. (e) No ideological, religious, or political commitment should be required or implied from individuals or families approaching the service. (f) Finally, no service is accessible to its intended users if they do not know that the service exists or have only partial information about its location, purpose, and characteristics. Consequently, all remedial services should be announced clearly and widely to the target population.

Main Policy Areas: Dual-income Couples and Their Families

As indicated earlier, a dual-income couple is one where both spouses are income-earners. I will refer to this type of couples, their children (if any) and their elderly parents (if they are supported by the income-earners) as dual-income families. In contrast to single-income families that typically have the husband as the sole breadwinner and the wife in charge of domestic duties, dual-career families face special problems on division of domestic work, decision-making, and time allocation, among others. Dual-career families also face different practical needs particularly in matters such as childcare for preschool children, child supervision, and performance of household tasks. Thus, dual-career families represent the most vivid example of the clash between the demands of economic development and family life.

Are dual-income families common in Asian countries in the 21st century? We need to make an educated guess. In the absence of direct figures on dual-income couples in the ten countries studied, the female economic activity rate as a percentage of the total male economic activity rate serves as a fairly reasonable substitute indicator, assuming that a large proportion of economically active women (defined as women who are working or looking for a job) in 2000 were married. With the average female age at marriage ranging from 22 to 28, and the high female economic activity rates for the age groups 25 to 49 as seen in Chapter 5, this assumption is acceptable.[18] Chart 7.8 shows three sets of figures: the total female economic activity rate; this rate as a percentage of the total male economic activity rate; and the GDP per capita.

CHART 7.8 ECONOMIC ACTIVITY RATES
AND NATIONAL INCOME, 2000

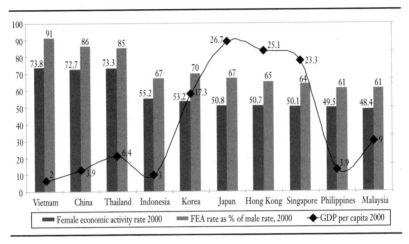

Source: United Nations Development Programme (2002). Female economic activity (FEA) rate refers to population 15 years old and above.

A striking feature of this cross-national comparison is identified when the level of national income is examined together with the rate of participation in the economy by men and women (Chart 7.8). The highest rates of female economic activity as a percentage of male economic activity (and thus, tentatively, the largest proportion of dual-income couples) are found in three countries with very low level of economic development, Vietnam (91 per cent), China (86 per cent) and Thailand (85 per cent). A significant proportion of these economically active women are found in the agricultural sector and related industries. The high participation of women in the economy in Vietnam and China is politically generated through their countries' ideological position on gender equality. But as indicated in Chapter 5, it appears that culture, not politics, provides the main boost in the case of Thai women, directing them to look after the financial security of their families as part of their traditional domestic role.

The proportion of economically active women as a percentage of the total male economically active rates is lower for the four countries with the highest GDP per capita, Japan (67 per cent), Hong Kong (65 per cent), Singapore (64 per cent), and South Korea (70 per cent). Thus, if the proxy indicator may be used again, these four high income countries have a lower proportion of dual-income families, just as the lower income countries Indonesia (67 per cent), the Philippines (61 per cent), and Malaysia (61 per cent). This feature is interesting because it differs from the trend towards an increasing presence of dual-income families in Western countries as a by-product of high economic development. For example, the female economic activity rate as a percentage of total male rate in 2000 was 89 per cent in Sweden, 86 per cent in Finland, 84 per cent in Denmark and Norway, 82 per cent in Canada, and 77 per cent in Australia.[19] A study of dual-income families in the United States reported that the proportion of one-income families fell from 55.5 per cent of all married couples in 1963 to 26.0 per cent of all married couples in 1997. Correspondingly, the proportion of dual-income couples went up from 21.1 per cent in 1963 to 43.5 per cent of all married couples in 1997.[20]

The general findings in Chart 7.8 and specifically the disparity in trends between the well-to-do Asian countries and their Western counterparts, reinforces the argument that the influence of traditional gender roles is very much present in Asia, irrespective of the level of economic development, as argued in Chapter 5 of this volume. Apart from official figures on female economic activity, women's work in agriculture and other sectors of the economy still tends to be considered domestic labour or remains unrecorded. They are the invisible workers. In rural communities, planting and harvesting seasons see women marching into the fields with their children on their backs to toil through the day. Yet, they also take charge of household chores and prepare the meals that the farming family and workers take during the day and interrupt their work only when their children need attention and feeding. Rural women are usually involved in cottage industries as well to supplement the family's income. Women in the urban lower and middle income groups are similarly involved in generating income for their families. A shopkeeper's wife works with him at the shop throughout the day with only the required interruptions to prepare the family's meals, look after the children, and complete the daily household chores. Unless she receives a salary or is officially recorded as co-owner of the business, this typical shopkeeper's wife would not be captured by the official records as a working wife or the couple as a dual-income couple.

In tandem with the increase in the participation of women in the labour force, many developed countries have emphasised the provision of childcare facilities. Singapore, Hong Kong, and other countries in Asia have commercial childcare facilities. But studies of family attitudes in Singapore indicate that, if given the choice, parents would prefer to look after their young children themselves or entrust their daily care to the children's grandparents. This preference is likely to be found in other Asian countries as well (Chapter 4). A more effective way of assisting parents (and particularly working mothers) to perform their family and job obligations is to introduce flexibility in job contracts and working hours. This involves adapting to the local situation practices introduced in developed countries such as flexitime, parental leave, and the redefinition of part-time and full-time contracts.

Flexitime has many versions and its applicability depends on the nature of the job in question. In its simplest form, it refers to the worker's option to complete the legally stipulated number of working hours per week in a manner that would suit the worker's family obligations. Parental leave is given to all workers who are parents irrespective of their gender and it refers to the right of paid leave to a worker to look after his or her sick child or newborn. In many countries part-time employees are excluded from career track positions, do not have promotion prospects, and are not covered by medical and other job-related benefits. In countries with full employment or low unemployment rates, female workers are more inclined than male workers to take part-time positions because this type of appointment allows them more time to meet their childcare and other domestic duties. Policy makers are in a position to urge and encourage employers to redefine the nature of part-time contracts so that working women in part-time positions may pursue their careers. Each of these options has been tested and improved in developed countries.[21] Policy makers in the region should study the experiences of developed countries and devise their own approach to ease the burden of working spouses and parents.

CONCLUSION

The preceding discussion identified the concepts and perspectives in family policy that dispute the three most common objections expressed by concerned observers to the formulation of family policy. First, some critics see social policy as the state's intrusion in the privacy of the family, but family policy need not be intrusive as it can be designed positively including built-in checks and balances. Second, some people fear that giving women education and equal access to jobs may lead to the loss of traditional family values. The principal traditional value that concerns both conservative and modern-minded people alike (but for different reasons) is the gender division of labour manifested in the dual role assigned to women: the role of income-earner and the domestic role as wife and mother. Because husbands are perceived as the main breadwinners and heads of household, the domestic and childcare tasks are assigned to the wife, whether or not she is holding a paid job outside the home.

The findings from this study suggest that the transformation of the traditional gender division of labour is lagging behind economic development and constitutes a burden particularly for women who are expected to deal simultaneously with both home and paid job obligations. This dual role of women is most pronounced in countries where the social pressures of tradition on the one hand and modernisation for economic development on the other hand, are both unrelenting. Therefore, some specific areas of concern for policy makers to assist dual-income families are recommended for countries undergoing a rapid pace of economic development.

Third, on the argument that families should be left alone to manage and solve their own problems, abundant evidence show that the state needs to contribute to family well-being at two levels: preventive and remedial. At the preventive level, the state must provide the necessary conditions for families to function and grow (for example, safety, political stability, employment opportunities, effective educational system). At the remedial level, while most families may be able to cope with stress and crises on their own, there are families whose needs are far greater than their resources. Families of this type are unable to recover from stress and to manage crises and thus, they require external help and resources of such nature and magnitude that only the state can mobilise.

Finally, the issues of family stress and dual-income families have been discussed separately for the sake of clarity but these problems are closely intertwined. Stress and conflict in the family are connected to financial need, overwork, rest deprivation, health problems, disparate career goals of spouses, and a host of other problems. Family policy,

217

therefore, must take a multi-pronged approach to the provision of alternatives that families may choose to alleviate or solve their problems.

The fundamental principle in family policy is help families to help themselves. Consequently, the comprehensive solution to the combination of family and work obligations requires a value change towards the partnership of husband and wife as equals in the family, and the treatment of men and women as equals in the labour force. In democratic societies, partnership between spouses and gender equality are social values that need collective acceptance and nourishment before they are reflected in social policies. Given the entrenchment of the traditional dual role for women, such value change may take time. Still, it is possible for political leaders to introduce social innovations successfully, provided that the leaders themselves have the political will to act.

ENDNOTES

1. The events and upheavals of the first three years of the 21st century have brought family and kin into a larger, more public perspective. Television screens and newspaper photographs blow-up the tears and pain of sons searching for the parents in the rubble of collapsed or burnt buildings, or people writing the names of their family members in long lists of missing persons. East and Southeast Asia experienced the SARS (severe acute respiratory syndrome) outbreak in the first half of 2003, and the importance of family love and support and the affective meaning of home and kin were once again publicly evident. But it is not only in pain that family comes to public view. On the brighter side, people receiving awards or being honoured are now proudly mentioning their parents, spouses, and children.

2. For a review of studies done on dual-income couples see Moen (2003).

3. See Firebaugh and Beck (1994); Marshall (1992); Smith (1991); Gottfried and Gottfried (1988); Moen (1989) and (2003); Gerstel and Gross (1987); Presser (1994); and Conger, Lorenz, et.al. (1993).

4. See Kahn (1969:131).

5. See Tallman (1979:470).

6. See Coleman (1990:584).

7. See Berger and Berger (1983:206-208).

8. See Quah (1990d:17).

9. See for example Sussman and Steinmetz (1987); Steinmetz (1988); and Boss (2002).

10. See Boss (2002:50-57). This section follows her framework, classification, and definition of stressors.

11. See Boss (2002:51 and 57).

12. See Pasley (1987); Boss (1988:72-85); Boss (2002:93-112).

13. See Boss (1988:139-141).

14. For the detailed computation of the HDI, see United Nations Development Programme (2002:253).

15. Taiwan is part of this group of rapidly advancing economies but, unfortunately, could not be included in this analysis due to the lack of comparable data.

16. See Reiss and Oliveri (1983).

17. See Reiss and Oliveri (1983:71-74).

18. It is important to note that the female economic activity rates for 2000 reported in Chapter 5 are figures from the International Labour Organization (2002) and that they differ from the 2000 female economic activity rates reported by the United Nations Development Programme (2002) discussed in this chapter. However, the trends are the same in both sets of figures.

19. See United Nations Development Programme (2002:234).

20. See Waite and Nielsen (2001:31).

21. See Ditch, Barnes and Bradshaw (1996b).

Bibliography

Abbott, D. A. and Walters, J. (1985). "Parenthood is a Question of Free Choice and There Should Be No Societal Pressure." In H. Feldman and M. Feldman (eds.), *Current Controversies in Marriage and Family*. Beverly Hills: Sage, 183-192.

Abroms, Lorien C. and Goldscheider, Frances K. (2002). "More Work for Mother: How Spouses, Cohabitating Partners and Relatives Affect the Hours Mothers Work." *Journal of Family and Economic Issues*, 23, 2, 147-166.

Adams, Bert N. (1986). *The Family: A Sociological Interpretation*. 4th Edition. New York: Harcourt Brace Jovanovich.

Advisory Council on the Aged (1988a). *Attitudes Towards the Aged*. Singapore: Committee on Attitudes Towards the Aged, Advisory Council on the Aged.

Advisory Council on the Aged (1988b). *Employment of the Aged*. Singapore: Committee on the Employment of the Aged, ACA.

Ahmad bin Muhammad Ibrahim (1984). *Family Law in Malaysia and Singapore*. 2nd Edition. Singapore: Malayan Law Journal.

Alcantara, Miriam C. (1995). "Childcare Arrangements of Working Mothers with Pre-School Children." In C.A. Florencio and F.C.F. Galvez (eds.), *Studies on Filipino Families*. Volume 1. Diliman, Quezon City: University of the Philippines.

Alpha Research (1994). *Thailand in Figures 1994*. Bangkok: Alpha Research Co.Ltd.

Altman, Irwin and Ginat, Joseph (1996). *Polygamous Families in Contemporary Society*. Cambridge, UK: Cambridge University Press.

Amornvivat, Sumon, Khemmani, T., Thirachitra, V., and Kulapichitr, U. (1990). *Thai Ways of Child Rearing Practices: An Ethnographic Study*. Bangkok: Department of Elementary Education, Chulalongkorn University.

Ang, Wai Hoon (1995). "Editorial." *Link*, July-September.

Arnold, Fred and Zhaoxiang, Liu (1992). "Sex Preference, Fertility, and Family Planning in China." In D.L. Poston Jr. and D. Yaukey (eds.), *The Population of Modern China*. New York: Plenum Press, 491-523.

Asahi Shimbun (2003). *Japan Almanac 2003*. Tokyo: Asahi Shimbun.

Asian Development Bank (2000). *Key Indicators of Development in Asian and Pacific Countries*. Volume XXXI. Manila: Oxford University Press.

Asis, Maruja (2002). "From the Life Stories of Filipino Women: Personal and Family Agendas in Migration." *Asian and Pacific Migration Journal*, 11, 1, 67-93.

Attorney-General Chambers (2003). *Republic of Singapore Statutes, Chapter 353, Women's Charter*. Singapore: AGC, Government of Singapore.

Bahr, Stephen J. ed. (1991a). *Family Research: A Sixty-Year Review, 1930-1990* Volume 1. New York: Lexington Books.

Bahr, Stephen J. (ed.) (1991b). *Family Research: A Sixty-Year Review, 1930-1990* Volume 2. New York: Lexington Books.

Bahr, Stephen, Wang, Gabe, and Zhang, Jie (1991). "Early Family Research." In S. J. Bahr (ed.), *Family Research: A Sixty-Year Review, 1930-1990* Volume 1. New York: Lexington Books, 1-23.

Barrett, Richard, E., and Li, Fang (1999). *Modern China*. Boston: McGraw-Hill.

Beauchamp, T.L. and Childress, J.F. (eds.) (1989). *Principles of Biomedical Ethics*. 3rd. Edition. New York: Oxford University Press.

Berger, Brigitte and Berger, Peter L. (1983). *The War Over the Family: Capturing the Middle Ground*. New York: Anchor Books.

Bernard, Jessie (1972). "Changing Family Life Styles: One Role, Two Roles, Shared Roles." In L.K. Howe (ed.), *The Future of the Family*. New York: Simon & Schuster, 235-246.

Bjornberg, U. (2001). "Cohabitation and Marriage in Sweden — Does Family Form Matter?" *International Journal of Law, Policy and the Family*, 15, 350-362.

Black, A. H. (1986). "Gender and Cosmology in Chinese Correlative Thinking." In C. W. Bynum, S. Harrell and P. Richman (eds.), *Gender and Religion: On the Complexity of Symbols*. Boston: Beacon Press, 166-195.

Blake, Myrna (1992). *Growing Old in the Malay Community*. Singapore: CAS/Times Academic Press.

Blumel, Susan R. (1991). "Explaining Marital Success and Failure." In Stephen J. Bahr (ed.), *Family Research: A Sixty-Year Review, 1930-1990* Volume 2. New York: Lexington Books.

Boh, Katja (1990). "The 'Optimum' Family: Policy Experiences in Eastern Europe." In S. R. Quah (ed.), *The Family as an Asset: An International Perspective on Marriage, Parenthood and Social Policy*. Singapore: Times Academic Press, pp. 355-377.

Borgatta, Edgar F. and McCluskey, Neil G. (eds.) (1980). *Aging and Society: Current Research and Policy Perspectives*. London: Sage.

Boss, Pauline. (1977). "A Clarification of the Concept of Psychological Father Presence in Families Experiencing Ambiguity of Boundary," *Journal of Marriage and the Family*, 39, 141-151.

Boss, Pauline (1988). *Family Stress Management*. Newbury Park: Sage.

Boss, Pauline (2002). *Family Stress Management: A Contextual Approach* 2nd Edition. Thousand Oaks, CA: Sage.

Boss, Pauline (1993). "The Reconstruction of Family Life with Alzheimer's Disease." In P.G. Boss, W.J. Doherty, R. La Rossa, W.R. Schumm, and S.K. Steinmetz. (eds.), *Sourcebook of Family Theory and Methods: A Contextual Approach*. New York: Plenum, 163-166.

Boss, Pauline, Doherty, W.J., LaRossa, R., Schumm, W.R., and Steinmetz, S.K. (eds.) (1993). *Sourcebook of Family Theory and Methods: A Contextual Approach.* New York: Plenum Press.

Bott, Elizabeth (1971). *Family and Social Network: Roles, Norms, and External Relationships in Ordinary Urban Families* 2nd Edition. New York: Free Press.

Braudel, Fernand (1973). *The Mediterranean and the Mediterranean World in the Age of Philip II.* Volumes I and II. New York: Harper & Row.

Broadbent, Kaye and Morris-Suzuki, Tessa (2000). "Women's Work in the 'Public' and 'Private' Spheres of the Japanese Economy," *Asian Studies Review,* 24, 2 (June), 161-173.

Brown, L. Neville (1966). "The Legal Background to the Family Court," *British Journal of Criminology,* 139, 139-49.

Buckley, Charles B. (1902). *An Anecdotal History of Old Times in Singapore, 1819-1867.* Singapore: Fraser & Neave.

Bumpass, Larry L. and Mason, Karen O. (1998). "Family Processes and Their Implications for Families in the Future." In K.O. Mason, Noriko O. Tsuya and Minja K. Choe (eds.), *The Changing Family in Comparative Perspective: Asia and the United States.* Honolulu: East-West Center, 237-253.

Bumroongsook, Sumalee (1995) *Love and Marriage: Mate Selection in Twentieth-Century Central Thailand.* Bangkok: Chulalongkorn University Press.

Burr, Wesley R. (1973). *Theory Construction and the Sociology of the Family.* New York: John Wiley & Sons.

Burr, W.R., Leigh, G.K., Day, R.D. and Constantine, J. (1979). "Symbolic Interaction and the Family." In W.R. Burr, R. Hill, F.I. Nye, and I.L. Reiss (eds.), *Contemporary Theories About the Family Volume 2: General Theories/Theoretical Orientations.* New York: The Free Press, 42-111.

Casey, James (1989). *The History of the Family: New Perspectives in the Past.* Oxford: Blackwell.

Chai, Ch'u and Chai, Winberg (1973). *Confucianism.* New York: Barron's.

Chaffe, John W. (1991). "The Marriage of Sung Imperial Class Women." In R.S. Watson and P.B. Ebrey (eds.), *Marriage and Inequality in Chinese Society.* Berkeley: University of California Press, pp. 133-169.

Challenge (2003). Singapore Civil Service Newsletter.

Chan, H. H. M. (1986). *An Introduction to The Singapore Legal System.* Singapore: Malayan Law Journal Pte. Ltd.

Chan, Susan (1997). "Editorial," *Link 1996.* Singapore: SDU.

Chan, Wing-Tsit (1963). *A Source Book in Chinese Philosophy.* Princeton, N.J.: Princeton University Press.

Chang, Chen Tung, Ong, Jin Hui, and Chen, Peter S.J. (1980). *Culture and Fertility: The Case of Singapore.* Singapore: Institute of Southeast Asian Studies.

Cheang, Molly D. (1985). "Family Court: Let's Have It," *The Malayan Law Journal,* May, cxlviii-cliii.

Chen, A.J. and Cheung, P.P.L. (1988). *The Elderly in Singapore.* Singapore: ASEAN.

Chen, P.S.J. and Chang, C.T. (1982). "The Elderly in Singapore." Singapore: NUS unpublished report.

Cherlin, Andrew (1988). *The Changing American Family and Public Policy*. Washington: The Urban Institute.

Cherlin, Andrew J. and Furstenberg, Frank F. (1992). *The New American Grandparent: A Place in the Family, A Life Apart*. Cambridge, MA: Harvard University Press.

Cherry, Kittredge (1991). *Womansword: What Japanese Words Say About Women*. Tokyo: Kodansha International Ltd.

Cheung, Chau-kiu and Liu, Elaine S.C. (1997). "Impacts of Social Pressure and Social Support on Distress Among Single Parents in China." In C.A. Everett (ed.), *Divorce and Remarriage: International Studies*. New York: The Haworth Press, 65-82.

Chi, Nguyentu (1991). "Preliminary Notes on the Family in Vietnam." In R. Liljestrom and T. Lai (eds.), *Sociological Studies on the Vietnamese Family*. Hanoi: National Center for Social Sciences, Institute of Sociology, 57-68.

Cho, Byung Eun and Shin, Hwa-Yong (1996). "State of Family Research and Theory in South Korea," *Marriage & Family Review*, 22, 1-2, 101-135.

Choe, Minja Kim (1998). "Changing Marriage Patterns in South Korea." In K.O. Mason, N.O. Tsuya, and M.K. Choe (eds.), *The Changing Family in Comparative Perspective: Asia and The United States*. Honolulu: East-West Center, 43-62.

Chu, Teo Seng (1960). "The Singapore Chinese Protectorate 1900-1941." Singapore: Unpublished Academic Exercise, History Department, University of Malaya.

Chua, M. and Theyvendran, R. (1990). *The Singapore Employment Act and Guide*. Singapore: Aequitas.

Chung, Young-iab (1989). "The Impact of Chinese Culture on Korea's Economic Development." In Tai Hung-chao (ed.), *Confucianism and Economic Development: An Oriental Alternative?* Washington: The Washington Institute Press.

Clark, Jon (ed.) (1996). *James S. Coleman*. London: Falmer Press.

Cochrane, S. H. (1982). "Education and Fertility: An Expanded Examination of the Evidence." In G. P. Kelly and C. M. Elliot (eds.), *Women's Education in the Third World: Comparative Perspectives*. Albany, New York; State University of New York Press, 311-330.

Coleman, James (1990). *Foundations of Social Theory*. Cambridge, MA: Harvard University Press.

Coles, R. (1986). "What's the Best Family Size?" In O. Pocs and R. H. Walsh (eds.), *Marriage and Family 86/87*. Guilford, Connecticut: The Dushkin Publishing Group, Inc., 110-111.

Condon, Jane (1985). *A Half Step Behind: Japanese Women Today*. Tokyo: Charles E. Tuttle Co.

Conger, R.D., Lorenz, F.O., Elder, G.H., Simons, R.L., and Ge, X. (1993). "Husband and Wife Differences in Response to Undesirable Life Events," *Journal of Health and Social Behavior*, 34, 1, 71-88.

Creel. H. G. (1949). *Confucius and the Chinese Way*. New York: Harper & Row.

Creel, H. G. (1962). *Chinese Thought From Confucius to Mao Tse-Tung*. London: Methuen.

Dai, Keijing (1990). "The Social Significance of Marriage and Parenthood in China." In S. R. Quah (ed.), *The Family as an Asset: An International Perspective on Marriage, Parenthood and Social Policy*. Singapore: Times Academic Press, 174-212.

Davis, G. (1982). "Conciliation or Litigation?" *L.A.G. Bulletin*, April, 11-13.

Ditch, J., Barnes, H., Bradshaw, J. (1996). *A Synthesis of National Family Policies 1995*. York: University of York European Observatory on National Family Policies.

Ditch, J., Barnes, H., Bradshaw, J., and Kilkey, M. (1998). *A Synthesis of National Family Policies in 1996*. York: University of York European Observatory on National Family Policies.

Doeblin, A. (1940). *The Living Thoughts of Confucius*. New York: David McKay.

Donzelot, J. (1977). *The Policing of Families*. New York: Pantheon Books.

Doolittle, Justus (1986). *The Social Life of the Chinese*. Volumes I and II. Singapore: Graham Brash. [Reprinted from the original published in 1895 by Harper & Brothers, New York]

Doyle, James A. (1985). *Sex and Gender: The Human Experience*. Dubuque, Iowa: W.C. Brown Publishers.

Ebrey, Patricia B. (1991). "Shifts in Marriage Finance from the Sixth to the Thirteenth Century." In R.S. Watson and P.B. Ebrey (eds.), *Marriage and Inequality in Chinese Society*. Berkeley: University of California Press, 97-132.

Economic Committee (1986). *The Singapore Economy: New Directions. Report of the Economic Committee*. Singapore: Ministry of Trade & Industry.

Economic and Social Commission for Asia and the Pacific [ESCAP] (2002). *Statistical Yearbook for Asia and the Pacific 2001*. New York: United Nations.

Edgar, Don (1990). "The Social Reconstruction of Marriage and Parenthood in Australia." In S. R. Quah (ed.), *The Family as an Asset: An International Perspective on Marriage, Parenthood and Social Policy*. Singapore: Times Academic Press, 96-121.

Edwards, J. N. (1989). "The Family Realm: A Future Paradigm or Failed Nostalgia?" *Journal of Marriage and the Family*, 51, 816-818.

Edwards, Walter (1989). *Modern Japan Through Its Weddings: Gender, Person, and Society in Ritual Portrayal*. Stanford, CA: Stanford University Press.

Ehrenreich, B. (1990). "Sorry, Sisters, This is Not the Revolution," *Times* (Fall), 15.

Elashmawi, Farid (2001). *Competing Globally*. Boston: Butterworth.

Erikson, E.H., Erikson, J.M., and Kivnick, H.Q. (1986). *Vital Involvement in Old Age*. New York: W.W. Norton.

Etzioni, A. (1993). *The Spirit of Community: Rights, Responsibilities, and the Communitarian Agenda*. New York: Crown.

Etzioni, A. (ed.) (1995). *The New Communitarian Thinking*. Charlottesville: University of Virginia Press.

Fawcett, J. T. and Khoo, S. E. (1980). "Singapore: Rapid Fertility Transition in a Compact Society," *Population and Development Review*, 6, 4 (December), 549-579.

Festinger, L. A. (1957). *A Theory of Cognitive Dissonance*. Evanston, IL: Row Peterson.

Fletcher, Ronald (1988a). *The Abolitionists: The Family and Marriage Under Attack*. London: Routledge.

Finer, Morris (1974). *Report on the Committee on One-Parent Families*. London: HMSO.

Firebaugh, G. and Beck, F.D. (1994). "Does Economic Growth benefit the Masses? Growth, Dependence, and Welfare in the Third World," *American Sociological Review*, 59, 5, 631-653.

Fischer, Claude S. (1982). *To Dwell Among Friends: Personal Networks in Town and City*. Chicago: University of Chicago Press.

Fry, C. G., King, J.R., Swanger, E.R., and Wolf, H.C. (1984). *Great Asian Religions*. Grand Rapids, Michigan: Baker Book House.

Fung, Yu-lan (1948). *A Short History of Chinese Philosophy*. New York: Free Press.

Fuse, Akiko (1996). "Status of Family Theory and Research in Japan," *Marriage and Family Review*, 22, 1-2, 73-99.

Gerstel, N. and Gross, H.E. (eds.) (1987). *Families and Work*. Philadelphia: Temple University Press.

Gies, F. and Gies, J. (1987). *Marriage and the Family in the Middle Ages*. New York: Harper & Row.

Gilmartin, Christina and Tan, Lin (2002). "Fleeing Poverty: Rural Women, Expanding Marriage Markets, and Strategies for Social Mobility in Contemporary China." In E. N. Chow (ed.), *Transforming Gender and Development in East Asia*. New York: Routledge, 203-216.

Glazer, Nathan (1988). *The Limits of Social Policy*. Cambridge, Mass.: Harvard University Press.

Goh, C. T. (1987). "New Population Policy," *Speeches*, March-April, Vol. 11, No.2, 1-6.

Gonzalez-Lopez, M. J. (2002). "A Portray of Western Families. New Models of Intimate Relationships and the Timing of Life Events." In A. Carling, S. Duncan and R. Edwards (eds.). *Analysing Families: Morality and Rationality in Policy and Practice*. London: Routledge, 21-47.

Goody, Jack (1990). *The Oriental, the Ancient and the Primitive: Systems of Marriage and the Family in the Pre-Industrial Societies of Eurasia*. Cambridge, UK: Cambridge University Press.

Gottfried, A.E. and Gottfried, A.W. (eds.) (1988). *Maternal Employment and Children's Development*. New York: Plenum Press.

Gottlieb, B. H. (ed.) (1981). *Social Networks and Social Support*. Beverly Hills: SAGE.

Government of Singapore (1994a). *Parliamentary Debates Singapore Official Report*. Volume 63, No.2, Monday 25 July.

Government of Singapore (1994b). *Parliamentary Debates Singapore Official Report.* Volume 63, No.4, Wednesday 27 July.

Greenhalgh, Susan and Bongaarts, John (1992). "Fertility Policy in China: Future Options." In D.L. Poston Jr. and D. Yaukey (eds.), *The Population of Modern China.* New York: Plenum Press, 401-419.

Gronseth, Erik (1973). "The Breadwinner Trap." In L. K. Howe (ed.), *The Future of the Family.* New York: Simon & Schuster, 175-191.

Habakkuk, H.J. (1974). "Family Structure and Economic Change in Nineteenth-Century Europe." In Rose L. Coser (ed.), *The Family: Its Structures and Functions.* 2nd Edition. New York: St. Martin's Press, 384-394.

Hansen, Donald A. and Johnson, Vicky A. (1979). "Rethinking Family Stress Theory: Definitional Aspects." In W.R. Burr, R. Hill, F.I. Nye, and I.L. Reiss (eds.), *Contemporary Theories About the Family.* Volume I. New York: Free Press, 582-603.

Hasegawa, K. (1986). *Japanese-Style Management: An Insider's Analysis.* Tokyo: Kodansha International Ltd.

Hassan, Riaz (2002). *Faithlines: Muslim Conceptions of Islam and Society.* Oxford, UK: Oxford University Press.

Heaton, Tim B. (1996). "Socioeconomic and Familial Status of Women Associated with Age at First Marriage in Three Islamic Societies," *Journal of Comparative Family Studies*, 28, 1, 41-58.

Henslin, J. M. (ed.) (1985). *Marriage and Family in a Changing Society.* 2nd Edition. New York: The Free Press.

Hewlett, S. A. (1987). *A Lesser Life: The Myth of Women's Liberation.* London: Sphere Books.

Higgins, Louise T., Zheng, Mo, Liu, Yali, and Sun, Chubg-Hui (2002). "Attitudes to Marriage and Sexual Behaviors: A Survey of Gender and Culture Differences in China and United Kingdom," *Sex Roles*, 46, 3 (February), 75-89.

Hoggett, Brenda M. and Pearl, Davis S. (1983). *The Family, Law and Society.* London: Butterworths.

Holmgren, Jennifer (1991). "Imperial Marriage in the Native Chinese and Non-Han State, Han to Ming." In R.S. Watson and P.B. Ebrey (eds.), *Marriage and Inequality in Chinese Society.* Berkeley: University of California Press, 58-96.

Hong, Daphne (1999). "Justice 21 @ The Family Court: The Role of the Court in Protecting Family Obligations in the new Millennium." *Family Court of Singapore.* Singapore: Singapore Government. URL: http://www.familycourtofsingapore.gov.sg/philosophy/paper_01.htm.

Horna, Jarmila L.A. (1990). "Marriage, Parenthood and Social Policy in Czescholovakia: A Look from the West." In S. R. Quah (ed.), *The Family as an Asset: An International Perspective on Marriage, Parenthood and Social Policy.* Singapore: Times Academic Press, 304-322.

Hugo, Graeme (2002). "Effects of International Migration on the Family in Indonesia," *Asian and Pacific Migration Journal*, 11, 1, 13-46.

Hull, Terence (2003). "Demographic Perspectives on the Future of the Indonesian Family," *Journal of Population Research*, 20, 1, 51-65.

Inoguchi, Takashi (2002). "Broadening the Basis of Social Capital in Japan." In R.D. Putnam (ed.), *Democracies in Flux: The Evolution of Social Capital in Contemporary Society*. Oxford, UK: Oxford University Press, 359-392,

Inoue, Shunichi (1998). "Family Formation in Japan, South Korea and the United States." In K.O. Mason, N.O. Tsuya, and M.K. Choe (eds.), *The Changing Family in Comparative Perspective: Asia and The United States*. Honolulu: East-West Center, pp. 19-41.

Institute of Social Research (1994). *Profiles*. Ann Arbor, MI: ISR.

International Labour Organization (2002). *LABORSTA on the WEB*. http://laborsta.ilo.org/ Geneva: ILO Bureau of Statistics.

Irving, Howard H. (2002). *Family Mediation: Theory and Practice with Chinese Families*. Hong Kong: Hong Kong University Press.

Jackson, Peter A. and Cook, Nerida M. (eds.) (1999). *Genders and Sexualities in Modern Thailand*. Chiang Mai, Thailand: Silkworm Books.

Jaspers, Karl (1957). *Socrates, Buddha, Confucius, Jesus: The Paradigmatic Individuals*. New York: Harvest Books.

Jencks, C. (1992). *Rethinking Social Policy*. Cambridge, MA: Harvard University Press.

Jernigan, H.L. and Jernigan, M. (1992). *Aging in a Chinese Society*. New York: Haworth Pastoral Press.

Joseph, Joe (1993). *The Japanese: Strange but not Strangers*. London: Penguin.

Jolivet, Muriel (1997). *Japan: The Childless Society?* London: Routledge.

Jones, Gavin (1994). *Marriage and Divorce in Islamic Southeast Asia*. Kuala Lumpur: Oxford University Press.

Jones, Gavin W. (2001). "Which Indonesian Women Marry Youngest and Why?" *Journal of Southeast Asian Studies*, 32(1), 67-78.

Jowett, B. and Loomis, L.R. (eds.) (1941). *Plato: Five Great Dialogues*. New York: Walter Black Inc.

Kahn, A. J. (1969. *Theory and Practice in Social Planning*. New York: Russell Sage

Kamerman, Sheila and Kahn, Alfred J. (1978). *Family Policy*. New York: Columbia University Press.

Kamerman, Sheila and Kahn, Alfred J. (1988). *Mothers Alone: Strategies for a Time of Change*. Dover, Mass.: Auburn House Publishing Co.

Kamerman, Sheila and Kahn, Alfred J. (1989). *Privatization and the Welfare State*. Princeton, N.J.: Princeton University Press.

Kelly, Emma (2002). "Can't Buy Me Love," *Japan Today*, Features Story 318. Tokyo.

Kelly, G. P. and Elliot, C. M. (eds.) (1982). *Women's Education in the Third World: Comparative Perspectives*. Albany, N.Y.: State University of New York Press.

Khuat, Thu Hong (1991). "Overview of Sociological Research on Family in Vietnam." In R. Liljestrom and T. Lai (eds.), *Sociological Studies on the Vietnamese Family*. Hanoi: National Center for Social Sciences, Institute of Sociology, 175-192.

Klein, David M. and Hill, Reuben (1979). "Determinants of Family Problem-Solving Effectiveness." In W.R. Burr, R. Hill, F.I. Nye, and I.L. Reiss (eds.) *Contemporary Theories About the Family* Volume I. New York: Free Press, 493-548.

Klein, David M. and White, James M. (1996). *Family Theories: An Introduction.* London: Sage.

Kling, Zainal (1995). "Background Characteristics of Malaysia," *Journal of Comparative Family Studies*, 26, 1, 43-66.

Knodel, John, Friedman, Jed, Anh, Truong-Si, and Cuong, Bui-The (2000). "Intergenerational Exchanges in Vietnam: Family Size, Sex Composition and the Location of Children," *Population Studies*, 54, 1, 89-104.

Kohli, Martin, Rein, Martin, Guillemard, Ann-Marie, and van Gunsteren (eds.) (1991). *Time for Retirement: Comparative Studies of Early Exit from the Labor Force.* Cambridge, UK: Cambridge University Press.

Komin, Suntaree (1991). *Psychology of the Thai People: Values and Behavioral Patterns.* Bangkok: National Institute of Development Administration.

Koopman-Boyden, Peggy G. (1990). "The Study of Family Policy: Sociological Approaches and Perspectives." In S. R. Quah (ed.), *The Family as an Asset:. An International Perspective on Marriage, Parenthood and Social Policy.* Singapore: Times Academic Press, 23-46.

Kua, E.H., Ang, P.C., Merriman, A. (1986). *Health Care in Old Age.* Singapore: Gerontological Society.

Kumagai, Fumie (1990). "Cross-cultural Perspectives and Policies." In S. R. Quah (ed.), *The Family as an Asset: An International Perspective on Marriage, Parenthood and Social Policy.* Singapore: Times Academic Press, pp. 213-246.

Kumar, Krishna and Raju, Sripada (1981). "Dependence in Sociology: An Empirical Study of Asian Countries," *Southeast Asian Journal of Social Science*, 9, 1, 100-122.

Kuo, E. (1987). "Confucianism and the Chinese Family in Singapore: Continuities and Changes." *Sociology Working Papers, No. 83.* Singapore: Department of Sociology, National University of Singapore.

Kuo, E. and Chiew, S. K. (1984). *Ethnicity and Fertility in Singapore.* Singapore: Institute of Southeast Asian Studies.

LaRossa, R. and Reitzes, D.C. (1993). "Symbolic Interactionism and Family Studies." In P.G. Boss et.al. (eds.), *Sourcebook of Family Theories and Methods." A Contextual Approach.* New York: Plenum, 135-163.

Ladurie, Emmanuel Le Roy (1978). *Montaillou, The Promised Land of Error.* New York: Basic Books.

Lai, Tuong (1991). "Introduction." In Rita Liljestrom and Lai Toung (eds.), *Sociological Studies on the Vietnamese Family.* Hanoi: National Center for Social Sciences, Institute of Sociology, 3-11.

Lasch, Christopher (1979). *Heaven in a Heartless World: The Family Besieged.* New York: Basic Books.

Lasswell, H. (1968). "The Policy Orientation." In D. Lerner and H. Lasswell (eds.), *Policy Sciences.* Stanford: Stanford University Press.

Lau, K. E. (1994). *Singapore Census of Population 1990, Statistical Release 6: Religion, Child Care and Leisure Activities.* Singapore: Department of Statistics.

Lavely, William (1991). "Marriage and Mobility Under Rural Collectivism." In R.S. Watson and P.B. Ebrey (eds.), *Marriage and Inequality in Chinese Society.* Berkeley: University of California Press, 286-312.

Law Commission (1966). *Reform of the Grounds of Divorce — The Field of Choice.* London: HMSO.

Law Reform Commission of Canada (1974). "The Family Court." *Working Paper No.1.* Ottawa: LRC Information Canada.

Law Society (1979). *A Better Way Out: Suggestions for the Reform of the Law of Divorce.* London: The Law Society Standing Family Law Sub-Committee.

Law Society (1982). *A Better Way Out Reviewed.* London: The Law Society

Lee, E. (1991). *The British as Rulers: Governing Multiracial Singapore, 1867-1914.* Singapore: Singapore University Press.

Lee, Gary R. (1979). "Effects of Social Networks on the Family." In W.R. Burr, R. Hill, F.I. Nye, and I.L. Reiss (eds.), *Contemporary Theories About the Family. Volume 1: Research-Based Theories.* New York: The Free Press, 27-56.

Lee, H.L. (1996). "What if Singapore Were Run Along Racial and Non-Meritocratic Lines?" ***Straits Times***, 28 August, 28.

Lee, K.Y. (1982). "The search for talent." In S. Jayakumar (ed.), *Our Heritage and Beyond: A Collection of Essays on Singapore, Its Past, Present and Future.* Singapore: NTUC, 1-11.

Lee, Swee Seng (2000). "Family Law for Non-Muslims in Malaysia," *Malaysian Law Journal,* August. URL: http://www.mlj.com.my/articles/sslee2.htm

Legislative Council of the Straits Settlements (1878 to 1884). *Proceedings for 1877 to Prodeedings for 1884.* Singapore: Government Printing Office.

Leong W.K. (1990). *Family Law in Singapore.* Singapore: Malayan Law Journal Pte. Ltd.

Leow, Bee Geok (2001a). *Census of Population 2000. Advance Data Release.* Singapore: Department of Statistics.

Leow, Bee Geok (2001b). *Census of Population 2000: Demographic Characteristics, Statistical Release 1.* Singapore: Department of Statistics.

Leow, Bee Geok (2001c). *Census of Population 2000: Economic Characteristics, Statistical Release 3.* Singapore: Department of Statistics.

Levitan, S. A., Belous, R. S. and Gallo, F. (1988). *What's Happening to the American Family?: Tensions, Hopes, Realities.* Baltimore: The Johns Hopkins University Press, Revised Edition.

Levy, A. (1965). "Machine Made Love," *Mademoiselle,* January, 60, 72-127.

Levy, M. J. (1949). *The Family Revolution in Modern China.* Cambridge, MA: Harvard University Press.

Levy, M. J. (1965). "Aspects of the Analysis of Family Structure." In A.J. Coale et.al. (eds.), *Analysis of Family Structure.* Princeton: Princeton University Press.

Levy-Strauss, Claude ([1957] 1974). "The Principle of Reciprocity." In Rose L. Coser (ed.), *The Family: Its Structures and Functions.* 2nd Edition. New York: St. Martin's Press, 3-12.

Lewis, Richard D. (1999). *When Cultures Collide.* London: Nicholas Brealey Publishing.

Li Fu Chen (1986). *The Confucian Way: A New and Systematic Study of 'The Four Books'.* London: KPI.

Liao, Tim Futing (1998). "Dealings with a Double Day: Role Strain among Married Working Women in Japan and South Korea." In K. Oppenheim Mason, N.O. Tsuya, and M.K. Choe (eds.), *The Changing Family in Comparative Perspective: Asia and the United States.* Honolulu: East-West Center, 137-154.

Liljestrom, Rita (1991). "Family, Gender, and Kinship in Vietnam." In R. Liljestrom and T. Lai (eds.), *Sociological Studies on the Vietnamese Family.* Hanoi: National Center for the Social Sciences, Institute of Sociology, 13-24.

Lim, S., Ong K.S., and R. Chandra Mohan (1985a). "The Family Court : Why Singapore Should Adopt It." *Singapore Law Review* Volume 6, 12-21.

Lim, S., Ong K.S., and R. Chandra Mohan (1985b). "Setting Up a Unified Family Court in Singapore : Some Aspects," *Singapore Law Review* Volume 6, 22-27.

Lincoln, B. (ed.) (1985.) *Religion, Rebellion, Revolution.* London: Macmillan.

Link (1988). "On the Pulse," July-September. Singapore: SDU [Quarterly magazine of the Social Development Unit].

Link (1996). "Activities and Services," January-March.

Link (1997). "Activities," Singapore: SDU [Annual Publication of the SDU]

Lu, M. (1983). *Confucianism: Its Relevance to Modern Society.* Singapore: Federal Publications.

Lu, Huey-fen (2000). "Family Types and Marital Power: A Field Study in Taiwan." Harvard University PhD Dissertation. Ann Arbor. MI: University Microfilms.

Mado-Sha (1990). *Karoshi: When the 'Corporate Warrior' Dies.* Tokyo: National Defense Council for Victims of Karoshi.

Magnus, Richard (2000). "The Citizen and the Family Justice Process." The Family Court of Singapore. Singapore: Government of Singapore. URL: http://www.familycourtofsingapore.gov.sg/philosophy/paper 02.htm.

Makihara, K. (1990). "Who Needs Equality?." *Times* (Fall), 35-36.

Mani, A. (1979). "Caste and Marriage Among the Singapore Indians." In E. Kuo and A.K. Wong (eds.), *The Contemporary Family in Singapore.* Singapore: Singapore University Press, 189-207.

Mann, Susan (1991). "Grooming a Daughter for Marriage: Brides and Wives in the Mid-Ch'ing Period." In R.S. Watson and P.B. Ebrey (eds.), *Marriage and Inequality in Chinese Society.* Berkeley: University of California Press, 204-230.

Mar, Pamela C.M. and Richter, Frank-Jurgen (2003). *China: Enabling a New Era of Changes.* Singapore: John Wiley & Sons.

Marshall, C.M. (1992). "Family Influences on Work." In S.J. Bahr (ed.). *Family Research: A Sixty-Year Review, 1930-1990.* New York: Lexington Books Volume 2, 115-166.

Martin, Philip (1997). "Japan's New Immigration Law," *Migration News*, Volume 4, No. 6 (June). Electronic version: http://migration.ucdavis.edu/mn/

Masinambow, E.K. M. and Swasono, Meutia (1985). "Indonesia." In UNESCO (ed.), *Sociology and Social Anthropology in Asia and the Pacific*. Paris: UNESCO, 177-217.

McDaniel, Susan A. and Tepperman, Lorne (2000). *Close Relations: An Introduction to the Sociology of Families*. Scarborough, Canada: Prentice Hall Allyn and Bacon.

McCubbin, Hamilton I., Sussman, Marvin B., and Patterson, Joan M. (eds.) (1983). *Social Stress and the Family: Advances and Developments in Family Stress Theory and Research*. New York: The Haworth Press.

Medina, Belen T.G. (1991). *The Filipino Family: A Text with Selected Readings*. Deliman, Philippines: University of the Philippines Press.

Merton, Robert K. (1968). *Social Theory and Social Structure*. Glencoe, IL: The Free Press.

Merton, Robert K. (1973). *The Sociology of Science: Theoretical and Empirical Investigations*. Chicago: University of Chicago Press.

Merton, Robert K. (1995). "Opportunity Structure." In F. Adler and W. Laufer (eds.), *The Legacy of Anomie Theory*. New Brunswick, N.J.: Transaction Publishers, 24-33.

Meyer, Donald (1987). *Sex and Power: The Rise of Women in America, Russia, Sweden and Italy*. Middletown, CN: Wesleyand University Press.

Middleton, Russell (1972). "Brother-Sister and Father-Daughter Marriage in Ancient Egypt." In Ira L. Reiss (ed.), *Readings on the Family System*. New York: Holt, Rinehart and Winston, 26-38.

Miyamoto, Makiko (2001). "Japanese Women Changing with the Times." *Japan Close-Up*, Volume 6 (32), No. 36, Issue 72 (375), 6-13.

Moen, P. (1989). *Working Parents: Transformations in Gender Roles and Public Policies in Sweden*. London: Adamantine Press.

Moen, Phyllis (ed.) (2003). *It's About Time: Couples and Careers*. Ithaca, NY: Cornell University Press.

Moore-Ede, M. (1993). *The Twenty-Four Hour Society*. New York: Addison-Wesley.

Mullan, Bob (1984). *The Mating Trade*. London: Routledge.

Murch, Mervin (1980). *Justice and Welfare in Divorce*. London: Sweet & Maxwell.

Nanakarage, Ako (1998). "Marriage in Japan: How It is Different," *Zephyr: Online Journalism for Northern Nevada*, Reynolds School of Journalism, University of Nevada - Reno, Edition 05.98.

Ng, S. Y. (1955). "Chinese Protectorate 1877-1900." Singapore: Unpublished Academic Exercise, History Department, University of Malaya.

Ngin, Chor-Swang and DeVanzo, Julie (1999). "Parent-Child Coresidence and Quasi-Coresidence in Peninsular Malaysia," *Southeast Asian Journal of Social Science*, 27, 2, 43-64.

NTUC [National Trade Unions Congress] (1996). *A Guide to Labour Legislation in Singapore*. Singapore: NTUC Legal Services Department.

Nye, F.Ivan. (1979). "Choice, Exchange and the Family." In W.R. Burr, R. Hill, F.I. Nye, and I.L. Reiss (eds.), *Contemporary Theories About the Family. Volume 2: General Theories/Theoretical Orientations*. New York: The Free Press, 1-41.

Ocko, Jonathan K. (1991). "Women, Property and Law in the People's Republic of China." In R.S. Watson and P.B. Ebrey (eds.), *Marriage and Inequality in Chinese Society*. Berkeley: University of California Press, pp. 313-346.

Ochiai, Emiko (1997). *The Japanese Family System in Transition: A Sociological Analysis of Family Change in Post-War Japan*. Tokyo: LTCB International Library Foundation.

Ogawa, Naochiro (2003). "Japan's Changing Fertility Mechanisms and Its Policy Responses," *Journal of Population Research*, 20, 1, 89-106.

O'Leary, K. D. (ed.) (1987). *Assessment of Marital Discord*. Hillsdale, N.J.: Lawrence Erlbaum Associates.

Olson, David H., McCubbin, Halminton I., and others (1989). *Families: What Makes Them Work* Updated Edition. Newbury Park, CA: SAGE.

Panopia, Isabel S. and Bennagen, Ponciano L. (1985). "Philippines." In UNESCO (ed.), *Sociology and Social Anthropology in Asia and the Pacific*. Paris: UNESCO, 218-264.

Parkinson, Lisa (1982). "Bristol Courts Family Conciliation Service," *Family Law*, 12, 13-15.

Pasley, Kay (1987). "Family Boundary Ambiguity: Perceptions of Adult Stepfamily Members." In K. Pasley and M. Ihinger-Tallman (eds.), *Remarriage & Parenting: Current Research & Theory*. New York: Guilford Press, 206-224.

Pasley, Kay (1993). "Applying the Social-Cognitive-Behavioral Model to Work with Stepfamilies." In P.G. Boss, W.J. Doherty, R. LaRossa, W.R. Schumm, and S.K. Steinmetz (eds.), *Sourcebook of Family Theory and Methods: A Contextual Approach*. New York: Plenum, 558-561.

Peden, Joseph R. and Glahe, Fred R. (eds.) (1986). *The American Family and the State*. San Francisco: Pacific Research Institute for Public Policy.

Phang Boon Leong, Andrew (1990). *The Development of Singapore Law: Historical and Socio-Legal Perspectives*. Singapore: Butterworths.

Phua, K.H. (1987). "Socioeconomic Implications for Care of the Elderly." In Gerontological Society of Singapore (ed.), *The Aged: Who Cares?* Singapore: Gerontological Society.

Pickering, W.A. (1885). "Annual Report on the Chinese Proctectorate for 1885." In *Legislative Council of the Straits Settlements, Proceedings for 1885*. Singapore: Government Printing Office, PC14.

Pierce, G.R., Sarason, B., and Sarason, I. (eds.) (1996). *Handbook of Social Support and the Family*. New York: Plenum Press.

Pimentel, Ellen E. (2000). "Just How Do I Love Thee?: Marital Relations in Urban China," *Journal of Marriage and the Family*, 62 (February), 32-47.

Pongsapich, Amara (1985). "Thailand." In UNESCO (ed.), *Sociology and Social Anthropology in Asia and the Pacific*. Paris: UNESCO, 135-176.

Poston, Dudley L. and Yaukey, David (eds.) (1992). *The Population of Modern China*. New York: Plenum Press.

Presser, H.B. (1994). "Employment Schedules Among Dual-Earner Spouses and the Division of Household Labor by Gender," *American Sociological Review*, 59,348-364.

Purcell, Victor (1956). *The Chinese in Modern Malaya*. Singapore: D. Moore

Putnam, Robert D. (2000). *Bowling Alone: The Collapse and Revival of American Community*. New York: Simon & Schuster.

Putnam, Robert D. (ed.) (2002). *Democracies in Flux: The Evolution of Social Capital in Contemporary Society*. Oxford, UK: Oxford University Press.

Quah, S.R. (1980). "Sex-role Socialization in a Transitional Society," *International Journal of Sociology of the Family*, 10, 213-132.

Quah, S.R. (1981). "The Impact of Policy on the Family: Can the Family be Strengthened by Legislation?" *Southeast Asian Journal of Social Science*, 9, 1, 33-53.

Quah, S. R. (1983). "Social Discipline in Singapore: An Alternative For the Resolution of Social Problems," *Journal of Southeast Asian Studies*, 14, 2, 266-289.

Quah, S. R. (1986). *Family Formation*. Research Report prepared for the Ministry of Health, Singapore, 143 pp.

Quah, S. R. (1988). *Between Two Worlds: Modern Wives in a Traditional Setting*. Singapore: Institute of Southeast Asian Studies.

Quah, S.R. (ed.) (1989). *The Triumph of Practicality*. Singapore: ISEAS.

Quah, S.R. (ed.) (1990b). *The Family as an Asset: An International Perspective on Marriage, Parenthood and Social Policy*. Singapore: Times Academic Press.

Quah, S.R. (1990c). "The Social Significance of Marriage and Parenthood in Singapore: Policy and Trends." In S.R. Quah (ed.), *The Family as an Asset: An International Perspective on Marriage, Parenthood and Social Policy*. Singapore: Times Academic Press, 247-289.

Quah, S.R. (1990d). "Family as Hindrance or Asset? An Overview of Current Controversies." In S.R. Quah (ed.), *The Family as an Asset: An International Perspective on Marriage, Parenthood and Social Policy*. Singapore: Times Academic Press, 1-22.

Quah, S.R. (1990e). "Family and Social Policy: The Shared Experiences." In S.R. Quah (ed.), *The Family as an Asset: An International Perspective on Marriage, Parenthood and Social Policy*. Singapore: Times Academic Press, 378-384.

Quah, S.R. (ed.) (1993). *Asian Sociologists at Work*. London: Current Sociology,

Quah, S.R. (1995). "Sociocultural Factors and Productivity: The Case of Singapore." In K.K. Hwang (ed.), *Easternization: Sociocultural Impact on Productivity*. Tokyo: Asian Productivity Organization, 266-333.

Quah, S. R. (1997). "Values and Development in Asia: A Historical Illustration of the Role of the State," *International Sociology*, 12, 3 (September), 295-328.

Quah, S. R. (1998). *Family in Singapore: Sociological Perspectives*. 2nd Edition. Singapore: Times Academic Press.

Quah, S. R. (1999). *Study of Singapore Families*. Singapore: MCDS.

Quah, S. R. (2003). "Ethnicity and Parenting Styles in Singapore," *Marriage and Family Review*, 35, 1 (in press).

Quah, S.R., Chiew, S.K., Ko, Y.C., and Lee, M.C. (1991). *Social Class in Singapore*. Singapore: Times Academic Press.

233

Radhakrishnan, S. and Moore, C. A. (1957). *A Sourcebook in Indian Philosophy*. Princeton, N.J.: Princeton University Press.

Rahim Ishak (1979). "Role of Women," *Speeches*, Volume 3, No. 4, 72-74.

Rapoport, Robert, and Rapoport, Rhona (1982). "British Families in Transition." In R. N. Rapoport, M.P. Fogarty, and R. Rapoport (eds.), *Families in Britain*. London: Routledge & Kegan Paul, 475-499.

Raquiza, Marivic (2001). "Coupling and Un-Coupling in a Land Without Divorce." *International Divorce Law Office: Philippines Divorce Law*. New York: Morley and Trager. URL: http://www.international-divorce.com

Ratarasarn, Somchintana T. (1990). "Marriage and Divorce in Thailand: Case Studies from Bangkok." In S. R. Quah (ed.), *The Family as an Asset: An International Perspective on Marriage, Parenthood and Social Policy*. Singapore: Times Academic Press, 290-303.

Rawski, Evelyn S. (1991). "Ch'ing Imperial Marriage and Problems of Rulership." In R.S. Watson and P.B. Ebrey (eds.), *Marriage and Inequality in Chinese Society*. Berkeley: University of California Press, 170-203.

Raymo, James M. (2001). "Spouse Selection and Marriage Timing in Japan." University of Michigan Dissertation Abstracts International - Humanities and Social Sciences.

Reiss, Ira. L. (1972). "The Universality of the Family." In Ira.L. Reiss (ed.), *Readings on the Family*. New York: Holt, Rinehart and Winston, 11-25.

Reiss, D. and Oliveri, M.E. (1983). "Family Stress as Community Frame." In H.I. McCubbin, M.B. Sussman, and J.M. Patterson (eds.), *Social Stress and the Family: Advances and Developments in Family Stress Theory and Research*. New York: The Haworth Press, 61-83.

Reith, G. M. (1907). *1907 Handbook of Singapore*. Singapore: Fraser & Neave.

Republic of Singapore (1981). *The Employment Act* (Chapter 122 of the Revised Edition). Singapore: Attorney-General's Chambers.

Rishi, W.R. (1970). *Marriages of the Orient*. Singapore: Chopman.

Rodgers, R.H. and White, J.M. (1993). "Family Development Theory." In P.G. Boss et.al., (eds.), *Sourcebook on Family Theories and Methods. A Contextual Approach*. New York: Plenum, 225-254.

Rosen, Robert, Digh, Patricia, Singer, Marshall, and Phillips, Carl (2000). *Global Literacies: Lessons on Business Leadership and National Cultures*. New York: Simon & Schuster.

Rossi, A. & Rossi, P. H. (1990). *Of Human Bonding: Parent-Child Relations Across the Life Course*. New York: Aldine de Gruyter.

Ryan, N.J. (1971). *The Cultural Heritage of Malaya*. Kuala Lumpur: Longman Malaysia.

Sandhu, K. and Mani, A. (1993). *Indian Communities in Southeast Asia*. Singapore: Times Academic Press.

Sasaki, Masahito and Wilson, Terry L. (1997). "Marriage and Divorce in Japan." In C.A. Everett (ed.), *Divorce and Remarriage: International Studies*. New York: The Haworth Press, 125-135.

Saw, S.H. and Wong. A. K. (1981). *Adolescents in Singapore: Sexuality, Courtship and Family Values*. Singapore: Singapore University Press.

Schvaneveldt, Paul L., Young, Margaret, and Schvaneveldt, Jay D. (2001). "Dual-Resident Marriages in Thailand: A Comparison of Two Cultural Groups of Women," *Journal of Comparative Family Studies*, 32, 3, 347-360.

SDU [Social Development Unit] (2003). *LoveByte Café*. Singapore: SDU. URL: http://www.lovebyte.org.sg/web/

Segaran, M. Kula (1999). "Why Malaysia Should Have its Own Independent Family Court," *DAP Malaysia Bulletin*, 30 September. URL: http//:www.malaysia.net/dap/bul568.htm

Shapiro, S. (1990). *The Law & Lore of Chinese Criminal Justice*. Singapore: Times Academic Press.

Shantakumar, S. (1994). *The Aged Population in Singapore*. Singapore: DOS Census Monograph No. 1

Sharifah Z.S. Hassan and Cederroth, Sven (1997). *Managing Marital Disputes in Malaysia: Islamic Mediators and Conflict Resolution in the Syariah Courts*. Surrey, UK: Curzon Press.

Shin, Eui-Hang (1988). "Marriages of the Business Elite Families in Korea: Homogamy or Marriage of Convenience?" Paper presented at the American Sociological Association Annual Meeting.

Shostak, A.B. (1987). "Singlehood." In M.B. Sussman and S.K. Steinmetz (eds.), *Handbook of Marriage and the Family*. New York: Plenum Press, 355-367.

Singapore Council of Women's Organizations (1989). *Report on Survey of Married Women in Public Housing*. Singapore: The Straits Times Press.

Singapore Department of Statistics (1992). *Yearbook of Statistics Singapore 1991*. Singapore: Department of Statistics.

Singapore Department of Statistics (1993). *Yearbook of Statistics Singapore 1992*. Singapore: Department of Statistics.

Singapore Department of Statistics (1994). *Yearbook of Statistics Singapore 1993*. Singapore: Department of Statistics.

Singapore Department of Statistics (2003). *Statistics on Marriages and Divorces 2002*. Singapore: Department of Statistics.

Singapore Ministry of Community Development (1987). *Survey on Family Life*. Singapore: Research & Information Department, Straits Times Press [Unpublished report].

Singapore Ministry of Health (1995). *Annual Report 1994*. Singapore: Ministry of Health.

Singapore Ministry of Health (1996). *The National Survey of Senior Citizens in Singapore 1995*. Singapore: Ministry of Health, Ministry of Community Development, Department of Statistics, Ministry of Labour, and National Council of Social Services.

Singapore Ministry of Labour (1987). *Guide to the Employment Act*. Singapore: Ministry of Labour.

Singapore Ministry of Labour (1989). *Report on the Labour Force Survey of Singapore 1988*. Singapore: Research and Statistics Department, Ministry of Labour.

Singapore Ministry of Labour (1997). *Report on the Labour Force Survey of Singapore 1996*. Singapore: Ministry of Labour.

Singapore Ministry of Social Affairs (1984). *Report on National Survey on Married Women, Their Role in the Family and Society.* Singapore: Research Branch, Ministry of Social Affairs.

Singapore Supreme Court (1997). *The Supreme Court and Subordinate Courts in Singapore. A Charter for Court Users.* Singapore: Supreme Court.

Smith, D.M. (1991). *Kincare and the American Corporation: Solving the Work/Family Dilemma.* Homewood, Ill.: Business One Irwin.

Snarey, J. (1993). *How Fathers Care for the Next Generation: A Four-Decade Study.* Cambridge: Harvard University Press.

Society of Conservative Lawyers (1979). *The Case for Family Courts.* London: Conservative Political Centre.

Sprey, Jetse (1979). "Conflict Theory and the Study of Marriage and the Family," In W.R. Burr,   R. Hill, F.I. Nye, and I.L. Reiss (eds.), *Contemporary Theories About the Family.* Volume II. New York: Free Press, 130-159.

Star, L. (1996). *Counsel of Perfection: The Family Court of Australia.* Melbourne: Oxford University Press.

Steiner, Gilbert Y. (1981). *The Futility of Family Policy.* New York: Brookings Institution.

Steiner, G. Y. (1985). "The Futility of Family Policy." In J. M. Henslin (ed.), *Marriage and Family in a Changing Society* Second Edition. New York: The Free Press, 493-499.

Steinmetz, S. K. (ed.) (1988). *Family and Support Systems across the Life Span.* New York: Plenum Press.

Stone, Wendy and Hughes, Jody (2002). *Social Capital: Empirical Meaning and Measurement Validity.* AIFS Research Paper 27. Melbourne: Australian Institute of Family Studies.

Straits Times (1988). "Matchmaking Shows Results," 15 August, 13.

Straits Times (1990a). "Ethnic Groups Asserting Their Identity A Healthy Trend." 17 November, 25.

Straits Times (1995a). "Volunteers Help in Family Court," 27 February, 20.

Straits Times (1995b). "Family Court Helps Settle Many Cases by Mediation," 4 September, 30.

Straits Times (1995c). "Pastels and Informality Make Mediators the Mainstay at the New Family Court," 6 March, 22.

Straits Times (1996a). "Family Court to Start Hearing Divorce Cases Within a Few Months," 7 January, 21.

Straits Times (1996b). "School Care Schemes to Receive Government Aid," 26 November, 1.

Straits Times (1998). "Matchmakers Losing Favour With Farmers," 3 October, 30.

Strauss, William and Howe, Neil (1991). *Generations: The History of America's Future, 1584 to 2069.* New York: William Morrow and Company.

Sugimoto, Yoshio (2003). *An Introduction to Japanese Society* 2nd Edition. Cambridge, UK: Cambridge University Press.

Sunday Times (1991). "Japanese Mums Unite to Match Their Children," 3 March, 12.

Sunday Times (1996a). "Family Court to Start Hearing Divorce Cases Within a Few Months," 7 January, 21.

Sunday Times (1996b). "District Court to Intervene Directly in Divorce Cases from Next Month," 17 March, 28.

Sussman, Marvin B. (1959). "The Isolated Nuclear Family: Fact or Fiction?" *Social Problems*, 6, 333-340.

Sussman, Marvin B. and Steinmetz, Suzanne K. (eds.) (1987). *Handbook of Marriage and the Family*. New York: Plenum Press.

Sussman, Marvin B., Steinmetz, S.K., and Peterson, G.W. (eds.) (1999). *Handbook of Marriage and the Family*. 2nd Edition. New York: Plenum Press.

Szompka, Piotr (ed.) (1996). *Robert K. Merton On Social Structure and Science*. Chicago: University of Chicago Press.

Tallman, I. (1979). "Implementation of a National Family Policy: The Role of the Social Scientist," *Journal of Marriage and the Family*, 41, 3, 469-472.

Tan, Shen (1996). "The Process and Achievements of the Study on Marriage and Family in China," *Marriage & Family Review*, 22, 1-2, 19-53.

Tan Y. L. K. (1985). "The Family, Social Policy and the Law in Singapore," *Singapore Law Review*, Volume 6, 2-11.

Tham, S.C. (1989). "Study on Aging and Retirement in Singapore." Singapore: National University of Singapore, unpublished manuscript.

Thatcher, Melvin P. (1991). "Marriages of the Ruling Elite in the Spring and Autumn Period." In R.S. Watson and P.B. Ebrey (eds.), *Marriage and Inequality in Chinese Society*. Berkeley: University of California Press, 25-57.

The Economist (2003). *World in Figures*. London: The Economist.

Thi, Le (1999). *The Role of the Family in the Formation of Vietnamese Personality*. Hanoi: The Gioi Publishers.

Ting, Kwok-Fai and Chiu, Stephen W.K. (2002). "Leaving the Parental Home: Chinese Culture in an Urban Context," *Journal of Marriage and the Family*, 64, 3(August), 614-626.

Tokyo Metropolitan Government (2002). "Family Register." Tokyo: TMG. URL: http://www.metro.tokyo.jp/ENGLISH/LIVING/

Tu, Wei-ming (1984). *Confucian Ethics Today: The Singapore Challenge*. Singapore: CDI

Turnbull, C.M. (1989). *A History of Singapore 1819-1988*. 2nd Edition. Kuala Lumpur: Oxford University Press.

Tyner, James A. (2002). "The Globalization of Transnational Labour Migtation and the Filipino Family: a Narrative," *Asian and Pacific Migration Journal*, 11, 1, 95-116.

UNESCO (1999). *Statistical Yearbook 1999*. Paris: UNESCO.

UNICEF (2002). *The Progress of Nations 2000*. Geneva: United Nations. UNICEF web page htpp://www.unicef.org/statis/

United Nations (2000). *Statistical Yearbook 1997*. New York: United Nations.

United Nations Development Programme (2002). *Human Development Report 2002: Deepening Democracy in a Fragmented World*. New York: Oxford University Press.

United Nations Population Division (1999). *World Population Prospects: The 1998 Revision Volume I – Comprehensive Tables*. New York: UN Department of Economic and Social Affairs.

United Nations Population Division (2000). *Global Population Policy Database, 1999*. New York: UN Department of Economic and Social Affairs.

United Nations Population Division (2002). *World Population Ageing 1950-2050*. New York: UN Department of Economic and Social Affairs.

United Nations Population Division (2003). *Fertility, Contraception and Population Policies*. New York: UN Department of Economic and Social Affairs.

United Nations Statistics Division (2002). *Common Database*. New York: UN Department of Economic and Social Affairs. [Electronic resource]

Waite, Linda J. and Nielsen, Mark (2001). "The Rise of the Dual-Earner Family, 1963-1997." In R. Hertz and N.L. Marshall (eds.), *Working Families: The Transformation of the American Home*. Berkeley: University of California Press, 23-41.

Waley, A. (1938). *The Analects of Confucius*. New York: Macmillan.

Wallerstein, J. S. and Kelly, J. B. (1980). *Surviving the Breakup*. New York: Basic Books.

Wallerstein, J.S. and Blakeslee, S. (1990). *Second Chances: Men, Women and Children a Decade after Divorce*. New York: Ticknor & Fields.

Ware, J. R. (1955). *The Sayings of Confucius*. New York: Mentor.

Warshak, R. A. (1992). *The Custody Revolution: The Father Factor and the Motherhood Mystique*. New York: Poseidon Press.

Weber, Max (1978). *Economy and Society*. Berkeley: University of California Press.

Weber, Marianne (1988). *Max Weber: A Biography*. New Brunswick, NJ: Transaction Books.

Wicks, M. (1987). "Family Matters and Public Policy." In M. Loney (ed.), *The State or the Market: Politics and Welfare in Contemporary Britain*. London: Sage Publications, 115-129.

Wilson, W.J. (1993). *Sociology and the Public Agenda*. Newbury Park: Sage.

Whitchurch, G.G. and Constantine, L.L. (1993). "Systems Theory." In P.G. Boss, W.J. Doherty, R. LaRossa, W.R. Schumm, and S.K. Steinmetz (eds.), *Sourcebook of Family Theory and Methods: A Contextual Approach*. New York: Plenum, 325-352.

Wolcott, I. (1991). "Mediating Divorce: An Alternative to Litigation," *Family Matters*, 28, 47-49.

Wolf, A. P. and Huang, C.S. (1980). *Marriage and Adoption in China 1845-1945*. Stanford: Stanford University Press.

Wong, A.K. and Kuo, E. (1983). *Divorce in Singapore*. Singapore: Graham Brash.

World Bank (2001). *World Development Indicators*. Washington DC: World Bank.

World Bank (2002). *World Development Indicators*. Washington DC: World Bank.

World Bank (2003). *World Development Report 2003: Sustainable Development in a Dynamic World*. Washington DC: World Bank.

Wolcott, Ilene (1991). "Mediating Divorce: An Alternative to Litigation," *Family Matters*, 28, 47-49.

Wu, Liu (1959). "The Chinese Protectorate III: Campaign against Social Evils," *Pinang Gazettee*, 22 March, 7-8.

Yang, C.K. (1959). *The Chinese Family in the Communist Revolution*. Cambridge, MA: MIT Press.

Yeo, Brenda, Graham, Elspeth, and Boyle, Paul J. (2002). "Migrations and Family Relations in the Asia Pacific Region," *Asian and Pacific Migration Journal*, 11, 1, 1-11.

Yi, Zeng (2002). "A Demographic Analysis of Family Households In China, 1982-1995," *Journal of Comparative Family Studies*, 33, 1, 15-34.

Zhang, Weiguo (2002). "Changing Nature of Family Relations in a Hebei Village in China," *Journal of Contemporary Asia*, 32, 2, 147-170.

Zimmerman, Shirley L. (1988). *Understanding Family Policy: Theoretical Approaches*. Newbury Park, California: SAGE.

Index